HERS

HERS

THROUGH WOMEN'S EYES

EDITED BY NANCY R. NEWHOUSE

VILLARD BOOKS NEW YORK 1985

Library of Congress Cataloging in Publication Data
Main entry under title:
Hers, through women's eyes.
    Essays from the Hers column of the New York times.
    1. Women—United States—Social conditions—Addresses,
essays, lectures. 2. Feminism—United States—Addresses,
essays, lectures. I. Newhouse, Nancy R. II. New York times.
HQ1420.H43 1985   305.4'2'0973   84-40605
ISBN 0-394-54461-7

Grateful acknowledgment is made to the following for permission to reprint previously published material:

Al Gallico Music Corp.: excerpt from lyrics to "The House of the Rising Sun." Copyright © 1964 by Keith Prowse Music Publishing Co. Ltd., London, England. All rights for U.S.A. and Canada controlled by Al Gallico Music Corp. Reprinted by permission.

Caleb Music Company: excerpt from lyrics to "The Universal Soldier" by Buffy Sainte-Marie. Copyright © 1963 by Caleb Music. Used by permission. All rights reserved.

Little, Brown and Company, and Collins Harville Ltd.: excerpt from "This Cruel Age Has Deflected Me" by Anna Akhmatova from *The Poems of Akhmatova* by Stanley Kunitz and Max Hayward. Copyright © 1972 by Stanley Kunitz and Max Hayward. First appeared in *Art News*. Excerpt from "Requiem" by Anna Akhmatova from *The Poems of Akhmatova* by Stanley Kunitz and Max Hayward. First appeared in *The Atlantic*. Reprinted by permission of Little, Brown and Company, and Collins Harville Ltd.

Manufactured in the United States of America
9 8 7 6 5 4 3 2

CONTENTS

Singular Women

The Married State

Being Alone

Having Children . . . and Raising Them

Person to Person

CONTENTS

INTRODUCTION

From its beginnings in March, 1977, the "Hers" column, written by fifty-two women to date, has had many different voices: serious, funny, factual, nostalgic, reportorial, inward-looking. It has offered brief but intense insights into whatever each author, in eleven or twelve hundred words, most wanted to tell readers. And it has evolved, from a time when writing about the pain of a divorce or the insult of salary discrimination seemed a kind of path-breaking, to the present, so attuned to the enormous changes in women's roles and expectations that have occurred in the last decade. As a society, in that same stretch of time, we have learned to talk much more freely about what's bothering us. So it is hard today to remember how new these women's voices sounded in 1977, particularly in the pages of a daily newspaper.

The "Hers" column was created as a forum for women to write, once a week for several weeks, about whatever they chose to. From the first, "Hers" columnists have spoken their minds. They continue to do so, with a candor and directness that have engaged readers in a special way.

Whether the subject being addressed is geriatric sex, or why girls must study mathematics, or the saga of being a single parent, or a recollection of Fulton Sheen, the audience keeps reading. When the voice at the breakfast table is compelling enough, a dialogue between reader and writer often ensues. It may be a purely interiorized conversation, or it may inspire clipping, a phone call, a letter. It is this sense of encountering the writer, of hearing from her in person, of caring about what she cares about, that is the special appeal of "Hers." Columnists have been overwhelmed at the strong reaction they have received from readers, person to person, if they live in New York, and in letters from around the country.

Betty Rollin, the television journalist and writer, observed of the response to her columns, "When you write about yourself honestly, you are, it seems, writing about other people too. At least that's what they tell you. Over and over they let you know that you are speaking for them. It makes you glad you exposed yourself." In response to Rollins' column on women's self-doubt and fear of failure, one reader wrote, "I practically scalded my tongue and fell out of my chair as your words on self-doubt leapt off the page."

"People I didn't know would come up to me and recite chapter and verse what I had said in a column," said Letty Pogrebin. "But what was most amazing was the length and intensity of the letters."

Men correspond as often as women. Perri Klass, writing about her tendency to cry under pressure in medical school, received the following letter:

"Dear Perri, I have just put down the Thursday *Times* to write this. Your piece in the 'Hers' column is why. . . . Crying, like laughing, needs no justification.

"In 1967 I sat in a tent one night in Tay Ninh, Vietnam, near the Cambodian border, and listened to a record I had never heard before. It was Buffy Sainte-Marie singing 'The Universal Soldier.' Some of the words went 'He's the one who lends his body as a weapon of the war, and without him all the killing can't go on.' I sat there and cried like a baby. . . .

"When I see news film of the Vietnam Veterans Memorial in Washington, the tears return. I usually fight them back. I know that I am saving them, so that some day, when, if, I find myself in the presence of that monument, I can cry, unchecked, for all those people, their loved ones, this nation, this world, and for myself. I look forward to that moment. (signed) Mike Sheller"

After recounting her problems caring for an aging but essential farm truck, Sue Hubbell received detailed instructions from a helpful reader on truck and car maintenance, including a nine-point guide to saving gas, clutch and the automatic transmission.

Nor is reaction limited to personal pieces. Covering current issues from teenagers and birth control to the exclusion of women from men's professional clubs, Susan Jacoby, who ignored my suggestion to unlist her Manhattan telephone when she was writing the column, regularly spent a portion of her Thursdays on the phone with readers who wanted to discuss her latest essay.

A meeting of the minds, of course, is not necessarily the rule. Among the columns sparking opinionated discussion were Joyce Maynard's impassioned defense of the nonworking mother and Alice Koller's pieces on living alone in winter-remote Nantucket.

Whether a particular author elicits disagreement, indifference or deep attachment (often some of each, depending on the reader), as a group the "Hers" columnists have provided a window into the special concerns of dozens of intelligent and articulate contemporary women. As the novelist and "Hers" columnist A. G. Mojtabai wrote to me recently, "I have always resisted the label 'woman writer.' And I have been consistently opposed to the notion that women write out of a life experience separate and distinct from that of men. When I write, I think of myself as *anyone*—man, woman, child, of any race or condition.

"In the process of writing the column, however, I reminded myself that I did have some experiences as a woman that men have not had. (I don't, for a moment, claim that a male writer, with the talent and the will, couldn't imaginatively create such an experience.) Here it was —waiting simply for me to pick it up, to acknowledge it as my own. It required no effort for me to describe the experience of, say, putting on a veil [pp. 71–74]. In doing so, I was reminded of my deep linkage with women everywhere."

The voices of women—their diversity, their richness, their contradictions—are the life of this column and this book. A beekeeper writes from her small farm in the Ozarks (Sue Hubbell); a freelance writer from her urban desmesne of Queens (Elin Schoen). An Indian journalist (Anees Jung) writes half a world away from a feminist in Fort Wayne, Indiana (Mary Kay Blakely), or an author in Hawaii

(Maxine Hong Kingston). One columnist is a professor at Wesleyan (Phyllis Rose), another an editor at *Ms.* magazine (Letty Pogrebin). The worldly resident of Hollywood and London (Jill Robinson) shares space with the sixth-grade teacher in Washington, D.C. (Faye Moskowitz). So far, the youngest columnist has been twenty-six years old (Perri Klass), the oldest, sixty-seven (June Wilson).

Separately, they have taken "Hers" in many different directions. The most powerful voices either have conveyed a larger vision— a humane and intelligent concern for the problems and contradictions of our society and the women in it—or have written about their own lives with an intimacy that approaches daring—the deeply revealing, as opposed to the confessional. Such pieces, the best of them, move us invisibly from the particular to the general. In a single Cambodian child we know the lot of all Southeast Asia's disinherited children; in a mother's farewell to a son who will not return, we remember our own wounds.

Together these women have devised a communal creation, a patchwork quilt of sorts, in bright and somber colors, piece after piece carefully worked and crafted. Stepping back to look for overall patterns may reveal something about the concerns of women today.

As editor of the "Hers" column, initially as editor of *The New York Times* Home Section, then as head of the department made up of the Home and Living sections and the Style pages, I have often been asked how columnists are chosen. Tempting as it would be to put forward a highly schematic system, the reality has been made up of chance, serendipity, and a few last-minute emergencies, as well as a substantial amount of "ideal method" advance planning.

Names have been suggested by colleagues, others by my own reading. I have approached well-known writers such as Gail Sheehy, Gail Godwin, Joyce Maynard, and Maxine Hong Kingston. Some distinguished writers have turned me down because they had current commitments; some simply said no. First books have come to me; this is the way I encountered Laura Cunningham, Mary-Lou Weisman, and others. Agents have sent in material; and an enormous amount of unsolicited submissions have come in. These are all read eventually, and a few have yielded columnists. Intangibles of juxtaposition and contrast also play a part in choosing writers: light after very serious, topical after personal, a Midwesterner after many New Yorkers.

Once a colleague came into my office with the enormous manuscript of an unpublished novel written by her cousin and asked me, with an expression of false innocence, if I would "look at it"; I could hardly lift it. It languished for a year. One Saturday, catching up on paperwork, I read it. To my delight, and some embarrassment, it was a fine piece of writing; I immediately signed up the author, Deirdre Levinson, for the column.

Good writing has been the governing principle in choosing columnists, and though many combine writing with another career, the overwhelming majority have been professional writers. Without exception, they have found the essay form a challenge, and, ultimately, a delight. Gail Godwin said the pieces were "an unforeseen pleasure for me to write. I could have gone on forever. There was something about that length—it just suited the thoughts as they came out." The essay, it seems, still works its spell on both writer and reader.

The "Hers" column came about when A. M. Rosenthal, the executive editor of *The Times*, attended a party in New York shortly after the first Living Section came out in November, 1976. Among the guests were some leading feminists, whose response to the new section was warm.

One of them, the author Lois Gould, said that what was really needed was a place in *The Times* that would be a special forum for women. At the time, most of what was published in newspapers was written almost exclusively from a male point of view.

The Home Section was then being planned, and Rosenthal and Arthur Gelb, deputy managing editor of *The Times* and Rosenthal's principal collaborator on the new sections, decided to create such a forum in its pages. Rosenthal foresaw a column different from the typical "women's column," one that would take a fresh approach to women's issues and women's lives. It would be written for men as well as women. "I didn't think of it as a column *for* women," said Rosenthal. "I thought of it as a column *by* women." Authorship would rotate periodically among writers not on *The Times'* staff. Fittingly, Lois Gould, who took part in some of the initial discussions, was the first columnist.

Since that time, in working with fifty-two columnists, I have been amazed by the unending freshness of their writing, and by the new talent that keeps coming to hand. It seems a justifiable fear that one day a column like this one will double back and start feeding on itself. So far, my experience has been the opposite; I sometimes feel that a small standing army of women writers has marshalled itself across the land, waiting for a trumpet to sound. Perhaps women simply have more to say than men these days—perhaps because more is happening to them. That "more" has been progress for women, in many areas, and it has also been dispiriting reverses.

But to receive columns from a twenty-six-year-old medical-school student at Harvard, who has a baby but nonetheless finds time to write about why she will be different from the male doctors around her, is to know change has occurred.

Although certain concerns of women have received seemingly endless coverage in recent years—the difficulty of juggling children and career, for example—change will create new concerns, or new versions of old concerns. And columnists, of course, will go back to the perennial subjects, too. These oft-told tales—of death, love, loneliness, divorce—surprise us even today by the power of their reincarnations in the hands of superb writers; several authors have written their strongest pieces about the death of a parent. As an editor, however, I strive for a balance between these timeless subjects and pieces that have current issues as a starting point. There is always a place, too, for the inspired digression, the musings of a narrator who hooks us with the lure of a truly idiosyncratic sensibility.

In a letter of April, 1981, to Arthur O. Sulzberger, the publisher of *The Times,* a reader in Chicago wrote to suggest that a "Hers" collection be published: "The overall content is interesting, beautiful, moving and relevant to human history in terms of the modern feminine sensibility; they should not be lost." Here is her book.

I am grateful to A. M. Rosenthal and Arthur Gelb for their continuing support and interest in "Hers," and to my colleague Dona Guimaraes, editor of the Home Section, for all that she has done in connection with the column. Above all, I want to thank the writers who have created the column and this book.

N. R. N.
January, 1985

A Question of Appearances

LETTY COTTIN POGREBIN

The membership committee of a business and professional club was considering what object might make an attractive bonus for new members. I suggested a canvas bag. "Men won't carry it" was the immediate consensus. At first I pushed my point. "Plenty of men carry Channel 13 bags," I argued. But even as I spoke, my mind's eye had trouble visualizing great numbers of men with bags in hand, while the image of women carrying all manner of totes was an easy one to conjure. I retired my suggestion and have since given a lot of thought to why it is that women—in Simone de Beauvoir's words, "the second sex"—are also "the schlepper sex."

Any informal street survey will tell you that many more women than men are carrying things around. First, and most obviously, women carry handbags. Purses and pocketbooks are essential because women's garments have skimpy pockets, if any, while men's wear is designed with copious pockets for a wallet, glasses, keys or whatever. As long as our culture deems it more important for women to follow fashion than function, we have to schlep handbags.

Second, you will notice that most of the babes in arms are in women's arms. Women carry babies because men are elsewhere doing other things with their hands and because the only way out of the house, short of abandoning one's children, is to take them along.

Third, your visual survey will yield many more men than women swinging their arms empty-handed. In a single minute on a mid-Manhattan street corner I counted twenty-two unencumbered males but only one female who carried nothing at all—and she was about six years old.

Finally, when men carry things, what they carry is usually associated with their work or leisure activities. Men in business suits carry attaché cases. Men in work clothes carry tool kits and lunch pails. Men in warm-up suits carry gym bags or tennis rackets. Of course, many women carry the same labor and leisure items that men do, but it is most likely that those women also carry loads of things that maintain and enhance the lives of others. Check the nearest street scene and you will see women carrying groceries, household supplies, laundry, baby bags and packages of assorted necessities.

For instance, trudging onto the No. 5 bus one evening was a well-dressed woman whose body was ballasted by the symbols of her double life. One hand lugged several boxes of disposable diapers tied together with twine, the other a bulging briefcase: portrait of a woman carrying family responsibility, unfinished work and guilt. A woman I know, a sewing-machine operator, always takes a net shopping bag to work. She says it's a rare day when she doesn't have to stop off on the way home to pick up a few last-minute items. She says her husband, a cutter at the same shop, goes straight home carrying only his newspaper.

Women who work in their homes rather than in offices or factories seem to do the most schlepping. In almost any part of town they can be seen pulling an overloaded shopping cart with one hand and pushing a stroller with the other; some carry an infant in a backpack, too. I have frequently noticed in airports, among the hordes of men with slender briefcases and compact suit bags, a woman juggling a squirmy two-year-old and the freight associated with said child's journey. It strikes me as a civic duty for business travelers to help such a woman with her bag of toys, coloring books and crayons, the stuffed animal, the bag of nursing bottles, the tote containing diapers and the baby's change of clothes, the woman's pocketbook and airline ticket, and the child who almost invariably refuses to walk aboard the plane under his or her own steam. But none of the juggler's fellow travelers seem to notice her.

When my children were too young to leave behind, I used to go marketing with them in tow. I remember many times when I felt close to tears because of the strain of carrying an armload of groceries and talking three toddlers safely across the streets. I remember how the men lounging in the playground and on the brownstone stoops, who otherwise flirted with or harassed me, just looked right through me when I was a schlepper with three children.

Schlepping doesn't only destroy one's sex appeal; it compromises one's dignity. This is why President Carter was roundly ridiculed for carrying his own garment bag. It is also why, a male friend told me, Margaret Thatcher looked more like a prissy matron than a prime minister when she attended summit meetings with a dangling pocketbook. Or why Representative Barbara B. Kennelly of Connecticut recently asked an onlooker to hold her purse while she was being photographed.

Several uniformed services have rules about who may carry what. New York City Police Department regulations term it "prohibited conduct" for a police officer to carry a package, umbrella or cane while in uniform except in the performance of duty. "Some captains don't even like cops to carry their lunch back to the precinct house in a paper bag," says Sgt. Pete Sweeney, a department spokesman. The United States Army Officer's Guide said until its 1949 edition: "There are long-standing taboos against an officer in uniform pushing a baby carriage, against carrying large and bulky bundles while in uniform on the street, and the carrying of an umbrella." In the guide's 1983 edition just the umbrella taboo remains—and it applies only to male officers. "Military customs reflect the values of the larger society," explained Joe Webb, a Department of the Army historian. "And carrying an umbrella doesn't fit the American macho image for a man."

Why does the Army care? "It's a question of maintaining proper military bearing," said a public-affairs officer, Lieut. Col. Michael H. Clark. "But under the old taboos it was improper for an officer to carry boxes and parcels because someone else was expected to perform that service for him."

That expectation still holds true for some civilians. An unmarried friend tells me she can usually pick out the single men in her neighborhood: "They're the ones carrying their own laundry." Married men schlep less because they have wives to do it for them. The masculine ideal allows a man to carry things in the act of making a living, having fun or performing special feats of chivalry or strength—such as carrying women or their furniture—but not to have routine burdens of his own. As with the Army officer, and the rich and the white colonialist, it is a measure of power and privilege to have others shoulder such burdens.

The ability to keep one's hands free implies not only status and economic privilege but real physical freedom. It is much easier for the unencumbered to use their hands, defend themselves, be mobile, run, or stand tall and retain their dignity whether uniformed or not. Historically and cross-culturally, women have been weighted down by babies in their arms and baskets on their heads while men, carrying only their weapons, move freely in the world. In modern society as in ancient cultures, noticing who schleps and carries tells us a lot about who is usually left holding the bag.

SEPTEMBER, 1983

LOIS GOULD

K imberley Ann, nine, has just decided what she wants to be when she grows up: a part-time cocktail waitress with frosted blond streaks. It is probably just a coincidence that Kimberley Ann's mother recently graduated from law school and lopped off her two-tone gold ringlets right at the dark roots.

Kim's classmate, Janice, who is still eight, has her heart set on becoming a file clerk who ties up her hair in a severe bun that can be shaken free, with a single lightning stroke, into a quivering mass of raven tendrils. (Janice's mother is a securities analyst, with a naturally frizzled pepper-and-salt pageboy.)

Nina, ten and a half, plans to be a schoolteacher with a firm grip and frosted blond highlights. And twelve-year-old Stephanie, the cynic, intends to become a frosted blond highlight, period.

Clearly, a fair number of feminists' daughters are having "role-model" trouble. The cause seems to be a sudden and widespread cultural confusion about the difference—if any—between a role model and a hair model. As I understand it, a role model is an adult person of your own gender whom you admire and want to be like: a president, an astronaut, a nuclear physicist, a private eye. Whereas a hair model is a stunning raven-haired president; a luscious redheaded astronaut; a blond bombshell of a nuclear physicist; a frost-streaked poster pin-up of a private eye.

It would be easy to blame the confusion on television's newest rage—the female "action-adventure" star who can either ride a motorcycle, toe-tap on a skateboard, shoot straight, do heavy lifting or figure out how to trap a criminal while wearing a dripping wet bunny costume. After all, no matter what else these new wonder women do besides wonders—and part-time file-clerking, schoolteaching, cocktail-waitressing—the thing they all do *best* is their hair.

. . .

So it would be easy to blame TV, but, as one of our stunning, raven-haired ex-Presidents used to say, "it would be wrong." The truth is, we have always had a little trouble spotting the subtle line between a heroine and a hairdo. In a highly unscientific recent survey, mothers of nine- to twelve-year-olds, selected solely on the basis of shampoo, color tint and permanent-wave length, were asked the following question: When you were nine to twelve years old, who was your "role model," and why?

• Seventeen percent answered "Esther Williams, the swimming star, because she could do fifteen minutes of flawless underwater side-stroke with gorgeous flowers twined in her braided coronet."

• Twenty-five percent named Brenda Starr, the comic-strip girl reporter, on the basis of her sensational headline set in bold-type curls the color of "a five-alarm fire," an "Irish setter," or a "saumon fumé."

• Twelve percent had idolized Sonja Henie, the Goldilocks of the ice, because she skated like a windup Christmas angel; her hair and feet set off "matching sparks of white light"; she was an "animated gold sequin."

• The remainder chose a wide assortment of heroines ranging from the Dragon Lady (dangerous mastermind set in a black curtain of silk hair) to Amelia Earhart and Dale, Flash Gordon's dauntless co-pilot, both of whom had their heads in clouds of wispy gold tendrils escaping from under their flying helmets.

Nobody had a role model with non-terrific hair.

Film historian Molly Haskell has noted that the long, sexy tresses of movie queens in the hard-boiled dramas of the 1940's was the female equivalent of a gun—an ultimate woman's weapon in a tough man's world of crime and carnality. The new "action" heroines of the seventies, operating in the same man's world, actually get to wield both weapons—the hair *and* the gun. But it's the same old game: Everything, including the girls, is still owned and operated by the fellow who runs the beauty parlor. Body, soul, gun and frost job, they are strictly *Charlie's* angels.

Armed with this valuable knowledge, I recently watched my first episode of the TV series *Charlie's Angels*, accompanied by two hard-core nine-year-old fans, Nicole and Sandy. Here's how it went:

Me: Tell me about the "angels."

Nicole: Well, first off you have to know which is which. Sabrina is the smart one, Kelly is strong, and Jill is beautiful. Mostly her hair.

Me: But they're *all* beautiful.

Sandy (patiently): Of *course*. But Sabrina is beautiful *and* smart. Kelly is beautiful *and* strong. Jill is *just* beautiful. Mostly her hair.

Me: Oh. (On the screen, three women are flashing guns, hair, sexy clothes and dazzling smiles, like armed stewardesses serving plastic filet mignon. Pause.) Which would you rather be—the smart one, the strong one, or the beautiful one, with the hair?

Nicole: Definitely not the beautiful one.

Sandy: Obviously.

Me: Why obviously?

Nicole: Because even if she has the most hair, she has the smallest part. (Sandy nods, solemnly.)

Me: What if you had a choice, I mean in real life? You could be smart and strong—or you could be beautiful. Which would you choose?

Sandy: Why couldn't we be all three?

Me: Well, first off, because hardly anybody gets to be all three. And hardly anybody even gets to have a choice. So I'm giving you a choice. Beautiful, but dumb and weak. Or smart and strong, but ugly. Ugly *hair*, especially.

Sandy (frowning): Hmmm.

Nicole (cocking her head so that her long mane of naturally frosty curls tumbles gently around her shoulders): *How* ugly?

MARCH, 1977

MARY-LOU WEISMAN

An over-forty feminist contemplates a face lift with the same ambivalence with which an environmentalist with bugs in his garden eyes a can of DDT. Such embarrassing encounters with hypocrisy, such uncomfortable moments of truth, are visited upon the passionately committed with awful frequency. Perhaps the point is to keep us humble.

Didn't we mean it when we declared that we would no longer contort or pervert our true female natures in order to conform to the oppressive desires of a dominant patriarchy?

Yet, here we are, more of us middle-aged women than ever before, touching the tips of our fingers to the tops of our cheekbones, giving little surreptitious upward tugs, assessing that new, smooth face through slightly Orientalized eyes and wondering, "Should I?"

Well, don't ask me. I've been standing in front of the bathroom mirror, hoisting my persona for the past two years, questioning my motives, and I still don't have the answer.

Some days I tug, and turn my head slowly, like the old MGM lion, examining my newly taut jawline until it pivots out of view, and scold myself for spending so much energy on what is nothing more than a trivial, privileged obsession.

Whom, after all, do I most admire—a serene, confident woman who would yield with grace to the natural aging process, or a frantic narcissist who would buy a ten-year reprieve by, quite literally, paying someone to slit her throat. I ought to be ashamed of myself, and I am. But not ashamed enough, it seems, to stop obsessing.

On other days, as I exact my pound of crepy flesh by grabbing at the nape of my neck, and look like Ronald Reagan in a wind tunnel, I see the absurdity of my obsession. Even as we live in a world where the population of middle-aged and elderly people is gaining on the young, still we do not take advantage of our numbers.

On my most idealistic, high-minded days, I want to fling myself against that impossible, oppressive youth cult. Someday, I tell myself, the vogue of trying to look young while growing old will, like other social fashions, spend itself and vanish. At times like this, I remind myself that yesterday's Rubenesque pulchritude is today's repulsive cellulite.

Ah, but can I wait? Can that brave, nascent sprout of self-worth and self-determination planted by feminism fifteen years ago take root and flourish in a predominantly alien environment?

On other days, I wonder if the face lift is a feminist issue at all. I suspect that there are increasing numbers of men, too, who, in the privacy of their bathrooms, lay down their razors and tug upward on their sideburns. Some of them, like some of us, tug out of sheer vanity. Other men, like some women, suspect—and they are probably right—that a face lift improves their chances in a marketplace world where the competition for jobs favors the young.

As for myself, I am not competing for a job in the marketplace world. I am sitting in the back room of my house, typing and growing dewlaps where no one who reads me can see me. Nobody cares how old writers get, or how old they look. The worst that can happen to you is that your publisher will leave your photo off the dust jacket.

I do not think, however, that too many men worry, as they tug after shaving, that their wives will leave them for a younger, smooth-skinned man. That mostly happens to women, and it happens a lot. And when it does, it is so severe a blow that even if she never wanted one before, she gets a face lift and ventures forth to compete with younger women for a man her own age, or older. So maybe that's the bitter extent to which the face lift is exclusively a women's issue.

But I am not looking for a man. My husband says he likes the way I look. He confesses that he sometimes looks at younger women, but then he reminds himself of how little he'd have to talk about with them, how shallow they'd seem, how boring.

"And vapid," I add too eagerly. "You forgot vapid."

And some days I indulge in rationalization. It's not that I want to look younger, I tell myself; I just want to look neater. But I cannot hide behind that little semantic fiction for long. "Neater," when it comes to skin, means "younger." I know of no old person whose skin responded to use and gravity by slipping upward and tucking itself in behind the ears with hospital corners. I must face it. I *do* want to look younger.

There is a place out West where the states of Utah, New Mexico, Colorado and Arizona meet. A stone is planted on that spot so that tourists can photograph each other. I remember getting down on my hands and knees on that stone, much to my children's delight, so that I could truly say I'd been in all four states at once.

Standing here in front of the mirror, I wonder if I am at a philosophic intersection where vanity, vogue, fear of aging and insecurity meet and collide.

I still have the map we used for that westward drive from Connecticut to California thirteen years ago. The children took turns drawing a heavy pencil line over every highway and rural road we traveled that lovely summer. There was a detour to show our older son the Baseball Hall of Fame in Cooperstown, N.Y. We laugh out loud whenever we look at that map and see that we started our trip west by heading due north.

Whenever we drive west, we use that map. It's fun to remember where we've been. Besides, an old map has other advantages. Thirteen years ago I struggled at the end of each day to fold the map closed and put it in the glove compartment; now it practically folds itself along well-worn lines. We've briefly discussed the obvious advantages of plotting future trips on a cleaner, neater map, but we prefer the old one. It has character.

. . .

Can I feel about my aging face the way I feel about that map? There is, written upon it, every gene I inherited, every smile I smiled, every scream, every frown, every cry; every time I squinted, every cigarette I smoked, every hour in the sun (before, and after, I knew it aged the skin); even every ambivalent tug I've tugged these last two years. It's all there—written all over my face. It is my legacy. It is my self.

On these days, standing at that philosophical intersection, it seems that the face lift is a frivolous issue, but a potent metaphor. It is a metaphor for no less crucial a question than how we face up to ourselves, as reflected in our lives as well as in our mirrors.

The bottom line, the ultimate wrinkle, is the integrity of the self. I wish I could face it down, but I can't. One must fight for one's self, even though the reward for waging that battle is often no more, but never less, than the cold consolation of integrity.

That's why I haven't gotten a face lift—so far.

NOVEMBER, 1983

LAURA CUNNINGHAM

t's now or never: You must get into that bikini by Labor Day or write off the summer season. The bikini, bought in March, will continue to languish with its price tag in the bureau drawer, be recycled as a neckerchief, or perhaps be stuffed into a picnic hamper as a convenient sling for carrying hard-boiled eggs. Now is the time to choose: You can give up the bikini idea, buy a commodious caftan and dive deeper in Häagen-Dazs, or you can take a deeper breath and start edging toward the pool, covered with a shred and a prayer.

It doesn't help that standards for bodies have never been so strict: If you can't run an eight-minute mile without your thighs quivering under the noonday sun, you're liable to feel like an eyesore on the public beaches. Not only are today's women warned against obesity, but we are told to be on guard against "the fat you can't see" (you can see it if you go looking for it). My advice is to listen to those experts who insist that cellulite doesn't exist (therefore it can't be dimpling behind your knees). Deal with only ordinary fat, and you stand a chance.

What can you do in these dog days of August? The first step is to determine your actual weight. You must use the correct scale. Avoid a doctor's scale. Those are so imbued with their own authority that they add an automatic five pounds. The best scale is your own scale: It knows your body, it will help you draw the line. Please use it correctly. Don't just stand on it. Approach it at a trot, jump on hard, tilt 45 degrees to the left, crouch forward, forehead almost touching the floor, and take a reading. This method guarantees the lowest possible figure and will give you the impetus to go on with your reducing program.

Now you're ready for the On-Scale Diet: Eat anything you want but only while standing on your scale. This way, you keep accurate track of how much you're really gaining or losing. If you must dine out, try to eat on a public scale. Railroad depots have the best.

Intrigued by all those one-food diets? You've probably tried the Grapefruit Diet, the Banana Diet, the Brown Rice Diet. Now, there's a new one: the Escargot Diet. It's so simple, you will never have to stop and think. Every meal is escargot. All the escargot you can eat for breakfast, lunch and dinner. Snails are a perfect diet food. One has only to see them nestled in their shells to know that. And because of the way your body metabolizes escargot, you can have all the butter and garlic sauce that you wish. You will notice the pounds slide away, a fact discovered eons ago by those svelte French escargot fishermen in Brittany who invented the Escargot Diet and kept it their own special secret for so long.

You will also want to use modern technology to help you thin down. The blender has become the dieter's best friend—the machine can whip up slimming treats in a froth. On the Purée-O-Diet, you can enjoy fabulously fattening foods that would be ordinarily forbidden. You are allowed to eat a complete French dinner simply by combining all the courses—a typical meal may include soup Senegal, salade Niçoise, blanquette de veau, crispy rolls, butter, crème caramel, petit fours—into the blender. Add two cups liquid (a good Bordeaux is permitted), liquefy on high speed. Result: Purée-O-Diet. Sip slowly, direct from the jar. Purée-O-Diet will quickly satisfy your appetite, and you will be surprised by how little you actually consume.

If a high-fiber diet is more to your taste, investigate the total fiber program. This program recommends those foods highest in cellulose: the rinds of canteloupe, shrimp tails, lobster backs, avocado peels and cherry pits. Almost negligible in cost (food can be found behind any neighborhood market), this diet puts the digestive system through a vigorous test that has already been established as healthier for the body than "a more refined diet."

If you must diet by the book, you may want to buy one of the best-sellers. Or try the classics that have been updated. When publishers realized that Tolstoy's *War and Peace* was lagging behind *The Scarsdale Diet*, a new edition was printed to include diet tips that now comprise the *War and Peace Diet* and the sequel, *The Siege of St. Petersburg Diet*. Both books feature basically the same fare: boiled potatoes, borscht and substitute King Sour for sour cream. Other "literary" diets are Melville's *Moby Dick Diet* (all seafood) and the Jean Rhys Liquid Diet: Pernod with every tiny meal.

No matter which diet you choose, you will benefit from correcting your knowledge of nutrition. The reason most people are overweight is that they were misinformed via typographical errors, by the first printed "Guidelines to Nutrition." Here now is the accurate information: We are not meant to have three meals a day. It was supposed to be three meals a *week*. There are not seven food groups, there are only three: yogurt, crackers and diet soda. Exercise does *not* burn off calories, as advertised, unless the exercise is performed *while* eating.

Here for the first time is the correct regimen: Exercise while you eat. Sample: Running burns 400 calories per hour. No one told us we had to run and eat simultaneously. Correct routine: Prepare a portion of french fries (the perfect running food). Run for one hour, eating 60 french fries (10 calories per french fry) one a minute as you go. Result: No weight gain. If you prefer to stay indoors, there is a new machine that can help: the Dine-a-Cycle, an exercycle that hooks under any dining table and allows you to pedal away as you consume caloric treats.

Emergency methods: You must get in shape for this weekend at the Hamptons, yet you have four pounds to lose by Saturday morning. What can you do? You can *run* to the Hamptons, 100 miles from midtown Manhattan. The run to the Hamptons will take roughly 1,500 minutes, or 25 hours. You will burn perhaps 15,000 calories getting there, which translates into a four- or five-pound weight loss. One stop at Riverhead, for juice, is permissible. Alternative: Swim to Martha's

Vineyard. Same principle: Your swim to the Vineyard, some 30 miles from Wood's Hole, should burn off eight pounds. You'll look great in your bathing suit as you arrive on the beach.

Let's say, for whatever reason, you don't make it. When diet fails, turn to disguise. For centuries women have dressed in black to look thinner (the House of Bernarda Alba School of Design). Today black is out but distracting accessories may minimize your girth. For years musicians have had their own secret for appearing thin. They carry their instruments. Nothing is as slimming for a woman as a cello.

Onward we waddle toward the first gray days of September. Until then bear up, and if you must try a geographical place diet, forget Scarsdale and Beverly Hills and consider something more egalitarian—the Flushing Meadows Diet. One slice of Entenmann's maple walnut crunch cake, washed down by sweetened coffee every half-hour. This diet has been the secret of the beauties of Flushing Meadows for more generations than anyone can remember. There is no guaranteed weight loss, but it gets you through the summer.

AUGUST, 1981

Mothers
and Fathers

ELIN SCHOEN

My mother died last month. She was my closest friend. She was also my father's closest friend, and his dream-sharer, his adviser on family policy, his unwilling but able first mate when they sailed, his sense of direction when he drove, his childhood sweetheart, his muse, his best audience, much more.

And he was as many things to her. But why enumerate, she would have said (although she was a constant list-maker, analytical, a filer-away of this and that with a special fondness for data such as the source of St. Pierre's finest bouillabaisse). Why enumerate? Because their perception of each other was total. Together, they formed a natural element. That was it.

To me, they were a single entity, a complex and, in some ways, mysterious organization with my mother as its liaison to the field reps —my sister and me. She was the filter through which news of my life reached my father, who had always found it difficult to grasp concepts such as freelance relationships. She and I had, from my father's vantage point, "this thing going." He watched, admiring, from the sidelines, occasionally refereeing with a sharp word about the rising cost of long-distance phone calls.

He was no more privy to our ongoing dialogue than I was to their ongoing romance. Yet he was, I always knew, the context in which that dialogue took place. And I, a product of that romance, was troubled sometimes by their interdependence. What would she do without him? What would he do without her? I once discussed this question with a cousin and I don't remember which of my parents we selected as most likely to succeed without the other. Probably we reached no conclusion. The likelihood of such an event's happening was simply unimaginable.

Four hours after it happened, my father met me at the airport and I hugged him very fast and then we grabbed hands and didn't let go until we got to the car. It was the first time, within recent memory at least, that my father and I had ever held hands. It was instinctive, easy in the giddiness of grief—but somewhere in the numbness I remember an ache of self-consciousness: I am holding my father's hand.

I felt awkward, too, responding when my father said (another first), "I love you" during a phone conversation later. I am being called upon, suddenly, to express feelings that have always been there but just never found their way into words or gestures. And things are shaky here in the unimaginable.

My father is reaching out to my sister, too, for the warmth, the grounding, that my mother's presence meant. But my sister is less available than I am since she is married, with two children. I am divorced, with a career. Over the weeks, my father and I have begun a dialogue. Oblivious to the rising cost of long-distance phone calls, my father consults with me about the color scheme of his new house, his business options and travel plans, whether he should sell his classic Volvo, all the things he would have discussed with my mother, and then something they never could have discussed—"my new oneness," he calls it.

"You know, I really admire your guts," he said.

"Guts?"

"Yes, I never appreciated before what it takes to be on your own, by yourself. And I just don't know if I can do it. You know, I'm a Sagittarius." (Another first: my father has heard of the zodiac?) "And that's not a domestic sign. I'm supposed to be the independent type." He laughed. "So much for signs."

"But you are the independent type, you always have been." Yes, within my mother's aura. The boldness, inventiveness, candor of my father flourished in that realm. What was so extraordinary was that it was their very dependence on each other, the reliability of that bond, that freed each of them to be themselves. Now my father, anchorless, broaches the subject of himself with me and I draw back a little because this means sharing myself.

Everything used to spill out so spontaneously with my mother. Now I am stalling, blocked. My father knows this. And, outspoken as ever—perhaps more so because he is determined to find his way in a foreign country, to master its language and customs—he wondered, one night, if I thought he would ever be "as important" to my sister and me as our mother was. I said he always had been: it was just—different.

Then I found myself trying to bridge the difference, testing for sameness: could he handle an intimation of immorality—the fact that the man I've been spending more and more time with is married. My father didn't think I was letting myself in for a lot of fun and games. But he was not shocked. I was shocked at how nonjudgmental he was, how cool. He passed the test, and with a certain smugness. "I know you think I'm a prude," he said.

"Who told you that?" (As if I didn't know.)

There will be other tests. My father and I are still in our old roles but moving forward, taking unexpected turns, speaking unrehearsed lines. We're both uneasy, although he's far more relaxed than I am. He's had thirty-seven years of practicing intimacy. My field is autonomy. He keeps getting back to it: "How do you do it? How do you live alone?"

I put a gloss on the surface, then slide along: living alone is just like marriage, really, except the person you're trying to get along with is yourself. You have your ups and downs, the times you adore yourself, the times you're furious with yourself. You communicate with yourself (but not, one hopes, out loud on the street).

I can go no deeper. I haven't found the secret formula, if there is one, for coping with plain loneliness and that other big area in which togetherness and solitude diverge: the fact that you can escape from another person but never from yourself. Nor can you have privacy from yourself.

I am not the loner my father thinks I am. But I wasn't ready to

tell him yet—it's that block about touching on real things with him—
that I live alone only because I will never settle for anything less than
what he and my mother had.

It might have made him feel better, had I been able to get the
words out, to know that I don't feel totally sorry for him, that I envy
him, in a way. I wanted to tell him, and couldn't, how lucky he is to
have earned the privilege of suffering like this.

SEPTEMBER, 1979

JILL ROBINSON

How difficult it is, at any age, to separate the longing for traditional mothering from the recognition of one's mother's ambitions. Such a difference there is between my daughter's acceptance of my writing and the way I felt about my mother's painting. I am not sure how much of this is due to social change, how much to the specifics of personality and circumstance. How I hated it when my mother would say, "I want you to know me as a person." I swore I would be a Real Mother. I based my definition not on mothers I knew, but mothers I saw in the movies. Even though as a child brought up in Hollywood I might have noticed those roles were played by some of the most driven women in the world, I never made that connection.

I am suddenly making all of these connections while standing in the National Gallery of Art in Washington, D.C. I have come here between appointments on a business trip my own daughter encouraged me to make even though she was ill at the time. "Just go," she said, "do your work and have a good time." I surprise myself being here. I turned away from art as a youngster mainly because my mother loved it. "Aggressions toward mother," my mother called it with a kind of a sad laugh.

As I watch painters here at the National Gallery, copying pictures, I want to reach out to them and have them turn to pay attention to me. I disliked the sign over my mother's studio: "M. Svet, Painter at Work: Disturb at Own Risk." I disturbed my mother whenever possible. She worked out a clever compromise. While I was complaining and telling her tall stories, she would have me pose. In this way she listened, silently, as we wished our mothers to do, and got her work done.

.   .   .

The smell of turpentine and linseed oil, the soft sound of the brush tapping, sticking an instant and leaving the canvas, became motherly smells and sounds, as, to other children, the smell of baking things might be. I watched my mother clean up—swirling the brushes about on a cake of Ivory soap—the way other children watched mothers doing dishes. Will the sound of a typewriter be a motherly association to my daughter, Johanna, and to my son, Jeremy?

I see paintings here by Rosa Bonheur, by Vigée-Lebrun and Mary Cassatt, and remember my mother telling me about them, that they were great painters. She longed to be one of them. I refused to listen when she complained they were not given recognition. What my mother liked I felt then could not be very good. But now I look at the arms on Cassatt's children. They make me sigh, they are so warm, so exquisitely painted. They also make me long to touch my daughter's firm young arm. To be home. Did my mother feel that pull—even as she forced herself to work every day. My mother despised "Sunday painters." I thought then, at least *they* drive station wagons and pick up their kids at school.

Now I am looking at a painting by Robert Henri, who was my mother's instructor when at eighteen, my daughter's age, she left home to study at the Art Students League. I can see that my mother's work is very, very good, cruelly unrecognized. As my mother said, during the years of the Abstract Expressionists, "My work will come into its own one day." Do I have the generosity of spirit yet to tell her she is right? Can I accept and recognize my mother's work as my children do mine? I turned to admiration and competition with my father because my mother's work was relegated to a second place. Shamed by her defeat and my failure to appreciate her excellence, I didn't even acknowledge the achievements she was able to make.

We talk of the expectations parents give children! My God—the expectations I had for my mother. Imagine: she was to be sexless, except that I should be her gently eroticized obsession. She would give me her total attention—but leave me alone, except when I needed her and then she was to be there instinctively. If my mother had troubles, I was not to hear about them, although she was to listen endlessly to mine, to offer only pleasing advice.

She was also to understand all of my troubles were of her own making. And yet she was not to be guilty because that would make me uncomfortable. She was to keep herself attractive, but to age—in an acceptable manner—so I would not feel she was in competition. She was to remain married, but to have a less perfect marriage than any of mine. It was clear she should have no sex life at any time, but at the same time was to understand and approve any sexual conversation I might throw her way.

In my daughter's and my son's eyes I see the toll their understanding has taken. I also see the rip in my mother's life as she fought ahead of her time to be herself. I want to acknowledge that understanding here. To ask forgiveness for the selfish denial of her excellence and frustration. I want to say to her as my daughter did to me, "Just go, do your work and have a good time." My mother gave me the license by showing me her own longing. But I am still caught. Surrounded by luminous paintings, astonished at how much my mother was able to teach me about understanding them, in spite of my resistance to every word—lessons which served me better than the pies she never made—I wonder if I will give her the pleasure of telling her that for relaxation now I turn to the world she offered me so long ago.

MAY, 1978

LAURA CUNNINGHAM

I began my life waiting for him. When other children asked, "Where is your father?" I had my mother's answer: "He's fighting in the war." For the first four years of my childhood, I grew into the anticipation: My father would come home when the war ended. In the interim, my mother and I moved in a holding pattern—from one relative's apartment to another, sleeping on sofas and collapsible cots. In the dark of different living rooms, we traded questions and answers that were always the same: "Did he see me before he left?" "Once. You were in your crib, sleeping."

How could I have slept? I wondered at age three. "Couldn't I have been wakened?" "You were fast asleep." I progressed from litany to interrogation—there was something wrong. I quizzed my mother for details, dates. "What did you wear to your wedding?" "A beige suit." "Why not a white wedding dress?" "There wasn't time. He had to fly overseas."

On national holidays, we hung a small flag out the window. At parades, we sang on the sidelines. My mother said my father had many medals, more ribbons than anyone and—this was my favorite part—his own fighting dog, a boxer named Butch, who was a gentle pet when he wasn't ripping apart the enemy. It was a red-white-and-blue story, told to the accompaniment of bugles. There was only one major flaw: While I waited for my hero father to return from battle, this country was not at war.

No war. I got the message when I was four. I rushed to tell my mother, who in 1951 assured me that World War II was not yet over. "Most of the soldiers have come back," she confirmed, "but there are still a few outposts that have to be captured."

While my father purportedly fought at his front, my mother and I lived in limbo. The interrogations continued: I collected information. His name was Larry. He was from Alabama. His hair was blond, his eyes blue. He was tall and handsome. He had met my mother in Miami, then been sent overseas. He could fly a plane, fire a machine gun.

By the time I was four, I noticed my mother blush when "Larry" was mentioned. I began to blush, too, whenever anyone inquired about my father. When the Korean conflict began, my mother and I both relaxed. No one looked at us strangely and asked "What war?" anymore.

But even Korea came to an end, and with it the first installment of my life without father. One afternoon, on a city street, as I demonstrated mock machine-gun fire—"This is how my daddy kills them."—my mother tapped me on the shoulder and led me a discreet distance away from the other children. As we walked, she said I shouldn't tell that story anymore. I guessed the reason: "The war's over." "In a way it is." She told me Larry would not be marching home after all. His body was already buried "overseas." I asked about the medals, the ribbons, perhaps his uniform? With a vividness of detail I can appreciate in retrospect, my mother explained why there was nothing left to be sent to us. "He was blown up in tiny pieces." His uniform was burned, his medals melted, the ribbons charred and lost forever.

"Butch?" Was Butch riding in the tank? No, he was not. "The Army needs dogs like Butch." Butch, I was told, had been reassigned. And so, it appeared, were my mother and I. No longer transient, we moved to our own "efficiency" apartment. We were no longer ladies in waiting, we were in mourning. My mother lit a memorial candle and placed it carefully in the corner of the bathtub, there to flicker in remembrance without becoming a fire hazard for twenty-four hours on each anniversary of my father's death.

Suspicion flickered, too: Why on the first day at school was I called to the office? "Why is your last name different from your father's?" I felt scalded. I didn't know. I said so, and felt as I still do sometimes that I was lying although I was telling the truth. By age seven, I was familiar with the sensation—that of being compressed into an upright, too-tight coffin—that accompanied any inquiries.

I believe my mother would have told me more about my father, but she died when I was eight. Her two younger brothers raised me. Fatherless for my first eight years, I spent the next eight under the care of two loving men.

When I asked my uncles for more information, they could not even verify the spelling of his last name. "We just don't know." Hadn't they asked my mother? No, they said, they had not. They respected her privacy: It is a discreet family. My mother, a tall brunette with a memorable smile, was thirty-five when I was born. She made her own way, she made her own choice. It was only the time—1947—and tradition that forced her to create the fiction.

Grown up, I exchanged one fantasy for another: My father was alive somewhere. I could find him.

My only problem with the new fantasy was that I rebelled at its maudlin nature. I don't like melodrama: It's not my material. A thousand soap operas played in my own mind. I was always walking into my father's office, surprising him. Why did I have to wear all white and that slouch hat? Having seen too many B movies, I ran with what clues I had. To me "the South" meant *Gone With the Wind* or *A Streetcar Named Desire*. I envisioned myself surprising my father on an antebellum porch, where we would soon fling ourselves into delicate frenzies of regret.

What happened was not romantic or melodramatic—it was tedious. I wrote to the Hall of Records. My letter was returned, stamped "INSUFFICIENT INFORMATION." I wrote again: How many Larry Moores could have been stationed in Miami in 1946? Too many, I was told. I would need the missing man's consent before his file could be released. Later requests to every imaginable authority were also denied. My father's name was "too common." I would have to give up.

I almost did. My efforts became erratic. I might not think of him for months, then see an out-of-state phone book and flip to his name. That was how I conducted my search—standing up, in fluorescent telephone "communications centers." Uncertain even of the spelling, I worked the combinations: Moore, Lawrence; More, Laurence; even Mawr, Laurenz. I studied the listings: Larry Moore of Flat Creek Road? I could see Larry Moore: There his face seemed, brooding over bourbon, staring down at Flat Creek. I invented detailed scenarios—his wife walks onto the veranda, her hands holding an empty vase: "Why, who's that, Larry?" she asks. "No one," he answers, his eyes meeting mine.

I never had the nerve (or perhaps the need) to telephone any of the hundreds of Laurence/Larry/Lawrence Moore/More/Mawrs. The closest I came was to draft a letter, to be copied, "Dear Laurence/Larry/ Lawrence, were you perhaps stationed in Miami in ——?" I explained that this was "not an emotional matter," but simple curiosity on my part. There would be no unpleasant scenes. It was not a case of anguish, I wrote, then realized I had misspelled the word "anquish." *Squish.*

I never finished the letter, never copied it, never mailed it. Still the potential drama lurks never too distant at the back of my mind. Hope is sneaky. It hides behind reason. As recently as three years ago, I might pause at a "communications center" to flip under the M's in the book marked Alabama. Then I stopped. Just quit. I didn't want to do it anymore: I wanted to come to terms with never knowing him.

His absence may have benefited me more than his presence: If my early life is a fiction, well, then, fiction is my trade.

The truth I feel is something stronger. I was raised by two men who cared for me. I'm their child, not his. And I owe my existence not to him, but to my mother, who risked more than usual to give me life. The ultimate revelation of being a love child is that it was my mother's love that made me. I am my mother's daughter. I am hers.

AUGUST, 1981

PHYLLIS ROSE

My mother has always said: "The daughters come back to you eventually. When the sons go they're gone." She has other favorite sayings—"A father's not a mother," "The beginning is the half of all things," and "De gustibus non disputandum est," which she translated as "That's what makes horse races"—all of which have become increasingly meaningful to me with time. Recently I told her that she was right in a fight we had twenty-seven years ago about which language I should study in high school. This came up because I had just had the same discussion with my son and took the side my mother took then (French). She laughed when I told her that she was right twenty-seven years ago. There have been more and more nice moments like that with my mother as we both grow older.

She is seventy-five, ash blond, blue-eyed, a beauty. When my father died three years ago she suddenly developed glaucoma and lost a lot of her vision. She says she literally "cried her eyes out." She can read only very slowly, with the help of a video enhancer supplied by the Lighthouse for the Blind. Nevertheless, her lipstick is always perfect. She doesn't use a mirror. She raises her hand to her lips and applies it. When I praise her for this, she says, "By now I should know where my mouth is."

She doesn't walk alone at night and during the day rarely gets beyond the area she can reach on foot, between 50th and 60th streets, First Avenue and Fifth. She loves to transgress those boundaries, so when I come in from Connecticut I usually pick her up in my car and drive her to distant parts of Manhattan: the Lower East Side, the Seaport, TriBeCa, SoHo, the Village. One of our favorite things to do together is to have Sunday brunch at a restaurant on West Broadway near Houston Street. We go there especially for the pecan pancakes and the scrambled eggs with salmon and dill.

. . .

One day this winter we went there for Sunday brunch. It was a particularly cold day and I was suffering from a pulled muscle in my neck. I walked with one shoulder higher than the other. My mother walked slowly and with a slight stoop. But as soon as we entered the door the restaurant buoyed us up. We were patrons, to be pampered. We had a reservation. We could share in the general atmosphere of youth, energy, chic, competence, success. The waiters were stylishly dressed with an accent of the 1940's. This was SoHo.

One young man, wearing a plaid shirt and pinch-pleated trousers, showed us to a table in a bright front section overlooking the sidewalk. This was excellent for my mother, who often finds restaurants too dark and carries a spelunker's light to read menus by. But we didn't need a menu; we ordered pecan pancakes and scrambled eggs with salmon and dill. When they arrived we split them and I began with the eggs. "Eat the pancakes first," my mother said. I didn't ask why. She's my mother. She has to tell me how to do things.

Three beautiful women dressed in black who were eating lunch at a table nearby finished eating, cleared their table and moved it aside. From the corner they took a cello, a violin and a flute, removed their covers and positioned themselves to play. They started with Schubert and went on to a medley of Strauss waltzes. My spirits soared. I looked at my mother to see if she was listening to the music. She was. I could see she was as ravished by it as I was, and for the same reason. Without exchanging a word both of us moved simultaneously thirty years backward in our minds and to another place.

"Palm Beach," I said.

My mother nodded. "Hoops, crinolines, strapless dresses with net skirts, white fox stoles. Each of us took three suitcases. Those days are gone forever."

In the 1950's my father, in his proud and powerful middle age, took my mother, my brother, my sister and me to Palm Beach for two weeks every winter until just after New Year's Day. We stayed at a hotel called the Whitehall; its core was originally the mansion of Henry F. Flagler, the railroad man and Florida pioneer. The lobby had floors of inlaid marble and variegated marble pillars.

The Whitehall dining room was a gigantic sunken area that, family legend said, was Mr. Flagler's indoor swimming pool. Whether it was or not didn't matter then, doesn't now. It was a magical place. The families as they came in for dinner and took their usual places were brilliantly dressed: fathers in the light-colored raw silk jackets appropriate for the Stuth; mothers in strapless dresses with wide skirts supported by hoops and crinolines; children, after a day on the beach and the tennis courts, scraped, peeling, but burnished for dinner. Nothing was casual. The hotel hairdresser was heavily booked. Elaborate sets and comb-outs several times a week were not unusual. Jewelry was not left in the vault at home. The room sparkled. There was general splendor, the result of all that effort and the discipline of dressing for dinner. And at the center of the room a quintet in black formal clothes played music throughout the four-course meal. Every night, usually during the clear consommé, they played a medley of Strauss waltzes.

My mother and I are tied together because we share the same memories. My brother and sister share them, too. We are a family because the Whitehall, a certain dude ranch in the Great Smokies, the layout of our house on Central Avenue and other recondite geographies exist in our minds and no others. We move in the same mental spaces. In some of our dreams we wander the same streets, trying to get back to the same house. One form of loneliness is to have a memory and no one to share it with. If, in twenty years, I want to reminisce about Sunday brunch in a certain SoHo restaurant I may have nobody to reminisce with. That will be lonely.

Often I feel I do not do enough for my mother. When I read *King Lear* I realize that I'd be flattering myself to identify with Cordelia. I have the awful suspicion that I am much more like Regan or Goneril—from Lear's point of view monsters of ingratitude; from their own just two women taking their turn at the top, enjoying their middle-aged supremacy. When these guilty thoughts afflict me a folk tale comes to mind.

There once was a bird with three young to carry across a river. She put the first on her back and, halfway across, asked, "Will you care for me in my old age as I have cared for you?" "Yes, Mama," said the first bird, and the mother dumped him in the river, calling him a liar. Second bird, same result. "Will you care for me in my old age as I have cared for you?" "Yes." "Liar." But the third bird, asked if he would care for his mother in her old age as she had cared for him, answered: "I can't promise that. I can only promise to care for my own children as you have cared for me."

It's a truthful response and it satisfied the mother bird, a philosophic spirit if ever there was one. But when I imagine my son saying the same thing to me—"I can only promise to care for my own children as you have cared for me"—I don't seem to find much comfort in it.

MAY, 1984

MARY-LOU WEISMAN

Are little girls forever exalted, forever doomed, to adore their fathers? My father died this fall at the age of seventy-eight from Parkinson's disease. It was the right time for him to die. His death was anticipated, even yearned for; his body had become as stiff and bent and useless as a discarded wire hanger. His keen mind occupied a ringside seat at his own body's undignified betrayal. It was the right time for him, but not for me, not for the part of me called "Daddy's girl."

The mature, forty-five-year-old woman, quite experienced in matters of life and death, knows that it was "for the best," but Daddy's girl, who hung onto his belt and danced fox trots on the tops of his shoes, cannot accept that Daddy is not here anymore. How could Daddy, the smartest of men, who ought to have been elected President, how could my hero die? How could he not be here for me anymore, even if I don't need him for anything I can say, even if I am a big girl now, even if I can take care of myself?

I wonder if the daughter's adoration of the father is a potent sociosexual prejudice that the women's movement will rectify in time, or whether it is an immutable behavior, coded into our chromosomes, its message to be interpreted for our times by Freud and Jung. Sometimes I think we're stuck with the Electra complex, that it even becomes us, that it is part of our female human nature. Sometimes I think the answer to Freud's question, "What do women want?" is "Daddy." Sometimes I think that Jung's "Great Father" will always glow with the magical aura of transpersonal overload.

But other times I believe that nurture counts, that the women's movement will modify, however slightly, a daughter's impossible passion for her father.

I like to think so. I want to believe that today's young daughters will outgrow their emotional Mary Janes before middle age. I want to believe that the impact of the feminist movement on the family dynamic will result in a parental domestic democracy, supplanting the kingdom where Daddy once ruled.

I know my mother and I conspired to keep my father larger than life. "Your father's had a hard day at the office." "I'm making your father's favorite dinner." "Ask your father when he comes home." She signed her letters "Gertrude Cohen (Mrs. Herbert L.)." I wooed him with birthday poems, knock-knock jokes and good report cards. We kept each other in a female-engendered, deferential thrall to The Big Man.

I watch today's feminist fathers, their daughters riding in Snuglis on their chests or in knapsacks on their backs, their sticky fingers plunged into Daddy's hair. I see fathers changing diapers, playing catch, dressing their daughters for school, feeding them, waiting at bus stops, teaching them manners and how to fix a car, and I wonder if these daughters who experience their fathers differently than I did will love them differently, too.

This heady love of father is a perilous love, a hubris that tempts the gods to vengeance. Just as there was no greater happiness than the pleasure of Daddy's approving smile, so there was no more horrible fate than his disapproval, hurled like thunderbolts from Zeus on high. Daddys' girls live on the razor's edge.

A perfect father leaves a tough legacy—an addiction to girlishness. It is a habit I have struggled to unlearn, a struggle, I suspect, that I will wage until my dying day. No sooner do I have the yeasty dough that is my father's memory punched down to proper proportions—so much admiration for his fine mind, so much for his sound values, so much for his good humor, so much, even, for his human limitations, so much, even, for the ways he disappointed me—than the loaf rises again, out of proportion, eclipsing reason, confounding reality.

. . .

What would our relationship have been like if Daddy had been obliged by his wife and times to do his fair share of the unheroic parenting, if he had dragged me down supermarket aisles, insisting upon oatmeal while I shrieked for Sugar Frosted Flakes? I might have feared his anger less if I had had the opportunity to witness my father come upon Crayola graffiti on the living room wall, seen him roll his eyes heavenward, and cry out in abject, impotent frustration, "God give me strength!" (Of all the traditional maternal tableaus I have acted in as a mother, or witnessed as a child, the pathetic "God give me strength" spectacle is the most humbling to the mother and the most heartening to the child.)

I might have gotten to know him better. I might have adored him less and loved him more. By giving him more than was rightfully his, I denied myself some of what was rightfully mine. I might have spared myself some of the stations of the cross at which adoring daughters must stop to make up for lost times. I might have spared myself the excessively heady high of falling in love, as well as the inevitable, plummeting crash of falling out.

I might have learned compassion sooner, and how to enjoy being married to someone who isn't as perfect as Daddy wasn't either. I might have thought it at least as important to compete at sports, to learn how to earn a living and read a road map, as to pass the hors d'oeuvres, play "Malaguena" and marry. I might have learned to be angry without crying, to disagree without apologizing, to be, if the situation required, displeasing.

As it is, his death, ironically, has brought him into closer range. It is as if, in death, he released to me my birthright. Because he is no longer here to keep me from harm, to protect me in some ultimate, fantastic way that only I, not he, ever imagined he could, I seem to be taking better care of myself. His death has opened up some space in me, and I am moving in and taking over.

I'm beginning to feel entitled. I leave the dishes in the sink when

I am late for work, with apologies to no man. As a result, my husband often does them, with recriminations to no woman. I dine out with friends, even on nights when my husband isn't going to be out for the evening. Was it always all right with him that I do that, or is it that it is finally all right with me?

NOVEMBER, 1983

JOYCE MAYNARD

My mother called last week to tell me that my grandmother is dying. She has refused an operation that would postpone, but not prevent, her death from pancreatic cancer. She can't eat, she has been hemorrhaging, and she has severe jaundice. "I always prided myself on being different," she told my mother. "Now I *am* different. I'm yellow."

My mother, telling me this news, began to cry. So I became the mother for a moment, reminding her, reasonably, that my grandmother is eighty-seven, she's had a full life, she has all her faculties, and no one who knows her could wish that she live long enough to lose them. Lately my mother has been finding notes in my grandmother's drawers at the nursing home, reminding her, "Joyce's husband's name is Steve. Their daughter is Audrey." In the last few years she hasn't had the strength to cook or garden, and she's begun to say she's had enough of living.

My grandmother was born in Russia, in 1892—the oldest daughter in a large and prosperous Jewish family. But the prosperity didn't last. She tells stories of the pogroms and the cossacks who raped her when she was twelve. Soon after that, her family emigrated to Canada, where she met my grandfather.

Their children were the center of their life. The story I loved best, as a child, was of my grandfather opening every box of Cracker Jacks in the general store he ran, in search of the particular tin toy my mother coveted. Though they never had much money, my grandmother saw to it that her daughter had elocution lessons and piano lessons, and assured her that she would go to college.

But while she was at college, my mother met my father, who was blue-eyed and blond-haired and not Jewish. When my father sent love letters to my mother, my grandmother would open and hide them, and when my mother told her parents she was going to marry this man, my grandmother said if that happened, it would kill her.

Not likely, of course. My grandmother is a woman who used to crack Brazil nuts open with her teeth, a woman who once lifted a car off the ground, when there was an accident and it had to be moved. She has been representing her death as imminent ever since I've known her —twenty-five years—and has discussed, at length, the distribution of her possessions and her lamb coat. Every time we said goodbye, after our annual visit to Winnipeg, she'd weep and say she'd never see us again. But in the meantime, while every other relative of her generation, and a good many of the younger ones, has died (nursed usually by her), she has kept making knishes, shopping for bargains, tending the healthiest plants I've ever seen.

After my grandfather died, my grandmother lived, more than ever, through her children. When she came to visit, I would hide my diary. She couldn't understand any desire for privacy. She couldn't bear it if my mother left the house without her.

This possessiveness is what made my mother furious (and then guilt-ridden that she felt that way, when of course she owed so much to her mother). So I harbored the resentment that my mother—the dutiful daughter—would not allow herself. I—who had always performed specially well for my grandmother, danced and sung for her, presented her with kisses and good report cards—stopped writing to her, ceased to visit.

But when I heard that she was dying, I realized I wanted to go to Winnipeg to see her one more time. Mostly to make my mother happy, I told myself (certain patterns being hard to break). But also, I was offering up one more particularly fine accomplishment: my own dark-eyed, dark-skinned, dark-haired daughter, whom my grandmother had never met.

I put on my daughter's best dress for our visit to Winnipeg, the way the best dresses were always put on me, and I filled my pockets with animal crackers, in case Audrey started to cry. I scrubbed her face mercilessly. On the elevator going up to her room, I realized how much I was sweating.

Grandma was lying flat with an IV tube in her arm and her eyes shut, but she opened them when I leaned over to kiss her. "It's Fredelle's daughter, Joyce," I yelled, because she doesn't hear well anymore, but I could see that no explanation was necessary. "You came," she said. "You brought the baby."

Audrey is just one, but she has seen enough of the world to know that people in beds are not meant to be so still and yellow, and she looked frightened. I had never wanted, more, for her to smile.

Then Grandma waved at her—the same kind of slow, finger-flexing wave a baby makes—and Audrey waved back. I spread her toys out on my grandmother's bed and sat her down. There she stayed, most of the afternoon, playing and humming and sipping on her bottle, taking a nap at one point, leaning against my grandmother's leg. When I cranked her Snoopy guitar, Audrey stood up on the bed and danced. Grandma couldn't talk much anymore, though every once in a while she would say how sorry she was that she wasn't having a better day. "I'm not always like this," she said.

Mostly she just watched Audrey. Sometimes Audrey would get off the bed, inspect the get-well cards, totter down the hall. "Where is she?" Grandma kept asking. "Who's looking after her?" I had the feeling, even then, that if I'd said, "Audrey's lighting matches," Grandma would have shot up to rescue her.

We were flying home that night, and I had dreaded telling her, remembering all those other tearful partings. But in the end, I was the one who cried. She had said she was ready to die. But as I leaned over to stroke her forehead, what she said was, "I wish I had your hair" and "I wish I was well."

On the plane flying home, with Audrey in my arms, I thought about mothers and daughters, and the four generations of the family that I know most intimately. Every one of those mothers loves and needs her daughter more than her daughter will love or need her some day, and we are, each of us, the only person on earth who is quite so consumingly interested in our child.

Sometimes I kiss and hug Audrey so much she starts crying—which is, in effect, what my grandmother was doing to my mother, all her life. And what makes my mother grieve right now, I think, is not simply that her mother will die in a day or two, but that, once her mother dies, there will never again be someone to love her in quite such an unreserved, unquestioning way. No one else who believes that, fifty years ago, she could have put Shirley Temple out of a job, no one else who remembers the moment of her birth. She will only be a mother, then, not a daughter anymore.

Audrey and I have stopped over for a night in Toronto, where my mother lives. Tomorrow she will go to a safe-deposit box at the bank and take out the receipt for my grandmother's burial plot. Then she will fly back to Winnipeg, where, for the first time in anybody's memory, there was waist-high snow on April Fool's Day. But tonight she is feeding me, as she always does when I come, and I am eating more than I do anywhere else. I admire the wedding china (once my grandmother's) that my mother has set on the table. She says (the way Grandma used to say to her, of the lamb coat), "Some day it will be yours."

APRIL, 1979

Aspects
of Feminism

LETTY COTTIN POGREBIN

Why do so many women who agree with feminist goals choose to disavow feminism? For me the question became urgent a few weeks ago when I read concurrent disclaimers from three prominent, strong women: Christine Craft, the television anchorwoman who sued her employer; Representative Geraldine A. Ferraro; and the actress Estelle Parsons. When I checked out each quotation, my question elicited very different but equally revealing answers.

Chris Craft, the outspoken TV anchor who sued the station that demoted her for being "too old, unattractive and not deferential to men," said in an interview in *The New York Times*: "I'm not a feminist." Yet her case seemed to epitomize women's struggle against sexism. Following the logic of the old punch line—if it looks like a feminist, sounds like a feminist and acts like a feminist, it is a feminist—I asked her if she'd been misquoted. "No," she said. "I hate being categorized. Objectivity has always been my goal. If I said I'm a feminist, I'd never get another job as a reporter. I mean no slap against feminism, but this is my battle and mine alone."

I suspect she resists being categorized because, despite more than a decade of women's movement activism on everything from child care to homemaker's rights, the category "feminist" still conjures for many an image of a narrow, negative fringe group. I can vouch for the power of those preconceptions: at virtually all my lecture appearances, believe it or not, someone says, "I thought you'd be bigger." At five feet four inches I delight in being a "decategorizing" force. Each of us who calls herself a feminist testifies that feminists come in all sizes, races, marital states and sexual persuasions. Admission to our "category" is by commitment only.

. . .

When Miss Craft cites her desire for objectivity as a reason to disavow feminism, I'm reminded of Gloria Steinem's civil rights parody of the equal-time rule: "O.K., we've heard from the black victims; now let's get the attack dogs' side of the story." It's as absurd to expect objectivity on racial brutality as it is to suggest there are two sides to the denial of human rights to women. Being a feminist—i.e., in favor of women's rights—should not stigmatize a woman reporter; it should mark her as a person with rudimentary human concerns and female self-interest. Put another way, would a black reporter be required to swear neutrality on the Voting Rights Act or apartheid before he or she could cover a story concerning such matters?

And if it's true, as Miss Craft maintains, that a feminist could not get work as a reporter, maybe she should challenge that situation in her next lawsuit.

Divide-and-conquer strategies get an assist when a public symbol like Miss Craft maintains that "this is my battle and mine alone." There was a time not long ago when youth, beauty and obsequiousness were generally accepted standards for female worth. But today—because of the moral and legal climate created by thousands of women before her —Miss Craft was able to argue the injustice of that standard and win $500,000 for having been victimized by it.

Ignoring those who marched, lobbied, went to court, took abuse and fought for every woman's right to be treated as a person, Miss Craft imagines that the battle originated at her news desk in Kansas City.

A few days later, *The Fire Island News* quoted Representative Ferraro as saying she did not consider herself a feminist "although she is in favor of the equal rights amendment and is pro-choice on the abor tion issue." Miss Craft had been an unknown quantity but Miss Ferraro's record matches nearly every item on anyone's feminist political agenda. Can she deny that she's a feminist?

She didn't: "I said that when I went to Congress in 1978 I did not run as a feminist or consider myself one. But I became a strong feminist when I got here and learned what is happening to women in this country. As Bella Abzug once tried to get across to President Carter, I'm trying to say that feminist issues are problems that affect women and they are very broad political and economic issues. Most people support feminism when they understand it."

The third disclaimer appeared in a *New York Times* interview with Estelle Parsons, star of *Orgasmo Adulto Escapes From the Zoo*, eight one-woman plays by Dario Fo and Franca Rame. Miss Parsons told the reporter that the plays are about "the condition of women"— and "how we're all prisoners of the male organ." That struck me as a fairly forthright, even radical, feminist summary. Yet she was quoted as insisting that she was "not interested in feminist messages."

I had seen her in *Miss Reardon Drinks a Little*, *Miss Margarida's Way* and the remarkable *Mert and Phil*—three plays with profound messages about "the condition of women." I knew that she belongs to a networking group that helps women get jobs in the theater; could Miss Parsons not be a feminist?

"I didn't realize I was one when I did the interview," she said on the telephone the other morning. "But these plays have led me into a lot of soul-searching about the patterns in my work and my life. Until now I didn't dare say myself what these plays are saying. I was afraid people would poke fun at me, so I withdrew from everything controversial. I've been wrong not to stand up and answer for my own commitments. It's not enough to just live your life. You have to recognize what you represent to other women. The women in the audience treat me as a feminist leader, but it is they who've raised my consciousness."

While I was pondering all this, Carol Kleiman, associate financial editor of *The Chicago Tribune*, told me that the opening comment by 90 percent of the businesswomen she interviews is "I'm not a feminist." "These women are not comfortable being woman-identified," she explained, "so they're trying to tell me how much they like men. Refusing to make common cause with feminism is a doomed effort to distance themselves from their sisters by making an alliance with the men who still, for the most part, control their destinies." Christine Craft continues to cultivate that alliance and disavow feminism no matter how she contradicts her own reality. Geraldine Ferraro and Estelle Parsons understand that facing women's reality makes a woman a feminist. They are in stellar company. Dr. Sally Ride, a true "first," credits other women for her success and even for the fact that back in 1977, she applied for astronaut selection because of a notice posted in the Stanford University Women's Center. If it wasn't for the women's movement, says Dr. Ride, "I wouldn't be where I am today." Can any woman truthfully disavow that statement?

SEPTEMBER, 1983

LOIS GOULD

My friend Pamela confesses she is no longer big on freedom of expression. In fact, when a man in her life recently mentioned, in a dismayed tone, that some misguided judge in Ohio had thrown a man in jail for seven to twenty-five years, just for publishing a "girlie" magazine, Pamela smiled one of her most delightful smiles and said softly, "Oh, that's wonderful."

I guess I have never gone quite so far as Pamela. But then, neither have I gone quite so far the other way as my friend Nancy the devout civil libertarian, who swears she would, if pushed to the typewriter, force herself to defend that publisher's right to air his disgusting magazine live and in color on prime-time TV, or on the 59th Street Bridge during rush hour.

Nancy also insists she would defend outrageous lies in advertising (even if the slogan went: "Ask Mommy to buy Old Tar cigarettes—they're good for kids!") and catchy racist epithets on the evening news, and free demonstrations of sado-masochism in front of Robert Wagner Junior High School, if not right in the science lab.

In the name of our First Amendment, Nancy says, we must simply learn—and teach our children—to avert the eyes, ears and nose, much as we acquire, and instruct the young in, the useful habit of stepping nimbly around other public nuisances that litter the crosswalks of life in a free country.

While I was pondering that, my telephone rang, and it was a pleasant young man calling on behalf of the very magazine whose publisher had just been thrown in jail. For a brief, crazy minute, I wondered if he was going to offer me one of their million-dollar "modeling" fees that went begging last year after Barbara Walters, Gloria Steinem, Caroline

Kennedy, Patty Hearst and other selected targets declined to answer the call. I remembered wishing at the time that they had all accepted —and then used the proceeds to buy the magazine and tear it up.

But that was not the subject of the young man's call. All he wanted was my name. Specifically, he wanted it on a petition expressing my concern at the jailing of his publisher. He assumed that no matter what I as a woman think of his product, I as a writer would force myself, like Nancy, to take up arms against his suppressors, lest they light out next week after Kay Graham or Adrienne Rich—or me. In other words, all us free-press persons should hold our averted noses and step in this public nuisance together.

By now I was feeling acutely uncomfortable. What if the fellow is right? What if they're *all* right? Pamela had to be right, because she knows that the magazine is much more than merely disgusting: it is also potent—a weapon and a textbook, not only for the very young, but also for the older and more dangerous. She knows that the thing it does is teach people that women are consumer goods—silly putty toys with replaceable parts, or snack foods with flavors enhanced by artificial spice and color.

On the other hand, Nancy had to be right, too, because she knows that the opposite of absolute freedom is, at least potentially, absolute tyranny, and because she has lived in the Soviet Union, where there is no porn to speak of, and where all sorts of writers are routinely thrown into jail.

Finally, I had to concede, the man from the magazine was right, because he knows that he's got us where we live—and what he sees fit to print has nothing at all to do with it.

Hmm, yes, well, I let my anxiety marinate overnight, and the next day I talked to my friend Charles Rembar, the attorney who escorted both Lady Chatterley and Fanny Hill to their triumphant American debuts, thereby spreading his cloak—and ours—in the mud puddle for a pack of porn hustlers. And I told him what was bothering me. I said that as a feminist I stood with Pamela all the way. But that as an American and a liberal, I stood with Nancy. And that as a writer, there seemed no place for me to stand but in the arms of a man who publishes a disgusting magazine.

"Uh-huh," said my friend, the libertarian attorney. "The First Amendment junkies are out pushing again." Junkies? I echoed. But I already knew what he meant. If the junkies really had their way, we would all O.D. on free expression—because there would be no stopping even the classic mad false-alarmist who yells "Fire!" in a crowded theater. But the junkies can give you their solemn word that they'd put up with anyone saying or writing or advertising anything they know they'll never have to make good on.

The minute our friend the publisher tried to unstaple his centerfold on TV, the network would bleep it—for fear of losing its license. And the minute he tried staging it on the 59th Street Bridge, he'd be safely hauled away for disrupting traffic. We've got the Federal Trade Commission and the Food and Drug Administration "censoring" the man who would say cigarettes are good for kids. And public nuisance laws keeping Lady Godiva from prancing through the midtown area, or Peeping Tom from gluing his eye to the keyholes in the Plaza Hotel. And the First Amendment junkies haven't been out waving their protest petitions to put a stop to any of it.

The truth is that we are already up to our averted eyes and ears in ifs and buts that stop us from expressing ourselves in a thousand disruptive or offensive ways. We are, after all, only relatively free. Which means that the rules can change as fast, or as slowly, as you can invent a newly printable four-letter word for a Supreme Court decision —or a disgusting magazine.

So there it was. Neither Nancy nor the magazine man could hold their freedom guns to my writer's head, and force me to embrace that publisher—or else. When my friend the attorney saved Fanny Hill from a fate worse than publishing death, he predicted that we would have to put up with a lot of bad things. But not with *everything*.

I just wanted Pamela to know that I'm not signing the ⅝¶&⅝! petition. And I wanted Nancy to know that my $c&! conscience is clear.

MARCH, 1977

BARBARA GRIZZUTI HARRISON

f there is one issue on which sane and reasonable people cannot agree to disagree, it is abortion. And even to say that is to make an inflammatory statement: People on both sides of the issue—pro-choice (or pro-abortion) and anti-abortion (or pro-life)—refuse, for the most part, to acknowledge that honor and decency can attach to anyone in the other camp.

You see what I mean: pro-choice/pro-abortion; anti-abortion/pro-life—even the semantics of abortion defeat dialogue. And to occupy a middle ground, to admit to being pushed in one direction, pulled in another, by the claims of conscience, compassion, and reality, is intolerable (others would say unconscionable): People call you names.

Smugness or stridency overwhelms rational discourse; and the voices we hear from most frequently—the loudest voices—are often both smug *and* strident, which is to say arrogant. The arrogance of (some) anti-abortionists is flagrant: to bomb a clinic is not an act conceived in humility. There is another kind of arrogance that expresses itself in the unwarranted assumption that anyone who takes a position against abortion is punitive, anti-sexual, lacking in compassion or mindlessly following an imperative imposed upon her by a "patriarchal" religion.

Partly in an effort to resolve my own psychic tug of war, I sought to hear the quiet voices of conviction from whom we do not often hear.

I thought, while I was at it, that I might as well start at home. I have a seventeen-year-old son, a sixteen-year-old daughter. My daughter said: "Abortion is murder." My son said: "The woman should decide for herself." My daughter, however, added: "It's different from other murders, though, because nobody means to do evil; there isn't any desire to kill."

She was expressing—without knowing it—a sophisticated theological concept: that of subjective, as opposed to objective, sin.

Catholics who do not oppose abortion take refuge in this theological loophole: Miriam Walcott, a lay leader, formerly Catholic chaplain at Brown University, says that while she is "personally repelled by abortion, it is specifically inaccurate to ascribe sin, such as murder, where none is intended within the conscience of the individual choosing to have an abortion."

Catholics for a Free Choice, a national organization with state and local chapters, quotes the Second Vatican Council Declaration on Religious Liberty, saying that people who possess "civil rights are not to be hindered in leading their lives in accordance with their conscience." Joan Harriman, of Catholics for Alternatives, whose activities include "nonjudgmental pregnancy counseling," says that "abortion is often the lesser evil in service of the greater good. I am concerned with when 'ensoulment' takes place; and second-trimester abortions are awful to contemplate. But I can't contemplate making a choice for another woman, either."

A friend I value for her generosity as much as for her integrity says adamantly that if my daughter were to have an abortion, she would refuse to drive her to a clinic: "I couldn't aid and abet you. I'm beginning to feel immoral because I don't try to dissuade friends who are choosing to have abortions. I allow the vehemence of my feelings to embarrass me, so my protest comes out sounding like a little romantic squeak."

My friend is Jewish, and secular; and she "couldn't care less when 'ensoulment' takes place. That's splitting hairs and focusing attention away from the kind of society we're creating. I see abortion as the worst kind of denial of our bodies. We *are* our bodies. If we deny the limits inherent in being a physical creature, society approaches an ideal of mechanical perfection. Mongoloid children or thalidomide babies can live happy and good lives. The trouble is that they are intimations of *our* mortality."

Another friend of mine, an active member of a mainline Protestant church, says, "I know how terribly destructive it is for a mother to give up a child for adoption; and how much adopted children suffer from a sense of identity loss. On one side guilt, on the other side longing. When my extended family gets together, I see three faces that probably would not be here if abortion had been legal twenty years ago—three adopted children. I love those children, and I'm glad they're alive. But I think of their mothers. How terrible it must have been—how terrible it is—for them."

Elizabeth Moore is a welfare mother of six who works for Feminists for Life. When anti-abortionists brought a fetus to a National Organization for Women conference on abortion, she publicly denounced their action on the ground that it was "hurtful to dialogue." Active in the civil rights movement and in the peace movement, she is opposed to "all forms of violence—handguns, nukes, capital punishment."

Clearly not an ultraconservative, she takes issue with what has unfortunately become known as the "pro-family" line: she supports the proposed equal rights amendment, day-care centers, shelters for battered wives and sex education in the public schools. "Abortion," she says, "is not an alternative to sharing jobs and wealth. Abortion does not cure poverty."

Pam Cira, also of Feminists for Life, says, "Feminism grew out of the anger of women who did not want their value to be determined by men. How can we turn around and arbitrarily devalue the fetus? How can I support a Nestlé boycott and turn around and support the destruction of life *in utero*?

"I wish we could talk to one another," she said. "This is a heartbreaking issue, and if we shout, the women's movement will be destroyed."

Some women are reluctant to speak. One very prominent religious reproaches herself for her silence: "A significant amount of blame must go to women like me who delivered the pro-life movement into the hands of people who care nothing about the hungry of the world, nothing about social justice, and who are not pro-life but merely anti-abortion.

"In talking about abortion," she continued, "we are talking about relationships: the relationship between the woman and the father, the relationship between the woman and the fetus, and our relationship to God, whose essence is creation and who calls us to be co-creators in the search for social justice. We say that a woman's body is her own, but we can't forget that moral decisions always come out of the perspective of being related. A human being is never *not* related."

"I was driving once with a group of poor Mexican-American women," she said, "and we passed a car with a bumper that said 'Abortion Is Murder.' By the time we reached our destination, every single woman in that car had admitted to having an abortion. They were scared to tell their husbands they were pregnant, and scared to tell them they were aborting. They had no options. Socially and economically, they saw no way out."

Like my daughter, I believe that abortion is murder. But I would drive my daughter to a clinic. I don't know how to fit this reality into a tidy moral or logical equation. But I do know that the arrogance one hears from the loud voices on both sides of this issue stems from the implicit assumption that the function of morality is to make one comfortable; whereas in fact the function of morality is to make one profoundly uncomfortable—it is only out of that discomfort, that spiritual or psychic itch, vexation and turmoil—that authentic ethical decisions can be made.

MAY, 1980

K. C. COLE

I know few other women who do what I do. What I do is write about science, mainly physics. And to do that, I spend a lot of time reading about science, talking to scientists and struggling to understand physics. In fact, most of the women (and men) I know think me quite queer for actually liking physics. "How can you write about that stuff?" they ask, always somewhat askance. "I could never understand that in a million years." Or more simply, "I hate science."

I didn't realize what an odd creature a woman interested in physics was until a few years ago when a science magazine sent me to Johns Hopkins University in Baltimore for a conference on an electrical phenomenon known as the Hall effect. We sat in a huge lecture hall and listened as physicists talked about things engineers didn't understand, and engineers talked about things physicists didn't understand. What *I* didn't understand was why, out of several hundred young students of physics and engineering in the room, less than a handful were women.

Sometime later, I found myself at the California Institute of Technology reporting on the search for the origins of the universe. I interviewed physicist after physicist, man after man. I asked one young administrator why none of the physicists were women. And he answered: "I don't know, but I suppose it must be something innate. My seven-year-old daughter doesn't seem to be much interested in science."

It was with that experience fresh in my mind that I attended a conference in Cambridge, Mass., on science literacy, or rather the worrisome lack of it in this country today. We three women—a science teacher, a young chemist and myself—sat surrounded by a company of august men. The chemist, I think, first tentatively raised the issue of science illiteracy in women. It seemed like an obvious point. After all, everyone had agreed over and over again that scientific knowledge these days was a key factor in economic power. But as soon as she made the point, it became clear that we women had committed a grievous social error. Our genders were suddenly showing; we had interrupted the serious talk with a subject unforgivably silly.

For the first time, I stopped being puzzled about why there weren't any women in science and began to be angry. Because if science is a search for answers to fundamental questions then it hardly seems frivolous to find out why women are excluded. Never mind the economic consequences.

A lot of the reasons women are excluded are spelled out by the Massachusetts Institute of Technology experimental physicist Vera Kistiakowsky in a recent article in *Physics Today* called "Women in Physics: Unnecessary, Injurious and Out of Place?". The title was taken from a nineteenth-century essay written in opposition to the appointment of a female mathematician to a professorship at the University of Stockholm. "As decidedly as two and two make four," a woman in mathematics is a "monstrosity," concluded the writer of the essay.

Dr. Kistiakowsky went on to discuss the factors that make women in science today, if not monstrosities, at least oddities. Contrary to much popular opinion, one of those is *not* an innate difference in the scientific ability of boys and girls. But early conditioning does play a stubborn and subtle role. A recent *Nova* program, "The Pinks and the Blues," documented how girls and boys are treated differently from birth—the boys always encouraged in more physical kinds of play, more active explorations of their environments. Sheila Tobias, in her book, *Math Anxiety*, showed how the games boys play help them to develop an intuitive understanding of speed, motion and mass.

The main sorting out of the girls from the boys in science seems to happen in junior high school. As a friend who teaches in a science museum said, "By the time we get to electricity, the boys already have had some experience with it. But it's unfamiliar to the girls." Science books draw on boys' experiences. "The examples are all about throwing a baseball at such and such a speed," said my stepdaughter, who barely escaped being a science drop-out.

The most obvious reason there are not many more women in science is that women are discriminated against as a class, in promotions, salaries and hirings, a conclusion reached by a recent analysis by the National Academy of Sciences.

Finally, said Dr. Kistiakowsky, women are simply made to feel out of place in science. Her conclusion was supported by a Ford Foundation study by Lynn H. Fox on the problems of women in mathematics. When students were asked to choose among six reasons accounting for girls' lack of interest in math, the girls rated this statement second: "Men do not want girls in the mathematical occupations."

A friend of mine remembers winning a Bronxwide mathematics competition in the second grade. Her friends—both boys and girls— warned her that she shouldn't be good at math: "You'll never find a boy who likes you." My friend continued nevertheless to excel in math and science, won many awards during her years at the Bronx High School of Science, and then earned a full scholarship to Harvard. After one year of Harvard science, she decided to major in English.

When I asked her why, she mentioned what she called the "macho mores" of science. "It would have been O.K. if I'd had someone to talk to," she said. "But the rules of comportment were such that you never admitted you didn't understand. I later realized that even the boys didn't get everything clearly right away. You had to stick with it until it had time to sink in. But for the boys, there was a payoff in suffering through the hard times, and a kind of punishment—a shame —if they didn't. For the girls it was O.K. not to get it, and the only payoff for sticking it out was that you'd be considered a freak."

Science is undeniably hard. Often, it can seem quite boring. It is unfortunately too often presented as laws to be memorized instead of mysteries to be explored. It is too often kept a secret that science, like art, takes a well-developed esthetic sense. Women aren't the only ones who say, "I hate science."

That's why everyone who goes into science needs a little help from friends. For the past ten years, I have been getting more than a little help from a friend who is a physicist. But my stepdaughter—who earned the highest grades ever recorded in her California high school on the math Scholastic Aptitude Test—flunked calculus in her first year at Harvard. When my friend the physicist heard about it, he said, "Harvard should be ashamed of itself."

What he meant was that she needed that little extra encouragement that makes all the difference. Instead, she got that little extra discouragement that makes all the difference.

"In the first place, all the math teachers are men," she explained. "In the second place, when I met a boy I liked and told him I was taking chemistry, he immediately said: 'Oh, you're one of those science types.' In the third place, it's just a kind of a social thing. The math clubs are full of boys and you don't feel comfortable joining."

In other words, she was made to feel unnecessary, and out of place.

A few months ago, I accompanied a male colleague from the science museum where I sometimes work to a lunch of the history of science faculty at the University of California. I was the only woman there, and my presence for the most part was obviously and rudely ignored. I was so surprised and hurt by this that I made an extra effort to speak knowledgeably and well. At the end of the lunch, one of the professors turned to me in all seriousness and said: "Well, K.C., what do the women think of Carl Sagan?" I replied that I had no idea what "the women" thought about anything. But now I know what I should have said: I should have told him that his comment was unnecessary, injurious and out of place.

DECEMBER, 1981

MAGGIE SCARF

"How's your wife been since the operation?" asked our family doctor, in the course of a routine physical. My husband looked at him in surprise: "My wife hasn't *had* an operation," he replied.

Later, we laughed about this incident. "Maybe," I proposed, "when a man is in his early forties, that's just a conversation starter. Instead of asking 'What do you think of this crazy weather we're having?' he asks how your wife is doing since her operation."

It was true, come to think of it, that if I hadn't had surgery it wasn't due to a lack of invitations. I, like many perfectly fit and healthy American women, had been duly offered a few "routine surgical procedures" during the course of my early and middle adult years.

Medical Scene: The Doctor and the Patient have been discussing various contraceptive options.

Doctor: Perhaps, Mrs. X, a longer view of the situation is in order. You are now in your latter thirties; tell me, are you and your husband considering having more children in the future?

Patient: Ever, you mean? (Pauses.) I suppose that we won't . . .

Doctor: Then I might advise a laparoscopic sterilization—what used to be called a tubal ligation, which was a more serious operation. The procedure's changed considerably; it's now very simple, very streamlined.

Patient: What would that kind of thing involve?

Doctor: Basically, just a tiny incision in the belly, which makes it possible for us to go in with an instrument which is, ah, something like a tiny periscope. Then, locating the tubes, and burning them with a brief, high-intensity heat. That's it then: no more need for contraceptives of any sort. But nothing else is changed—the ovaries function, menstruation continues and so forth. (He smiles encouragingly.)

Patient: Still . . . making that incision—doesn't that involve anesthesia? (She looks doubtful.) And going to the hospital?

Doctor: Yes, but just for a day for the procedure and one for recovery, then you'd have the whole thing behind you. (He smiles again.)

Patient: But general anesthesia—isn't that supposed to be dangerous?

Doctor: Depends. In a medical facility like ours, one needn't worry—no problem.

Patient: Still, I have a funny feeling; it's almost as if one were a machine, with a lot of disposable spare parts or something. It just seems odd to mess around like that, to say: "Well I'm done having children, so let's chuck this useless organ out."

There is a short, uncomfortable silence.

Doctor (stiffly): As I said, this is a very simple, conservative procedure. Just that brief burn and that's it. The normal monthly flow, everything, continues as usual.

Patient: My husband felt that way, too. I mean, he was considering a vasectomy and he just . . .

Doctor: Well, he was right. That wouldn't be a wise idea.

Patient: A vasectomy? Why not?

Doctor: Because you, at your age, probably should not have more children. But he, at the same age, could—safely.

Patient (astonished): But, we're *married.*

Doctor: Yes, now. But suppose there were some sort of an accident —say you and your children were in a crash of some kind, a year from now, a month from now. And all of you were killed? He might wish to remarry, to start another family—and he'd have ruined his chances of doing so.

Patient: I don't think that would be a problem.

Doctor: You can't predict—unforeseen things do happen.

Patient: What I meant was that my husband probably wouldn't want another family.

There is a long, uncomfortable silence.

Doctor (annoyed): My own wife is a year younger than you are. And we're having our first child in a few months. And she is having a laparoscopic sterilization, right after the baby's birth.

Patient (rising to leave): Well, that's her body, and her decision, I guess.

The physician, in this vignette, obviously had his own agenda. He was offering his patient—correctly—a surgical contraceptive option; but incorrectly, he had made her decision in advance. He was, moreover, characterizing the surgery in terms of benefits alone; he wasn't allowing any real discussion of risks. And he was, finally, offended when his patient failed to follow his clear directive: he behaved as though his competence were under attack.

This doctor's view of the "good patient" (and probably of the "good woman" as well) was that of someone much more docile and compliant. And many female patients do, undoubtedly, behave in ways that he would have found far more appropriate: they follow orders, without raising questions that might seem mistrustful or demanding.

"What stupefies me," said Dr. Burton B. Caldwell, an endocrinologist and assistant professor of obstetrics and gynecology at Yale University, "is how many women will simply go to a doctor and do whatever it is he tells her to do even though she may just have heard about him from a friend or even walked in from the street, knowing nothing whatever about him. The next thing you know the person's in surgery, having a D and C. She's putting her life on the line."

Female patients, either because they're intimidated by the superior knowledge of the physician or because they want to be seen as cooperative, are often uninformed about the actual risks to which they are being subjected. That laparoscopic tubal sterilization, for example: one woman in every 10,000 dies during the procedure (not a big risk unless you're that one). There are, also, a number of associated morbidities: the surgeon might hit a blood vessel, the uterus, the bowel or the bladder by mistake. Errors happen.

"The operator is working with a tiny periscope—the laparoscope —which he must insert blindly," Dr. Caldwell said. No matter how skilled the surgeon, there are risks to the individual.

There are, certainly, situations in which benefits will outweigh risks: if, for example, a woman has found no other form of contraception that is effective and she's approaching forty—a pregnancy at age forty involves risks to her that are even greater. The patient ought, however, to insist on examining both sides of the medical ledger in advance.

The ubiquitous D and C (dilation and curettage) is another case in point. According to Dr. Nathan Kase, professor of obstetrics and gynecology at Yale, the great majority of therapeutic D and C operations are unnecessary. There are office procedures that are less costly, less dangerous and yield the information that is needed.

"D and C surgeries are often a knee-jerk reaction to heavy bleeding," he said. The problem, though, is often hormonal in origin and so scraping the lining of the uterus will do nothing beneficial. What it does do is lead to another D and C and another, and finally to a hysterectomy. "It's now necessary," said Dr. Kase, "because the normal basal layer of the uterus, the endometrium, is gone."

Hysterectomy is, of course, major abdominal surgery—and America is the hysterectomy capital of the world. A woman living in this country is more than twice as likely to have her uterus removed surgically than is a woman living in Great Britain.

I don't, by any means, want to write the paranoiac's guide to surgery—to suggest that every operation is, ipso facto, one that isn't necessary. But I do believe it would be wiser if we called a surgery a surgery —not a "small procedure"—and stopped to understand the reasons for its happening. We should look hard before we leap upon the table.

JANUARY, 1981

MARY KAY BLAKELY

I used to be an unbeliever. I questioned the integrity of an economic system that valued women's work only half as much as men's. I was—and this seems almost preposterous to admit now—dissatisfied with the lot of women.

Before I reached enlightenment, I suffered from a common form of math anxiety caused by statistics from the Department of Labor. I was easily susceptible to depression whenever the words "supply and demand" came up in conversation. I kept getting lost in the void of the earnings gap. Years of investigation about women revealed many things to me, but didn't make sense of those numbers: Women earn 59 percent of what men earn. Until last week, I was like a haunted woman—devils of injustice chasing me, demons of inequity plaguing me.

My conversion happened unexpectedly, during a business meeting with a highly placed administrator. I had noticed—because skeptics habitually pay attention to damning facts—that the women employed by his prestigious institution were being paid much less money than the men. Like most unbelievers I was there to complain about the inequity. That's the major problem with those who don't have the gift of faith in our economic system. They have their visions trained on the temporal facts of their lives.

The discussion began predictably enough. With benign paternal tolerance, he reviewed the intricate principles of economics, the baffling nuances of budgets, the confounding factors behind the salary schedules. With the monosyllabic vocabulary educators use to address slow learners, he explained the familiar platitudes.

He invoked the dogma of salary surveys—the objective instruments used to determine what "the market will bear." They prove, beyond a shadow of doubt, that women workers are "a dime a dozen." That's reality, he reported almost regretfully, that's how life is outside

of Eden. Practitioners of sound business—the members of the faith, so
to speak—can in good conscience pay them no more. If he didn't adhere
to the precepts of salary surveys, it would cause economic chaos. Other
women, in other institutions, would begin to think they were worth
more, too. The brethren in other administrations would expel him from
the faith.

"You have to think about what the job is worth, not the person in it,"
he cautioned me. It always gets you into trouble, thinking about what
a person is worth. He warned me against engaging in the fallacy of
"comparing apples and oranges," a comparison odious to the members
of the faith. It is only the unbelievers, the kumquats, who try to argue
for the fruits of their labors. Mixing the categories would produce
uncontrollable hybrids on the salary scale. Men are men and women
are women and their paychecks are just further evidence of their vast
biological differences, the powerful influence of the X and Y chromosomes.

I confess, I had heard these tenets of the faith many times before.
It was the kind of conversation that might inspire the vision of a lawsuit. So it wasn't with an open heart that I asked the question one more
time. How could he accept women's invaluable contributions to the
success of his institution, witness their obvious dedication, and withhold
their just rewards?

He paused, regarding me carefully, deliberating, apparently, on
whether I was prepared to hear the truth, to embrace the amazing
mystery of women's wages. Then slowly, respectfully, he revealed the
fantastic reason.

Women came seeking positions with an intense longing for work,
but with a paucity of credentials and experience. They were filled with
gratitude when they were offered a job. They worked in a pleasant
environment, doing meaningful work, and had the privilege of writing
the name of the prestigious institution on their résumés. They received
such an extraordinary sense of well-being, it would be almost a violation

of female sensibilities to compensate them with cold, hard cash. Instead, they received something much more valuable; they earned a "psychic income."

I heard my voice becoming hysterical. Hysteria is not at all un-common during conversions. I was loud—perhaps I was even shouting —when I asked him how much of his income was "psychic." Like many doubters, I didn't immediately see the light. I thought one of us was mad.

But not an hour later, enlightenment came. I was in a car dealership, chatting with the amiable mechanic who had repaired my transmission. He seemed to enjoy his job, especially when he handed me the bill. I gasped, knowing that the balance in my checkbook wouldn't cover the charge. Then I remembered my "psychic income" and that people who love their work, who are dedicated to it, are better paid with congratula-tions and a pat on the back. I told him what a wonderful job he did, how much I appreciated it. And then I wrote a "psychic check."

Suddenly, I was filled with the spirit. A happiness, a release flooded over me. I realized that every act of spending my "psychic income" was an act of faith. I had so much catching up to do. I worked steadily to increase my state of grace. Immediately, I applied for a loan at the employee credit union at the prestigious institution, authorizing payments through "psychic payroll deductions." I used my "psychic credit cards" to charge two pairs of spiritual Adidas for my kids, whose real toes were poking through their real tennis shoes.

I was filled with a fervor to spread the Word. At a rally of work-ing women, I brought them the message of "psychic incomes," and many converts came into the fold.

Nurses, who had an extraordinary love for their work, felt "psychic bonuses" coming to them. Their sense of self-esteem expanded miraculously, and they no longer bowed down to the false gods in the hospitals.

Clerical workers grasped the theory of "psychic work for psychic pay" and began typing only intangible letters, filing transcendental folders, and making celestial phone calls.

Prior to their conversions, working mothers thought they had to do all the housework, because their earnings were only half of their husbands' salaries. But when they learned how to bank on their "psychic incomes," they never cooked dinner again. They served their families supernatural pot roasts.

Of course, everyone will not accept the gift of the Word. There are those who will try to persecute us for practicing our faith. We must learn to smile serenely at the unfortunate creditors who lack the vision. We must have a charitable attitude toward the bill collectors whose interests are rooted in temporal assets. Beware of the pharisees who pay spiritual salaries but still demand physical work.

And judge not the angry women who file the interminable lawsuits, who still rail against the status quo. Their daily struggle to exist prevents them from accepting the good news. Remember that there, but for the gift of "psychic economics," go we.

MARCH, 1981

A. G. MOJTABAI

Question: *You are guilty, you know.*
A: Undoubtedly. What is it this time?
Q: *Of compromise, conciliation, yes, I'd even say of collaboration with the oppressor.*

A: Which particular oppressor? Would you mind—I mean, what exactly did I do?

Q: *When you lived in Iran—and that was long before the present regime—you put on the veil.*

A: I did.

Q: *Not just once, either. You can't tell me you put it on just to see how it felt.*

A: I put it on as often as required. I was a foreigner trying to fit in. You know? When I went into a Catholic church, I covered my head. So it's the same sort of thing. In Iran, when the situation called for it, I put on the chador. I thought of it as nothing more than one of those little concessions to circumstance that social life exacts from each of us now and then. It was nothing more than having a sense of occasion. I put on the chador for funerals, as did all the women in the family (whether young or old, old-fashioned or Westernized). When visiting a mosque or shrine that was not open to tourists, I put on the chador.

Q: *Funerals I can understand, but for anything else you could have chosen not to.*

A: I *could* have, I could have stayed away. But the chador was my passport to what otherwise I would not have been privileged to see. And it isn't that oppressive as garments go. It's more like a body-length kerchief than anything else I can name. It is a bit inconvenient, though, I must admit. The problem is in its lack of fastenings. So the ends are either bitten together and held with the teeth (cure for an idle tongue), or clutched together (keeping one hand out of mischief). It was holding or biting the thing closed, while managing to walk or talk, that was a nuisance.

Q: *All diversionary. The problem—the question before us—is your putting on the veil, not once but repeatedly. I'd like to suggest a certain amount of self-deception, bad faith, play-acting.*

A: There was some of that. Play-acting, I mean.

Q: *That's right, admit to the lesser charge.*

A: Well, let's at least look at the play-acting part. Sure, it's there. It's part of the reason that men in drag take to the chador. And prostitutes. Although, with prostitutes, it's also for self-protection. But coquettish women also use the chador to great effect. Beautiful eyes, but so-so nose? Banish the nose and expose the eyes; let the rest be inferred from the eyes.

In Pakistan, where women are often completely veiled, wearing either little gauzy curtains over the face, or a cover of heavy, coarse fabric with only a crocheted grillwork for the eyes to peep through, I was struck by the fact that hands and feet were elaborately ornamented, even bejeweled, and intricately painted with henna. And, given these conditions, how provocative the slightest exposure becomes! Where the erotic is denied release, *everything* becomes suffused with erotic feeling. And the prohibition gives it all an extra poignancy. Only think what the sight of a woman's ankle once meant, and then think of nudist camps.

Q: *You seem to be straying again. The point at issue is the veil and you. You and the veil. You put on the chador. I would go further —you enjoyed it. Hmmm? Just a little bit?*

A: Well—I have to confess to a little of that. It was something of a masquerade. I was no one, I was anyone I wanted to be, I was a native —I belonged. And then, you have to remember, unlike so many women *condemned* to the chador, I could take it off when I chose. For me, it was always something of a costume. For my mother-in-law, it was something very different, something closely bound up with her sense of self. It was more than the fact that she was a devout Muslim. The chador seemed to be a sort of second skin for her. She even wore the chador in the house, toga-fashion, although it is never required in the privacy of family quarters.

During the reign of Riza Shah Pahlevi, father of the recently deposed Shah, there was an effort to modernize Iran as Kemal Ataturk had modernized Turkey, and there was an active campaign to eliminate the chador. Gendarmes were stationed in the bazaar to spray acid on the chadors of the women passing through. The drive was not a success; women, especially poor women, refused to change. My mother-in-law simply changed to a floor-length dress and scarf, at once complying with the letter of the new directive and dissenting from its spirit. The point, after all, had been modernization.

For poor women, who have few clothes, the chador is a great equalizer, a sort of uniform; it matters little what you are wearing underneath. But you were asking?

Q: *You enjoyed it.*

A: A little, yes, in spite of every scruple. I didn't enjoy it in the heat, when every added layer was a burden. I didn't enjoy it in the wind, or stepping into places where foreigners entered at peril, when I had to hold on for dear life. But when the covering held secure, and I gazed out, safe in my anonymity, that was something. I felt—somehow beyond reproach, invulnerable, snug, enclosed. I felt curiously *free*. Dead to the world, I was all alive.

It was a little like that old dream of invisibility. You know—wishing for moments when you can see without being seen? Doesn't everyone have that fantasy at one time or another? It's partly a dream of superiority, looking out, judging everyone you see, while remaining beyond judgment yourself. But it's also, in large part, motivated by genuine curiosity. And it's a writer's dream, isn't it, to become a nothing, a transparency, a clear lens—no longer a murky, distorting medium? The less intrusive you are, the more the people around you can be themselves.

But, of course, I could put off the veil largely when I chose; I was not doomed to invisibility—I mustn't forget that. And, in Pakistan, I did not put on the *burqa*, ever—I never covered my face. But, then, Pakistan wasn't a real test for me; I wasn't a native-by-adoption there, and was not expected to conform to local custom.

Q: *You have some qualms about covering the face?*

A: Yes. There, I think, I'd draw the line. And the custom of blackening the faces of women in news photographs, recommended by the Saudi Arabian Government in its tightening of Islamic law—that chills me through and through. Blacking out the face—canceling out— the sense that a woman's presence in the outside world can only be a disruptive force, *that* I find frightening.

Q: *Yet you put on the chador?*

A: Yes, but you see, the matter wasn't simple.

Q: *It never is.*

A: One small concession, as I said.

Q: *Which leads to yet another, and another.*

JUNE, 1980

NORMA ROSEN

My friend B has a tighter schedule than most but has always enjoyed it. She is up at 5 A.M., runs to a jogging track on the grounds of a neighborhood school, runs there from 5:30 to 6:00 A.M., then runs home and breakfasts with her school-age children, drives to her full-time job at a school in Queens, is home in time to swim a half hour's worth of laps in a Y pool, then to supper and the evening chores of a parent and householder and the paperwork of a junior-high-school science teacher.

A minor physical impairment that would make this day impossible for her is mitigated and controlled by the adherence to the regimen of physical exercise. The necessity becomes a pleasure, too; she enjoys the exercise and the first bloom of morning it reveals to her. Her body rewards her with health and stamina, and her friends have learned not to telephone after 9, when she's more likely than not to be asleep.

One day while B was jogging in the dawn she felt strong arms fling themselves from behind about her neck and drag her down. At first, without thinking, she fought back. She and her assailant fell to the ground and B kept moving. A saying from her childhood sounded in her head, from the time when boys made sneering remarks about rape—"You can't thread a moving needle"—and she kept moving with all the strength of her excellent muscular body.

She screamed and fought so long and hard—rolling, kicking, biting—that it must have become clear to her assailant that he would have to kill her to prevail. Suddenly he was up and sprinting. She leapt to her feet without seeing anything about his appearance except, in one horror-struck instant, that he was a jogger, too.

He ran to the lot, she to the road. As in a nightmare she knew that she had been released only to be trapped again. She would have to be swifter on foot than he in his car, which in his rage he would surely use to run her down. But she reached the road before him, encountered a woman jogging there in time to warn her from the track and saw a car race by, unidentifiable in the semidarkness of dawn.

If B had not been in fine physical shape, if she were not a runner and a swimmer, she could not have been that "moving needle." She would have been overcome. We have, alas, great evidence now; we know what can happen physically and psychically to a woman who is overcome in this way. But B got away, narrowly. How does an escape this narrow affect a life?

In B's case, this was not immediately discernible. First, her schedule had to be fulfilled. By the time she reached home, bathed, dressed, breakfasted with children, her husband was descending the stairs to begin his morning. She had barely time to tell him what had happened before she took off for work, where an early conference, the first of several in a tightly packed teaching day, was waiting.

Finally a colleague noticed her bruises, her trembling. Pressed, she told the story again, briefly, en route to another appointment. She must call the police, she was told, even though no identification was possible. She must talk about it, to someone who would understand the psychic harm.

So she telephoned her husband at his office and asked him to report the event to the police because she had no time. Nor had she time for a therapist. That evening she received a dozen guests at her house for a prewedding dinner for her oldest son, his bride- and in-laws-to-be. At odd moments she ran upstairs to her bedroom, shut the door and sobbed, then washed her face and came down again. She spoke to no one there about what had happened, for in three days her son was to be married and not only was there no time, there was also no tone of voice in which she felt it could be said.

She decided that she would not—could not—change her schedule. Or give up her beautiful mornings. Or ruin her health. Or cripple her psyche with fear. So she began to run again, same place, same time. Except of course that nothing is the same—the bloom is off the morning. She runs in fear that her assailant may wait for her, watch her, know where she lives and where her children are home alone after school. Nevertheless, she runs—with her dog, a golden retriever. We know what they are: if they had ten tails to wag and twelve tongues to lick with, that would not be enough to show all the friendliness in their unsuspecting hearts.

"If someone jumped me," B says, "the dog would probably leap up and kiss him. But I know he wouldn't run off. I wouldn't be alone. That helps."

When I ask, like others, why she doesn't see a therapist to help her over this period, her eyes fill with tears and she answers that there's no point in taking the time since it won't help apprehend her assailant.

The shame women once felt in speaking up about rape has been largely routed. My friend is not ashamed; she hasn't the time to speak. What women set out to do they have done: they engage with the world as strenuously as men; they have banished the image of themselves as weaker beings. B knows very well that when trauma assaults the psyche anyone may become for a while, woman or man, a weaker being, deserving of shelter and respite. But she will not—cannot—stop to make her own claim on that healing. It is as if she is saying: "I've had to fight to pull the pieces of my life into some kind of balance. If I linger over this trauma everything might fall apart."

Some people say, "Running is my life," but that's hyperbole. In B's case it's true. Running is built into her schedule because there's no room for walking. She has had to run for her life and she can't stop running now.

There was a time when a woman who grew exceedingly uncomfortable in a bad situation could quietly slip from her chair in a graceful fall to the floor. In a twinkling she would be removed from a room that had grown too full of boring or offensive speakers. She was considered to have done an honorable thing—fainted—and would not be expected to return to the scene of her distress.

There was a time when a woman could grow melancholic or unaccountably invalided (one thinks at once of those nineteenth-century figures Elizabeth Barrett or Alice James) as another form of response to unbearable situations. They paid a price, of course—melancholia and disability extract their own cost—but in an age of little real shelter for women from child-bearing and heavy domestic and social duties, even among the well-to-do, these were shelters of a kind. Within them Barrett could write poetry, James could be a memorable diarist.

Who is the modern woman? She faints not, neither does she grow melancholy. Her price is far above rubies. She keeps on running.

JANUARY, 1983

Between
the Sexes

ERICA ABEEL

Out of circulation since a year ago Christmas and stalked by animalish urges, Jane asked around among her friends not hoarding men if they knew any suitable ones. They answered no. Finally Xenia the worldly said she did know a man who was in town from Minneapolis, where he was a part-time surrogate for a sex clinic. Should she, Xenia asked Jane, send him round. Though in no position to be difficult, Jane unhesitatingly answered. No. Maybe. Jane reflected. Here at last was the bottom line difference between men and women: A needy (or greedy) man might resort to a lady of pleasure or freelance surrogate (even enjoying it, to judge by testimonials). But a needy woman would stop just short of corresponding expediencies, which, to be sure, aren't often available, there being no call for them, except among characters in *The Delta of Venus*.

Then, too, Jane just couldn't picture a surrogate in her living room. The children in their pajamas would tootle in with a trayful of assorted teas, offering the surrogate a choice of Pelican Punch or Red Zinger, straight up or with honey, then show him their *Faeries* book, and—oh dear, *no*.

Pleased to have by-stepped neurotic indecision, Jane had yet to solve, like so many women, the larger problem: how to manage a libidinous appetite over which she had as much control as Phaeton over the maddened steeds of Apollo's chariot.

Male sex drive, without an object of its affections, is a widely acknowledged fact of life, respectable even, catered to in the best neighborhoods. But female sex drive without an object is not nearly so acceptable as today's verbal egalitarianism might suggest. In fact, female sexuality is thought not to exist at all until summoned by a princely embrace. (Perhaps this misapprehension is encouraged by the fact that there's no icon of female lust equivalent to a man's.) And if it does exist? Unseemly, sordid, inadmissible. Women still do not have permission to be abstractly sexual—and women themselves often withhold the permission.

Jane's friends, for example, wonder why she can't just concentrate on career and children; they call her a man junkie. And when Jane says that Freud was mistaken, that she's unable to sublimate libido into creativity, that she's more creative when gratified, her friends say: Pshaw, it's love you want, not sex (No, protests Jane, for now it's sex); or they say, Think of all the women who went through the war.

Of course, anatomy is, if not destiny, a factor: men, said Freud, are born with more libido than women are. In adolescence, concurs the sex therapist Helen Kaplan, the male sex drive is the more powerful. But by forty, that drive is subsiding; he is becoming, she said, "more stimulus-dependent, more easily dissuaded." While the woman's drive, at forty, is peaking. And since blessedly exempt from man's curse, the performance imperative, she may well have a greater potential for sensuous pleasure than he.

You'd think that the sensuous woman, perking with potential, could actively instigate encounters of the close kind. Doubtless, men of the age of John Travolta would welcome such overtures, and an occasional riper fellow might, too, if only because a) it relieves him of the relentless burden of taking the initiative (although at least that consumed calories); b) it's flattering, especially if he's no Robert Redford; and, best of all, c) he wouldn't, for once, risk rejection.

But many more men find a sexually assertive woman pushy, or at best "amusing." For a stubbornly entrenched etiquette sentences women to passivity. Let's not be deluded by literary licentiousness. If the lusty heroines of *Blue Skies, No Candy, Scruples* or *Sweet Savage Love* stepped off the pages into the world, frankly pursuing gratification, they'd be more welcome on the 42d Street strip than in the L-shaped rooms of presentable men. The mating dance, in which the male still gets all the fancy steps, is not very different from the way

Freud's disciple Marie Bonaparte perceived it some fifty years ago: "The role of everything female, from the ovum to the beloved, is a waiting one."

But some women lack a vocation for waiting. Like Crazy Jane, whose better-adjusted friends find it worrisome that a person of such colossal naïveté is loose, so to speak, in New York. First she flung herself at a sensitive philanderer who had been involved with numerous women in media. But after much verbal foreplay, he confessed he was liberating himself from the conquest mentality and didn't want sex without love. Next she came on to an overweight wizard of finance, only to learn he was attending a sex clinic due to lack of desire.

Jane envies the simple life of the lady firefly, who simply flashes her light to get things rolling.

Xenia has tried to explain to Jane that unalloyed female hunger acts as anti-musk, and is not only unappealing but grotesque. That the active, aggressive men she favors want to make the moves, that she shouldn't steal their thunder, that she should, instead, seduce, invite, exude receptivity. "*That* old game? On the eve of the eighties?" Jane asks. "Exactly," sighs Xenia, wondering if Jane has lived her life in Outer Mongolia—"*That* old game. What your mother taught you."

But Crazy Jane only finds all this incomprehensible. After all, she, like many women at different stages of their development, likes lusty men. François Truffaut was not merely wishfully thinking but right on target in *The Man Who Loved Women*: A compulsive womanizer, neither handsome nor successful, is irresistible to women. On ideological grounds, of course, these fellows on screen or off are disgusting. But women's yen for the ardor, the eagerness and, above all, the *knowingness* of the libertine lies beyond, or, rather, beneath, ideology. The flesh has its reasons.

Incorrigible Jane now stagnates in a swamp of unrequited desire. Such remedies as running around the reservoir and cold showers, because so physical, only up her libido. The world exists to suggest—

from the gray snowlight of Sunday morning to the smiling complicity of last night's string quartet. She'd be better off, Jane thinks, minus her midsection, from solar plexus to kneecap, as in some Magritte-style painting.

Fortunately, most women are better adapted to the sexual inequity of our times. Like Xenia, they feel aroused only when there's a viable man in their lives. In fact, Xenia is so well synchronized her libido plummets, she has noticed, when the viable man goes out of town on business. (Theoretically, his plummets, too, though this has not been verified.) Xenia jokes that she is just like the female rabbit going hippity-hop in the forest: it only ovulates in the presence of the male.

Xenia has also explained to Jane that even after they've launched the affair, men find flagrantly sexual women taxing, the office being demanding enough; that they flee the highly sexed woman by taking refuge in sports, participatory and spectator. She, Xenia, having lived and suffered, figured all this out after a lover told her, "Though I adore your appetite, it would scare most men"—and then jogged out of her life. Hippity-hop.

FEBRUARY, 1979

LINDA BIRD FRANCKE

I t was the kind of party where everyone knew everyone else, except no one knew me. Deciding to utilize my assertiveness training, I clenched my muscles and aimed for a tanned, mustachioed blue-eyed man, whose T-shirt alligator rippled on a most beguiling ridge of muscle. We hit it off immediately, bantering, laughing, cracking entre-nous jokes before we even had an entre-nous.

My popularity ego, whose pendulum swing can flash from "nobody loves me" to "everybody loves me" in the time it takes to say "white wine," soared to a new high when we were joined by an even more attractive man, whose white-milk teeth and sun-wrinkled brown eyes positively enveloped me in warmth and interest. Heady with proof of my alluring femininity, I left the party reluctantly, determined to unearth the phone numbers of my newfound swains. The next day I discovered why they had been so warm and cozy. For some time the two had been a couple and that very day they had just bought their first house together.

I have almost come to the conclusion that there just aren't any men left these days that are worth the salt to put on a pigeon's tail. In more incidences than I care to remember, the men to whom I've been irresistibly attracted would have been more attracted to my brother, had I had one. The reason is obvious. I am drawn to them because of the absence of sexual tension, a cease-fire in the war between the sexes. They are attracted to me for the exact same reason—which all adds up, in an ongoing relationship, to absolute zero.

. . .

A woman can't look for peace in a relationship with a man because if she finds it, she doesn't have a man. And vice versa. The trick is to organize the war games so that the body count is minimal.

In some cases, the war is undeclared, and, like Vietnam, the outcome indecisive.

In the early morning sunshine last week, I overheard a conversation on the tennis court between two married women who apparently hadn't seen each other in a while. Knowing it was not only insensitive but out of it to say "How's Ralph?" the server asked instead, "Are you still married?" "I don't know," the receiver replied. "What about you?" "Well, sort of, I guess," the server said before double-faulting. Though the divorce rate has spiraled, the numbers of semi-marriages that don't fit anywhere on the statisticians' charts has probably passed the undiagnosed plague level of the Middle Ages.

Where the rules of the war games are articulated, if not the strategies, the men appear to have left the bargaining table altogether. As women have come bursting out of their kitchens, armed with determination, degrees and Title IX to protect them against discrimination, men seem to be climbing over each other's backs to get out of the way.

My old friend Sally, who has made a name for herself in educational films in New York, had dinner in Los Angeles recently with another old friend, who has made a much bigger name for himself in television. Settling down over late-night brandies, she was stunned when he turned to her and said, "You know, I can't imagine being married to you. I'd panic and run." Why, Sally asked, hurt that their friendship, which had never even touched on the subject of marriage, seemed suddenly flawed. "You're a star," he said. But, Sally pointed out, he was the one getting quoted in *Time* and *Newsweek* and was probably earning $100,000 a year to her $20,000. "Maybe so," he said declaratively, "but underneath it all I think you're smarter than I am."

.   .   .

What lurking terrors possess men when their women achieve success on their own? Oh, we've read to a newsprint fault about Bella and Martin and Mary and Harding and Farrah and Lee, but what about my pal Lucy, who has achieved considerable stature in publishing and whose equally successful husband has retreated to bed in a seemingly terminal state of depression?

And then there is Maggie, of whom I am very fond, who got along just fine with her executive husband until, with his support, she went back to work and quickly ascended the corporate ladder. Her husband, though he appeared to be proud of his Galatea in public, was evidently quite the opposite in private, and for the last three years of their marriage had not slept with her. "It was fine until I got my expense account," said a still puzzled and recently separated Maggie. "He couldn't stand it when I took him and some of my clients out to dinner. He said he felt like my wife."

The truth of the matter is, that in spite of Virginia Slims, we haven't come such a long way, babies. Oh, on the surface things have changed with D-day speed. There are girls in the Little League and the Boy's Club, and women welders working on twelve-story steel skeletons. But when these women come home to their men, there is a lurking unease and things haven't changed so much. Scratch almost any man, and you'll find wistful memories of his mother darning socks and cooking Sunday lunch and sending his father off in the morning with swept lapels and always, but always, being there to support and encourage her family. Women are still doing most of those things, but they are leaving the problem of lapel lint to the suit-wearers and racing for the front door themselves.

It's a brave new world and the rules have changed, if not the participants. "Independent" and "assertive" have become threatening words in this new war, where the body count is mounting. "Linda," my mother worried me when I told her I'd been promoted at *Newsweek*, "you've got to learn to be more dependent."

It's no wonder, really, that so many men have turned to other men for solace and sport, becoming conscientious objectors in a war they prefer not to enter. But what is puzzling is why so many heterosexual men—successful and highly visible men—are opting out of the skirmish as well, when presumably the liberation of women was to be their own liberation, too. Humpty Dumpty has had a great fall. And neither the king's women nor the king's men can figure out how to put Humpty together again.

SEPTEMBER, 1977

JENNIFER ALLEN

am eight or nine years old, and my brother's friend Phil is sleeping over. Phil is as tall as a tree, with huge feet and hands and a prematurely deep voice that make him seem, at thirteen, almost like a grown man. Like my brother, Phil loves rock music. He wants to buy a motorcycle. He dresses like a slob. He is my dream man.

Phil rarely speaks to me, but he and my brother and I have pillow fights whenever he sleeps over. On this night, we are in the basement pummeling each other with our bed pillows. My brother gets distracted by something, so Phil and I go at it, one on one, holding onto our pillows and thwacking away. Phil smiles when he starts tickling and pummeling me and I, up too late, giggling too loud, flattered beyond belief, am in a state of bliss close to frenzy. Suddenly, with a force that stops me dead, I have a thought: This activity could get me pregnant. I am so stunned that I blurt it out loud: "I might get a baby from this!"

I knew the accepted wisdom as to where babies came from. I had had some sex education in school; my mother had read me a library book that covered the basics. In the book, sex was a show of affection, harmless as a bear hug, but remote. First you had to fall in love, get married, decide to have children. In sex education, it was more antiseptic but just as distant. Intercourse. Ovulate. Penetrate. Ejaculate. Fertilize. Vocabulary-test kinds of words. Formidable, maybe, but dry, not scary. Intercourse was part of being an adult, like having a job.

But that wasn't the whole story. Any child growing up in the early sixties couldn't help getting wind of the first rumblings of the sexual revolution. Popular culture was saturated with it; the signs, the words, were all around us, in ads and movies and magazines, on the tongues of older siblings. Sex. Sexy. Sex appeal. Sex drive. Orgy. French kiss. Fruit. Fairy. Topless beach. Bikini. Blue movie. *Sex and the Single Girl.* Go-go girl. Sexpot. Sex kitten. Ski bunny. Stewardess. Slut. *Peyton Place.* Fourth base. Bachelor pad. Promiscuous. Playboy. Swinger. Animal. Rapist. Sex maniac. Sex fiend. Sex pervert. Kids co-opted words from the adult vernacular—you screamed "sex maniac!" for example, at any boy who chased you during recess. Husbands never said to wives, proudly, "Well, you're looking like a sexpot today." They seemed satisfied with Intercourse. To this day, a small part of me thinks that dirty movies are tinted blue, that stripteasing involves sticking your tongue out as you take your clothes off and that a bachelor's apartment is furnished in wall-to-wall pillows that turn it into one big pad, the better to French-kiss sexpots.

You didn't have to be a genius to see that sex was much bigger than a soundless, discreet activity like Intercourse. Intercourse was self-contained, it never left the bedroom; sex was insidious, it snuck in everywhere. If sex was invisible but pervasive, like air, wasn't it possible to catch it, or take part in it, without knowing it? Maybe Phil and I were having some form of sex, invisible to the naked eye, that just looked like a pillow fight. Maybe sex was like rubbing two sticks together. Phil and I were the sticks; somehow, unseen sparks might pass between us, like germs, and I would have a baby growing inside me. Conjured out of thin air.

It was no use asking any adult about sex. Enlightened as they were on the subject of sex education, they seemed in favor of Intercourse, opposed to sex. They never talked about sex appeal, never said French kiss or sex kitten or slut. They seemed satisfied with Intercourse. Any manifestation of sex, or the body, or private parts, made them nervous. My mother had a reminder that she used to deliver to my sister and me: *Protect your modesty.* "Protect your modesty," she would say when we sat with our skirts hitched up, knees wide apart, and we would know to straighten up, draw our legs together.

Though they never mentioned it, you got the message: Adults didn't like sex. But the phenomenon stared us in the face, far more real than Intercourse. Protecting your Modesty seemed profoundly beside the point.

So I put my radar out for sex, was fascinated by what I could not understand. At eight, ten, twelve years old, we had it at our fingertips. Playboy bunnies did much more than have Intercourse. They had sex—with their ears on, perhaps at *orgies.* Go-go girls were almost certainly promiscuous—maybe that was why they were kept in cages to dance for customers. Jack Paar was probably a *swinger.*

But the most compelling references to sex were in rock-and-roll. All you needed was an older brother who filled the house with a more sinister brand of rock. *Light my fire, light my fire, light my fire.* Jim Morrison offered the chant, over and over. I would close my eyes and try to think of what "light my fire" could mean; all I could see was a bonfire. But it meant more than that, of course: The way Morrison sang it, shouted it, made me think of a coyote howling at the moon. Animal. *Sex maniac.* What was it about sex that made him want it so badly? The words "light my fire" were a code, and I couldn't crack it. The Animals sang a song that chilled me: "There is a house in New Orleans, they call it the Rising Sun. It's been the ruin of many a poor boy, and God, I know I'm one." Eric Burdon, the Animals' lead singer, looked haunted, and had a waxy complexion. Ruined. Sex went on at that house, sex so dangerous, so monstrous, that by the time you stumbled out, as the sun rose, you had been ruined.

Sex could do worse than ruin you. It could kill you. Marilyn Monroe had killed herself—after realizing, as I understood it, what she really was. A sex kitten. A sexpot. A slut. It had made her want to die. (Monroe's death so upset my mother that she broke her silence on the subject of sex: Monroe had died because "men" had forced her to pose naked for years; now she wouldn't have to do it anymore.)

There were plenty of real-life sex crimes, too—you could read them in papers and magazines. I followed a series on the Boston Strangler with ghoulish fascination. Why did all the Strangler's victims let him in, when they knew there was a killer on the loose? The magazine said he had hypnotic eyes. Aha, I thought, this was the magazine's code for *sex appeal*. That was it: he got through the door on sex appeal and by then it was too late. A person could have sex appeal, then, but be a *sex fiend* underneath. Could you learn to tell the difference?

I grew up a little, I got to be fourteen, fifteen, sixteen. I developed serious crushes on a couple of eighteen-year-olds and learned what going weak in the knees meant. I began to see what the fuss was about; sex lost some of its morbid, fantastical edge. But it stayed dangerous. I skimmed for the Good Parts in the few suggestive books I found and knew this did not speak well for my character. I found a copy of Terry Southern and Mason Hoffenberg's *Candy*, which was one long Good Part, and felt sickened and in need of a bath after speeding my way through it. *Candy* confirmed what I'd thought all along: that sex was a toppling from grace into a messy world. But more important, had I put the book down? Had I made any move to Protect my Modesty? No! I hadn't been able to tear myself away. I was as filthy-minded as Candy, or worse. I had fallen, irretrievably; I could never turn back.

I took a look at *Candy* the other day. It is a period piece, spottily funny, way too long. It would be a chore to read through. But I resisted looking at Terry Southern's dust-jacket photograph. I didn't want to remember what he looked like, this man whom I had gone to fourth base with. He hadn't even touched me, but it had happened. Sure and invisible as air.

I don't think sex, or most sex, is grubby, or deadly or dire. I think, though, that the notion of sex I grew up with had one resounding element of truth. Sex *is* everywhere, informing everything we do. You can have sex without realizing it at all, seduce and not know it, be attacked and never touched. It is insidious, mutable, in ways that still astonish me; a tyrant sometimes, a traitor at others.

And another thing. While I think sex has a great many qualities —sublime, infuriating, farcical, electric, exhausting, crazy-making—it is never, to its credit, even remotely as banal as a bear hug. Even a child knows that.

MAY, 1982

BARBARA LAZEAR ASCHER

Well, I can tell you what I'd do if I discovered that my husband was having a love affair. I'd go get a gun. None of the pertinent information would filter through the buzzing sound that fills the brain when the heart is hurt. I would forget the facts: that I adore him, that there's a family to consider, that he makes a better living than I, that criminal lawyers are expensive. The possibility of widowhood, poverty or prison would not deter. Infidelity is reason enough for strict gun control.

It's hearts like mine that have put laws on the books and the question in the minds of judges and juries: "Is infidelity sufficient provocation to reduce a charge of murder to manslaughter?" Yes, according to eighteenth-century case law, if the killer commits the act "in the first transport of passion." Yes, according to the 1977 English case of *Mossa* v. *the Queen*, if the defendant has been told by his wife, "I've had intercourse with every man on the street" and then throws a telephone at him. Yes, said the law of New Mexico in 1963, it is a *complete* defense if the accused witnessed the adulterous act. How the defendant would prove this was left to our imaginations (which is probably why the law was repealed in 1973).

I realize that there are people who appear to act rationally in the face of infidelity. Most of them exist in nineteenth- and early-twentieth-century fiction. Consider Maggie, for instance, in Henry James's *The Golden Bowl*. Upon learning that her husband, the Prince, was romantically involved with her best friend, who was also her stepmother, she devised a plan that was a work of art. Arms negotiations could not match the complexity of bringing Maggie's husband back to her. It worked, but it seemed to take forever. Few of our hearts are strong enough to cling to flotsam that long—to wait for the whim of current to carry us back to shore.

. . .

Consider Leonora, the wife of Edward Ashburnham in Ford Madox Ford's *The Good Soldier*, who facilitated her husband's known infidelities by keeping the object of his affections close at hand. "I suppose," muses Ford's narrator, "that Leonora was pimping for Edward."

Models of restraint. But the lady from Oklahoma wins my admiration. The year was 1927, Manhattan was a long train ride from Tulsa and there were three little children playing about her knees when her sister-in-law approached with grave news. Her husband, the father of these children, was keeping company in New York with a certain actress. Our young mother sent the children off with their aunt and took the next train east.

She went to his hotel, and finding him in the dining room in the company of the lovely miss, stood before the entire crowd of diners and announced: "Samuel, you are either coming home with me immediately or you are never coming home again. You are either raising our children with me or I will do it alone, in which case, you will never see them again." My friend, the now-sixty-five-year-old daughter of this woman, smiles. She is proud of her mother. "He came home," she says.

Of the people who sit it out with honor, who wait for their spouses to "get over" extramarital infatuation, who martyr themselves for the cause of marriage, family or economics, I would want to know, was it worth it?

I have an eighty-year-old friend who tells me, "The hardest time in my life was when my husband had a love affair, and it lasted many years." I ask her, "Why didn't you leave?" revealing myself to be a member of the "me" generation, ill-equipped to handle frustration or psychic pain for more than a week, let alone years. "Oh, I thought of being passionate, of walking out the door," she replies, "but I had to think of the welfare of the family as a whole."

As I look at her family as a whole—the grandchildren, the companionship of husband and wife over the dinner table—I am almost persuaded. But then I don't know the price she paid: conceiving, bearing and raising his children, knowing all the while that his heart and passions were elsewhere. If these weren't intensely private matters, I would ask her, How long did it take for warmth to return to your body? To your heart?

In spite of the latest *Playboy* survey, which would have it that infidelity is a matter of fact of life—48 percent of men and 83 percent of women questioned said they were or had been engaged in extra-marital affairs—infidelity is no fair. Somebody is left out. Somebody else is having all the fun. And even that isn't quite true, because guilt hovers about the door of even the most carefree transgression. If you're very lucky it won't knock louder than your heart or knees when you are in that illicit embrace.

It is that embrace that is visualized by anyone who has ever been betrayed: one's beloved in the arms and bed of another. Imagine it and tell me that your heart doesn't go belly up like a dead fish.

Some of us struggled to understand the hippies' generosity of spirit. If they were willing to share spouses and lovers, we asked, why weren't we? After all, we had so much in common: make love not war—we agreed there; eat grains not flesh—that's cool. We thought that our desire for fidelity must be small and selfish, some tight little knot in our hearts, a nasty wart on our souls.

Now, I wonder, how much did the flower children really know about love? In infidelity someone is the outsider. Being an outsider hurts. Memories of birthday parties we weren't invited to, teams we weren't chosen for, being a child in a world run by and for grown-ups. Betrayal dredges up all these old feelings, raw and fresh as if age had neglected to install a protective layer of insulation between childhood and adulthood.

So I question the honorable selflessness of James's Maggie, who desires not only the return of her husband but that he be protected from guilt and loss of honor. I question the hippies' magnanimous gestures. I question those who say of their "unsuspecting" spouses, "He (or she) will never find out." "It had nothing to do with you."

That's like a pickpocket leaving behind a note saying, "Nothing personal." It may not be personal, but all the same you've been robbed. You've been had.

In *The Good Soldier* and *The Golden Bowl* hearts and circumstance failed to mesh. The Prince married Maggie because he couldn't afford to marry his true but penniless love. Obligations of their parents bound Leonora and Edward. In the enlightened 1980's it is hoped that we marry for love.

A friend of mine, divorced for ten sexually active years before remarriage, tells me: "I never knew that fidelity would feel so good. There is something lush about each encounter when you both know that each of you is the only one."

I would describe it as a feeling of being alone in the world without loneliness. Of being complete but uncrowded. Of total peace and security. Like finding yourself under a tropical sun in February, or listening to Stern and Rose play Brahms' Double Concerto, or having your newborn, still connected by a cord, stare straight into your eyes. Nothing to give up without a gun.

FEBRUARY, 1983

SUSAN JACOBY

Readers tend to snicker at newspaper stories with quotations attributed to taxi drivers because the anonymous "cab driver quote" is a device much favored by reporters who are too lazy to ask any real people for their opinions. But I swear that the following story is an account of a real conversation with a real New York cabby.

He was a talkative widower of sixty-eight with an unsentimental view of relations between men and women. In the fifteen minutes of driving time between La Guardia Airport and my home, he told me exactly why older women get a raw deal in this society.

"I'm no prize to look at, right?" (Right. He had a paunch, thinning hair and bad teeth.) "I tell you in all honesty that I could have remarried at least a dozen times in the last five years. But I don't want to. I like going out a few times a week, enjoying myself, maybe staying over with a lady on a Saturday night. The women I take out are all in their forties and they look good."

I asked if he ever went out with women his own age.

"Never. You think that's unfair, right? Well, it is unfair. I don't want to go out with women in their sixties. I'll tell you why—their bodies are just as flabby as mine. And, see, I don't have to settle for that. I got a good pension from twenty-five years in the fire department on top of what I make driving a cab. Gives me something to offer a younger woman. Oh, I know they aren't going out with me because I'm so sexy looking. A woman my age is in a tougher spot. See, she looks just as old as I look but most of the time she's got no money and no job. The way I figure it, you gotta have something else to offer when the body starts falling apart. Right?"

I see older women everywhere these days—I never really looked at them when I was in my twenties—and their loneliness chills me. A letter from Florida chronicles the sterility of life in a condominium with "1,500 other single women." A widow in my building returns at least one food purchase to the grocery store each day; the clerks are sympathetic, because they understand that she desperately needs the extra minutes of human contact. As for the women I know best—my mother-in-law and grandmother, whose husbands have been dead several years; a friend whose longtime lover died of a heart attack—I can hardly confront their sense of loss.

Sooner or later, their aloneness will be mine. As a woman who loves men—the sight and touch and sound of them, and the fights I have with them—I dread the thought of growing old as I dread nothing else.

I can hear some feminists pointing out that there are many women who choose to live without men and manage to do so quite happily. But each decade of life removes the free choice from more women. Men die younger; one out of every six American women over the age of twenty-one is a widow. The divorce rate has increased most dramatically among couples married twenty to thirty years, and the tendency of men to seek out younger women means that a wife—even when she wants a divorce—is much less likely to find a new partner than her husband is.

It is often assumed that older women are at a disadvantage simply because their bodies are less appealing that those of younger women, but this notion encompasses only a part of the truth. On the crudest level, my taxi driver was saying that you need money to buy love if you haven't got your youth and your looks (regardless of whether you are a woman or a man). On a more sophisticated level, he was saying that money and a job he happened to like—driving a cab and talking his head off—conferred a sense of worth, in his own estimation and in the estimation of women. This sense of worth offset the sexual debit of his expanding paunch.

However cold this equation may seem, it holds out hope for women who do not want to grow old without men. There is nothing that the feminist movement, or any other social movement, can do about aging bodies, but there is a good deal to be done about the lack of worldly esteem that makes middle and old age so bitter for so many women.

Many women complain that "everyone thinks a forty-year-old man is gorgeous, while a forty-year-old woman is considered over the hill." I wonder if everyone, or anyone, really thinks that forty-year-old men are "gorgeous" in comparison to forty-year-old women. Is a man's bald head any more attractive than a woman's graying one? Is a man's potbelly sexier than a woman's flabby thighs? Does anyone who looks at other human beings seriously doubt that the slow process of physical decay begins at about age twenty-five in both sexes?

What is sexy about middle-aged men is not their gorgeous physiques but the worldly accomplishments and status that are, for many women, more of an aphrodisiac than the firm flesh of youth. Society is ordered so that men in their forties and fifties are at the peak of their professional competence and influence and earning power. If similar possibilities were open to more women, there is no doubt in my mind that more men would become interested in sexual partners closer to their own age.

I am not enough of a Marxist to think that improvements in the economic status of older women will render men insensible to the sight of a twenty-one-year-old in a size 8 bikini. But I am not enough of a romantic to think that money—or the lack of it—plays no role in the mystery known as sex appeal.

For millions of women, being left without a man means being reduced to a niggardly standard of living that could hardly enhance anyone's sexual attractiveness. Six out of ten American widows live below the official poverty line. In *The Economics of Being a Woman* (Macmillan), Dee Dee Ahern and Betsy Bliss point out that only 2 percent of widows are receiving private pension benefits from their spouses' working years. The average private pension for retired women in 1976 was only $81 a month.

Small wonder, then, that my sixty-eight-year-old cab driver prefers forty-year-old women to sixty-five-year-old women. He not only gets a younger body—he also gets a woman who is capable of earning her own living.

No amount of money or achievement can compensate for the loss of a beloved man, and no improvement in the overall status of women can nullify the mortality tables decreeing that most of us will spend the closing years of our lives without a man. But I do think that a woman with substantial economic and professional assets is less likely to be passed over for someone twenty or thirty years younger. As the man said, "You gotta have something else to offer when the body starts falling apart."

MARCH, 1978

JANE ADAMS

What, he asked, do women want? Six of us, winners and losers in the Relationships Sweepstakes, gathered in a television studio on the East Side to enlighten the affable and genuinely perplexed talk show host. Between the game shows and the soaps, we clamored for attention. We interrupted him, we interrupted one another, and we interrupted the commercial breaks, to tell whoever watched and listened exactly what it is that women want today.

We want men to share their deepest, most secret feelings with us, we proclaimed. We want them to take more risks for the sake of greater intimacy, we suggested. We want them to let down their defenses and allow our love to come in, we repeated. Above all, we said, we want men to be "vulnerable."

Men, being human, are of course vulnerable, as are we all. Vulnerable as women are to pain, disappointment, uncertainty and anxiety. Vulnerable to loneliness, to fear, to rejection. Vulnerable to the loss of love or to its absence in our lives. We have always known that. But we are tired of agreeing only among ourselves; now we want men to confirm that they are vulnerable, too.

That women are vulnerable must come as no surprise to anyone who has skimmed a current magazine, read a recently published book, watched a television drama filmed in the last year, listened to a live radio call-in show or seen a contemporary movie anytime in the last decade. For at least that long, women have been sharing their innermost insecurities with one another; indeed, with the world.

And so we should all realize that men have been listening to us. They could hardly have avoided it, so incessantly have we talked, so dedicated have we been to exploring our emotions with our best friends, finding real intimacy with casual acquaintances, and risking rejection by anyone else within the sound of our individual and collective voices.

In the eighties our prayers have at last been answered—the current model of the Vulnerable Man was at the showrooms, or at least on the big screen. Burt Reynolds was even more vulnerable in his version of Cinderella Gets Divorced, *Starting Over*, than Jill Clayburgh was in hers, *An Unmarried Woman*; he has an anxiety attack in Bloomingdale's to prove it. Boy meets girl, boy risks girl by exposing his fears, lack of potency and basic insecurity—and boy gets girl. Gary Cooper must be spinning in his grave—the Duke certainly is—but Burt has won our hearts.

The lesson is not lost on even the most macho; more men are talking about more feelings than at any time in recent history. And not just in the movies; on the uptown bus, I heard a man of middle years announce to his male companion (or perhaps to a perfect stranger, for it's hard to gauge the relationship of straphangers to one another): "I'm afraid, and I'm not afraid to say I'm afraid." Two women sitting across from him smiled and nodded their heads in approval, while the bus driver cursed in a steady monotone and narrowly missed colliding with an oncoming taxi.

Men still reticent about admitting their vulnerabilities are being coaxed into full disclosure, and none too gently, by the women in their lives, with prodding from men who have already come out of hiding. The recalcitrant are fixed with level stares, and accused of cowardice if they refuse. Be brave, we demand. Take risks. Only a sissy would be afraid to sound like one.

Bravery was simpler for men a few years ago. They knew what courage required; risking something that mattered for something that mattered even more. Today we demand that they risk their manliness to win their humanity; what we really mean, though, is that we can dilute our own fears by adding theirs to ours. In mutual insecurity, we are all equally secure.

Seized by the solidarity of the panel—six of us to one of him—I forgot all the times that I would have been just as happy if a man had kept his feelings to himself. The time one shared his fear that life was passing him by; as I recall, that was just before he followed a sweet-faced girl half his age (and mine) to the Coast. The time another one shared his feeling that I just didn't turn him on anymore; it was his problem, he assured me, not mine, but he wouldn't be honest if he didn't mention it. The time another felt as if he needed space—which turned out to be a fair distance from my own. The times a man shared his feelings that my ankles were too fat, my children too unruly, my needs too great, my independence too threatening. You get the idea.

Those, of course, weren't the feelings that the television panel of women had in mind at all. The feelings we wanted our men to express, to share, are different. What we're after is the feeling that no one else in the world understands and accepts them like we do. The feeling that they're the luckiest men in the world because we love them. The feeling of wanting to spend the rest of their lives with us—or at least the next weekend.

What women really want to hear, to share, to touch, are not men's vulnerabilities at all, but their invulnerabilities. Not their insecurities, but their certainties. Not their pain, but their happiness in us. We don't want their doubts, we want their reassurances. We want to be told that we matter; we want them to make our fears that we do not go away.

Some of us, I reflected after the show, are getting more than we begged, pleaded or bargained for. We hardly laugh these days at the punch line in the joke about the woman who kept asking her husband, day after day, if he loved her. Of course I do, the man kept replying, day after day. Until one day he looked up from his newspaper and remarked, "Now that you mention it, I'd like a divorce."

If the tree falls in the empty forest, does it make noise? If feelings aren't shared, don't they exist? Of course they do; but occasionally, if they are not dislodged from wherever they've been hiding and held up to the light for painstaking examination, they have been known to pass. And life—and love—have continued. Sometimes, in fact, improved.

There may still be time to close Pandora's Box before it's too late. For once we've reassured ourselves that men are just like us, we may not want them; nor they us. Once they've started to talk, they may never shut up. Once they're vulnerable, we may be more so.

SEPTEMBER, 1980

JOYCE MAYNARD

The first call came around 9 o'clock one night ten years ago. I was living alone in the country, unmarried, twenty years old. Watching whatever happened to be on TV, finishing my second bowl of ice cream, when the phone rang. The man talked like a cowboy, said he lived in Oklahoma and his name was Jim. He'd read a book I wrote. He wanted, he said, to be my friend.

I thought it was a joke. But there was also the odd way this call had come at a moment when what I needed badly was someone to call me up and say he'd be my friend. There were things he said that made me feel he really knew who I was. He had a Hank Williams record that I owned too playing in the background. He used to work at a Campbell's soup factory just because he wanted to see the tomato soup he loved being made. He talked about books he read, promising to send me about a dozen he mentioned: American history, obscure short-story collections, movie-star biographies. He was a birdwatcher. Hank Williams was singing all this time: "Jambalaya," "Your Cheatin' Heart," "I'm So Lonesome I Could Cry."

"Come on," I said finally. "Who is this really?" Your friend Jim, he said. From Oklahoma. I said, All right then, what's the Oklahoma state bird? "Scissortail flycatcher."

The next day I looked up the answer in an almanac, and of course he was right. A week later came a package containing the only picture I ever saw of him (cut from his high school yearbook, showing a very handsome dark-eyed boy, the varsity basketball center), plus the books he'd promised—each one elaborately inscribed with my name in oversized capital letters on the first page. "Property of . . . Hands OFF. KEEP OUT!!!" Now and then, reading along or slipping through the pages, I'd come across a comment in the margin. In a biography of Vivien Leigh, her birthday (the same as mine) circled in red, with exclamation points all around it. Something about birds or country music. And over and over again there were the words "Don't Forget, You Can Always Count on Me."

I know what all this sounds like. (Psychopath twisting the phone cord. Unhappy young woman alone in the woods.) My mother, hearing about Jim, made no comment, then called back a day later to say: "I can't stop thinking about that man in Oklahoma. I'm scared for you." I told her, told myself (and the many people I entertained with the story of his increasingly frequent phone calls) that I was getting into this because it made such a good story.

And though he called me, by now, twice a week (very often after the old *Mary Tyler Moore Show*, which he and I both loved), I never phoned him. At some point, though, I realized that if he disappeared I'd miss him. Even his strange form of communication (exchanging precious little information about the basic facts of either person's daily life, work, family) made an odd kind of sense to me. Never mind that he was thirty-eight and I was twenty, that his passion was the Oklahoma Sooners football team and I built doll-house furniture. The very fact that our two lives held so little in common seemed to me, now and then, to suggest the presence of some much deeper form of kinship.

Of course it seemed crazy that I was sitting in my house in the middle of a New Hampshire winter (and then another one) on a Saturday night, talking for an hour with a man I'd never met, who lived 2,000 miles away. But every now and then I'd go to a party or visit friends at college, where I'd find myself face to face with some young Ivy League type, and I'd ask him what his major was, and he'd tell me about applying to medical school, and all the social rites and customs we'd go through, on the way to absolutely nothing more than the cheese and crackers platter—it all seemed just as crazy to me as what was going with Jim. Maybe more so.

He sent me strange, wonderful presents. A deluxe two-key harmonica (with the request that I learn how to play "Red River Valley" in time to perform it, over the telephone, for his birthday in May). A pair of blue cowboy boots and an Oklahoma football jersey. A four-record set of bird calls, a pair of apple-head dolls made by Oklahoma Indians. An antique green velvet doll-sized chaise longue. One of the first American Cuisinarts, with a gold plaque attached to the side inscribed with my name and the words "HANDS OFF!!!" He sent so many books I had to buy two sets of shelves. And anytime an article I had written showed up in *The Ladies' Home Journal* or *Seventeen* he'd know about it. He was keeping a scrapbook about me, he said.

Once in a while he'd make some remark about paying me a visit in New Hampshire. There were one or two times, real low points in my life, when I felt I had to go away somewhere, and Oklahoma came to mind. But it was easier to be brave on the telephone than in real life. In real life I left my house in New Hampshire and got a job in New York. Had a few appropriate-seeming boyfriends who weren't nearly as interesting or funny, as good company or as devoted to me as Jim, and whose names and faces I can't now recall. Jim still called on Saturday nights—though sometimes I'd be out and come home to find his message on my new answering machine. He never got the hang of waiting for the beep.

Then I met the man who's now my husband. And even though, between Jim and me, over the four years since he'd started calling, not one word of love or commitment had been spoken, still I felt guilty and two-timing the next time he called me with Steve there in the room. I meant to tell Jim about Steve that night, but he wanted to talk about a tape he'd made for me of the last episode of *The Mary Tyler Moore Show* which he was sending, enclosed in a five-pound can of macadamia nuts. I wrote Jim a letter (easiest of all to be brave on paper) telling him that I was getting married. He wrote back to say he'd always be my friend, but that he probably shouldn't call me anymore.

. . .

I heard from him, after that, only on Vivien Leigh's and my birthday and at Christmas, when he'd send our daughter a red-and-white Oklahoma Sooners jersey in her current size and some hugely extravagant toy. A three-foot-high stuffed elephant. A baby doll with a thirty-piece layette. That one arrived on a Christmas when we had so little money that our gift to her came from a secondhand store; Steve wrote to Jim, after that, to say, Please, no more presents.

Over the years, in our various periods of hard times, we've sold most of Jim's presents to me, though I still have the personalized Cuisinart. I still think of him now and then (when I'm grating carrots and, sometimes, rereading an old book, when I come upon a reference to Tammy Wynette or red-winged blackbirds, underlined in red). And sometimes, when I'm feeling fed up with my real-life seven-year-old marriage to a man I love who gives me meat thermometers and dish towels on my birthday—who loves me, but is not about to keep a scrapbook documenting my life's work—I think about how much easier it is to carry on a romance with someone if you've never met him.

FEBRUARY, 1984

Singular Women

MARY CANTWELL

"All of a writer that matters is in the book or books. It is idiotic to be curious about that person." She says that in *Smile Please*, an unfinished autobiography, but I would not have paid any attention had she written it before we met. I wanted to talk with Jean Rhys.

Let me describe her. To put it simply, too simply perhaps, Jean Rhys, who was described ten years ago as "the best living English novelist," is the obverse of Colette. Both lived in paradise, Colette in her mother's house, Jean Rhys on a West Indian island, and lost it. Both performed in music halls and had—one hates to use the word now—mentors. Colette's was her first husband, Willy; Jean Rhys's was her patron, Ford Madox Ford. But their work is very different. Open a book by Colette and you walk into light. In Jean Rhys it is always the hour of the wolf and it is always cold. Colette's women love their lives; Jean Rhys's women only inhabit theirs. And if Colette plays hide-and-seek with the reader, Jean Rhys stands still for the camera. Asked about her heroines, she inevitably answered, "I. . . ."

Having discovered in 1974 that Jean Rhys, whom I adulated and assumed dead, was alive, I wrote and asked to interview her. Her publishers said she was a recluse who would not answer. Instead I heard immediately: I suspect she looked forward to having a guest. So I flew to England, through a friend's pull, first class, and, my head swimming with ports and cognacs not drunk (it was the possibility that intoxicated me) and sleep masks and courtesy slippers, I took a train to Devon. And I drove to a very small house in a very small village, carrying a bottle of champagne.

I had dressed for the occasion. Clothes meant a lot to Jean Rhys—

who can hurt you if you're armored in good clothes?—and I wore a gypsy kind of get-up with a scarf wrapped around my head. She too had dressed for the occasion, in a long skirt and a black-and-gold lamé jacket, and she wore one of those rings that turn blue or lavender or pink depending on where you face it. "Look," she said, turning it this way and that, "isn't it pretty?" "Oh, yes," I said, and showed her the topaz that had belonged to my great-aunt. I think it fair to say we got along.

We spent two days together. She was a bit deaf so I moved my chair close to hers while we spoke, rising only to turn the electric fire on or off. When she rose it was to splash more soda into her vermouth (she'd given me Scotch, a good one, she said), her hand almost too frail to press the syphon. I took notes in longhand because tape recorders made her nervous, and we thumbed through piles of photographs. "There is a conspiracy among photographers," she said, "to make me look mad as a hatter." Occasionally I stopped my questions and we just chatted. We spoke, for instance, of husbands, and when I, who had had one to her three, murmured something about courage, she said, "It wasn't courage, but an obstinate decision to be happy."

The next-door neighbor, a red-faced woman whose big smile revealed three teeth, came in to see if Mrs. Hamer (Jean Rhys's married name) would like anything from town. Her daughter, a stocky Dutch-woman, arrived unexpectedly and opened the champagne while her mother blanketed her ears and I, who fear the flight of corks, louvered my eyes. The daughter laughed, we all laughed. Jean Rhys was flattered that someone had come all the way from New York to write about her but seemed more pleased by the companionship than by praise. She knew how good she was. It is probably the only thing she did know for sure.

Five years later Jean Rhys died. She'd been living in London, I read, drunk and as disorderly as you can get if you're eighty-nine, and trying on hats and wigs in Harrod's and its brothers. The details aren't important: they're all of a piece with the rest. She would never belong, she wrote once, and she never did. "Writing," she said, "took me over. It was all I thought of. Nothing and nobody else mattered much to me."

Now I am reading *Smile Please*. It is a jumble, written when she was very old and when time was as palpable as rain or wind. But once again Jean Rhys snaps me. In the midst of a dialogue between herself and two inquisitors, the Prosecution and the Defense (typical of Jean Rhys not to have imagined herself as partnered by either), she says, "If I stop writing my life will have been an abject failure. . . . I will not have earned death."

To earn death. The command staggers. For Jean Rhys it meant wringing from herself all she had to say. One hopes for her sake that she died written out. But the rest of us?

One seldom has the chance to earn death. That is the tragedy of dying young: one goes with so much juice left. Or of dying old but without ever having been called upon: again, one goes with so much juice left. Better to die a husk.

To earn one's death. I think of it as a kind of parlor game. How, I shall ask my friends, would you like to earn your deaths? And how would I like to earn mine? The question is strangely liberating, implying as it does action, energy, choice. In fact, it has an unexpectedly American ring: death as First Prize. I like it—it makes the nights less frightening.

Not all nights are frightening. Most nights are not, and I have a talent for sleeping, and when, rarely, I cannot, I turn on my right side toward the window and watch the big dog whose shadow I can see against the blind across the way. Or I look up and try to find a star or two, or I walk to the kitchen for milk, happy because the refrigerator is purring and the stove is sleeping and it is three o'clock in the morning and I own the world.

But there are other nights, those four or five a year when my bed falls into the center of the earth. There is no sound and the darkness is impenetrable and I am terrified. On nights like those it is good to have a charm, some kind of magic like "how earn . . ." because with the question comes a multitude of answers.

I played the game the other night, effacing mortality with fantasy, conjuring the things I must do, the sights I must see, the projects to start and the starts that must be finished. But then I slept, and dreamed that a very young and beautiful boy was kissing me. My subconscious, stronger than my imagination, was battling death with Eros. It was a dream that came unbidden and unwanted, and it reminded me of something Jean Rhys had said.

We were speaking of the inconveniences of getting old, and I, not yet of an age to know many, said: "There is one thing I miss already. It's that look of pleasure on a man's face when you are young and pretty and he realizes you are to be his dinner partner. That's a silly thing to think of, but . . ."

"Not silly," she interrupted. "I miss it still."

MARCH, 1980

BARBARA LAZEAR ASCHER

"My hobby is acting out Civil War battles," the commuting businessman tells his fellow passenger on the New York-to-Pittsburgh run.

"What do you get out of it?"

"Well, you know how you get the feeling that you just want to blast a guy? I get to do that every weekend." His enthusiasm reaches volcanic proportions. "Guys come from all over. We have real Yankees, real Rebels and real cannons."

I am on my way to Erie, Pa., to interview Sister Joan Chittister, O.S.B., Ph.D., prioress of the Benedictine Sisters of Erie, who sees in the nuclear arms race "all the male values of the society run amok." Like our born-again Civil War hero.

I boarded this plane after hearing talk among church leaders and peace groups that it was Sister Joan's protest that brought the bishops back to the table to strengthen the stand they had taken in the first draft of the Bishops' Pastoral Letter on Nuclear Disarmament. "I don't know if anyone ever read what I wrote," she is to assert. "But their second draft does address every issue I raised."

Upon arrival I am greeted by a forty-six-year-old woman with brown curly hair who is not in a habit. Her bright eyes fasten on mine and lock them in place. There is no ignoring this presence. She throws her arms around me in welcome, grabs my hand and runs to breakfast to meet a group of sisters eager to hear about her recent week of meetings with some of the country's foremost feminists at Stanford University. Her own feminism she describes as "not antimarriage, antimothering, antimale, but a commitment to the dignity and equality of opportunity of all people."

She laughs with the pleasure that seems boundless in her soul. "Before I arrived at Stanford some of the women were concerned that a nun would not be able to cope with the high intellectual demands of the meetings." The rest of the sisters whoop with glee, for they know that their prioress is a genius.

She also has the energy of a race horse and unshakable commitment. "I'm very hard-nosed," she said of herself. "You can't call me a romanticist. I won't permit that kind of flattery. I'm just entirely too mean and too stubborn to allow the corruption of military thinking to go unchallenged."

Although she has been a major force in the Roman Catholic Church as president of the Conference of American Benedictine Prioresses, past president of the Leadership Conference of Women Religious and a delegate to the White House Religious Conference on SALT II, it was her article in the August 1982 edition of *Commonweal* and the bishops' purported response to it that have brought her national attention.

She took the bishops to task for failing "to be morally absolute in their repudiation of the manufacture or use of nuclear weapons." She wrote that she was troubled by the contrasting ease with which they were able to take a clear stand against abortion. "What is a woman to think?" she asked. "That when life is in the hands of a woman, then to destroy it is always morally wrong? But when all life is in the hands of men then destruction can be theologized?"

Did it take great courage for a nun to challenge bishops in this way? She responds: "We must all become models of holy disobedience. We must say that 'Peacekeeper' is a lie for 'Death Reaper.' "

When asked about separation of church and state her eyes flash, she begins to walk around the room. "When bishops bless bombs, salute the flag and pay taxes, nobody says the church shouldn't be involved in politics. But when a church begins to talk about the destruction of the planet, then they say, bishops, religious and priests should stay in the pulpit, should mind their prayers, should concentrate on mercy and forget the obstacles to justice. Tell that to Jeremiah and Daniel, to Deborah and Judith for me."

I am reminded of a comment by Sister Mary Lou Kownacki, who says of her prioress: "When she articulates a point it's helpful to imagine a Roman candle that starts with a slow burn, quickly bursts into a series of sparks and then shoots into the sky, exploding into myriad colors."

That's what is happening before my eyes as we sit in her study and discuss deterrence. She pulls a chart down from her bookshelf lined with treatises on monasticism, feminism, pacifism and oil wells (one dug on the convent property had a strike). "This was drafted by Geier and Green for Christianity and Crisis, December 13, 1982," she said. "It is a typology of the present nuclear environment." She points to a page that consists of 121 dime-size squares, each filled with dots. Each dot represents three million tons of TNT, the amount of firepower used in all of World War II. The total number of dots, 6,000, represents the number of megatons existing in the world. She points to three encircled dots: "These represent the firepower of one American Poseidon submarine, or the equivalent of three World War II's. It is capable of destroying the major and minor cities of Soviet Russia. We have thirty-one Poseidons.

"Geier and Green say that if you put a dime any place on this chart, you will have identified enough firepower to destroy the entire planet." She leans toward me so that there is no chance that her words might get lost in the space between us. "Tell me," she asks, "what will you do with the rest of your dimes?"

Although she cannot pinpoint what brought her to this calling, this conviction, the elements become apparent as we talk. She was a sensitive and bright child growing up in a world that had just experienced the Holocaust and the dropping of the bomb on Hiroshima. She remembers being told when she was in fifth grade that if a bomb were dropped, there would be no escaping it. "And then my teacher said, 'Isn't it lucky that we are the only ones who have the bomb?'

And I remember thinking, 'No, because we dropped it.' To this day, whenever I hear that we will never use nuclear weapons, I always think: 'But we did, we did.'

"We can now eliminate a culture as easily as the Nazis exterminated the Jews," she comments. "But *this* time I want there to be evidence that some Christians said no."

Her Benedictine tradition demands a commitment to peace. "It was Benedictines who provided sanctuary during medieval wars," she said. "It is Benedictines whose most ancient motto was 'Pax.'" She has come to realize, she says, "that to be monastic is not to be cloistered but to have burning eyes and a steel voice. As a Benedictine I am compelled to face the nuclear issue." It's a nice image—a nun bringing the military complex to its knees.

She departs for a news conference in town. The black community has asked various local leaders to attend the conference in support of a black woman lawyer whose appointment to the County Commission of Industrial Management has been stalled. All but Joan refuse.

Everyone is terribly polite. The local N.A.A.C.P. representative assures the commission and the press that this is not a racial issue. Sister Joan, who has been growing increasingly agitated, suddenly jumps to her feet: "Of course it's racial! And furthermore, it's sexist. The world is not white and the world is not male, and when institutions don't reflect the various perspectives of the communities they purport to represent, then they are institutionally racist and sexist."

She is amazed by the standing ovation that begins and does not end. She later explains her outburst: "I just can't stand pussyfooting." As she moves to leave, the audience parts to open a path, arms reach out to pat her on the shoulder. An elderly black woman steps forth, embraces her and says, "You're some woman, Sister Joan. You are *some* woman!"

MARCH, 1983

GAIL SHEEHY

"I'm old news," Gloria Steinem said. "Why don't you write about leaders like Carolyn Reed and Koryne Horbal?"

"Who?"

That was just the point, of course. Everybody who lived through the last decade's earthquake in gender knows the name Gloria Steinem —a buzzword for the women's movement all over the world. But the more I coaxed, the more deftly she tried to duck an interview: "Just say that my form of leadership is to put forward other women who are not as well known."

That is Gloria Steinem inside and out.

On the outside, functioning as the stage manager, she recognizes that if the movement is to have a long run, women must be represented not by a few stars but by a full cast. Despite the fact that her style is not imitable—one can stand in the dressing room for hours trying to be Gloria Steinem and come out looking like just another aviator needing a haircut—she is tireless in her attempts to transfer her own star power to other women.

But her reluctance to be interviewed is also a clue to the inner Steinem. The champion of equal standing for women is, by her own admission, "very afraid of conflict."

How could that be, when leadership demands that one deal with conflict, embody it, mediate and shape it? "I've never been prepared to take it on the chin," she insisted. "I'm still not."

Her very demeanor—she sat folded in, the curtains of hair characteristically drawn halfway across the sides of an otherwise strong jawline—together with the hesitant "I means" and "I don't knows" with which she prefaced otherwise cogent answers throughout our three-hour interview, lent credibility to her self-criticism.

Back when her first articles on feminism in *New York* magazine stimulated many requests for television appearances, at least two networks boycotted her. Not because she was controversial but because, she confessed, "I used to panic the night before and cancel out."

"Why is conflict frightening?" I asked.

"I think it's a female thing," she said. "We're supposed to make nice, not conflict."

The handicap that deterred Gloria Steinem from developing a fighter's instincts was imposed by her girlhood and appears to be with her for life. How she compensates for that handicap, without being ruled by anger or bitterness, is a source of hope profound in its implication for other potential women leaders.

One careless caravan between Florida and California with a jolly, free-spirited father who never held a job, never wore a hat, never sent her to school but always let her share his dreams, delicious pipe dreams of inventing the jackpot orange drink or getting back a giant check for sending off ad slogans—this was Gloria Steinem's childhood until the age of eleven, painting out the tragic shadow of her mother. A near-invalid who sank often into funks of depression, Gloria's mother had become very early Gloria's child.

"I never felt angry," she said, at pains today as then to put herself in her father's shoes, to blunt the fact of his abandonment when she was twelve.

"He was really trying but he just—" She swallowed hard. "Because of the way he lived, I mean, he was unconventional and wonderful and," she laughed, "like a child."

Alone with the scratch of rats in the walls of a ramshackle house where water froze in the glass before morning because the furnace was always being condemned, shunned by the Polish and Hungarian working people who looked upon hers as the only family in the neighborhood on its way down—that was Gloria Steinem's adolescence. That and "a blind emphasis on getting out," she said, "whether it happened through becoming 'Miss Capehart TV' or joining the Radio City kick line or going to college."

She could not confront her father—he was the child who ran away—or her mother, for whom she bore total responsibility. And so Gloria Steinem learned how to empathize and forgive.

She never actually said no to the programming followed by all the other girls—marriage and pregnancy right out of high school. "I just kept putting it off: 'I will definitely do that. But not right now.'"

College didn't fit, but remarkably, her mother sold the house and sent Gloria to Smith, where, close to graduation, she became engaged.

"I didn't know how not to get married, so I went to India."

The two years in India were catalytic. Burning with the refusal to accept the poverty and inequity she had discovered in the world, she returned convinced that no one else knew. ("I must have been a terrible pain in the ass.") Over the twenty years since, she has journeyed prolifically from writer-investigator-explorer to activist to transformational leader.

But Gloria Steinem also had to sail enough worlds away from her personal disappointments to globalize them, to dissolve them in the cries of all the powerless and impoverished. Rather than sinking into self-absorption, she has become a transformational leader, one who reaches into the existing value structure and excites men and women to support the higher values: justice, equality, individual dignity.

Still, she fears face-to-face confrontations.

"What gives you confidence," she said, "is the sense there is a clear injustice. Trying to change that gives you a shared purpose with other people."

The leader of any outgroup must be prepared to take some "trashing," another of the guises of conflict faced by Gloria Steinem and one for which she has no disarmament techniques at all.

"A woman who has not been allowed to like herself will say,

'How dare she do that? She's just a woman, like me.' That self-hatred in women is the most dangerous thing," she said sadly. "You just have to wait until finally they have enough confidence to be generous to other women."

The Redstockings, a radical feminist group introduced to the public, approvingly, by Miss Steinem herself, has for the past five years been peddling charges that back in the fifties she worked for the Central Intelligence Agency. Miss Steinem denies it categorically. It is not beside the point that no one would recognize the names of her tormentors: four women, apparently obsessed with discrediting her, who pursue like a recurring bad dream.

"Here's what I've learned," said Miss Steinem, exhibiting one of her best defenses, a gift for conceptualizing private hurts into broader social pertinence. "We live in a country in which it's more painful to be accused of working for our own government than for someone else's."

To avoid the burn-out that often desiccates those who work too long, too close, on social issues, she took last year out to stop and read and listen: "More women are realizing we are going to be part of this movement not for just a few years, but the rest of our lives. That means we pace ourselves differently."

Next comes a stage in which Miss Steinem means to analyze the effect of changes talked about by the women's movement, in order to be fortified for the depth—and global breadth—of opposition that she expects.

"We're demanding reproductive freedom as a right, like freedom of speech," she said. "What are the implications? It weakens nationalism. A basic necessity of nationalism—whether it's right, capitalist or Communist—is that a central authority can control population, and decide how many more soldiers are needed, or workers, or White Russians to offset the explosion in Asian Russians. The right-wing way is to force women to have children. The feminist way is to say, 'Individuals should make that decision, not the men in power.' "

"Do you mind being a buzzword?" I asked at the end. She paused, thought, smiled and came back strong: "Being a buzzword for half the human race is pretty diverse."

JANUARY, 1980

PHYLLIS ROSE

Nora Astorga is a heroine of the Sandinista revolution. In 1978, when the dictator Somoza was still in power, she attracted one of his chief officials, the notoriously brutal Gen. Reynaldo Pérez Vega, second in command of the National Guard. General Pérez pursued her and she resisted until one day she called his office and left the message that something the general was very interested in and had long been asking for could be his that day. She would be at home. When he showed up she had him send away his bodyguards. In her bedroom he took off his firearms. Then he was set upon and killed by Sandinista guerrillas who had been hiding there. Later Nora Astorga sent a photo of herself in guerrilla fatigues to the newspaper *La Prensa* and took full credit for her role.

In March 1984 the Government of Nicaragua decided to appoint its Deputy Foreign Minister, Nora Astorga, as Ambassador to the United States. Last week the nomination was rejected by the State Department as inappropriate. Is she an accomplice to murder or a savior of her country? Was the action slaughter or revolutionary justice? We are willing to acknowledge that murder is sometimes justified by politics, otherwise war would be impossible. But political killing off the battlefield is morally ambiguous in the extreme. On the verge of assassinating Julius Caesar, Brutus—as imagined by Shakespeare—announces that he should be seen as a "sacrificer," not a "butcher." The ambiguity remains, however. You know the figure that from one angle looks like a vase and from another a witch? Same with Brutus: from one angle a noble idealist willing to assume the terrible guilt of murder to rid his country of a tyrant; from another a self-indulgent fool who deludes himself into thinking there is an excuse for murder.

Still, however uncomfortable we are with political murder, we recognize that it exists in a different moral category from murder for personal gain or murder from passion. How you feel about it—whether you can imagine it as justified—tends to depend on two things: how long ago it happened and whether you agree with the killer's politics. The two are connected. If the assassination took place long enough ago, you are more willing to sympathize with the assassin's cause.

In Nora Astorga's case there is another important element: She is a woman. Political murder may be more than usually problematic when a woman is implicated. Two crimes are being committed—a murder and a betrayal of expectations about female behavior.

The Bible tells the story of Jael, wife of a nomad chief, who killed the Canaanite general Sisera. After a battle in which his forces were routed by the Israelites, Sisera took shelter in the camp of Jael's husband, officially neutral but allied to the Israelites. Jael made Sisera at home in her tent, covered him with a blanket and soothed his jangled nerves with a drink of milk. When he was asleep she drove a wooden tent peg through his forehead. The next day she proudly acknowledged what she had done, and she is praised in the Book of Judges for her righteousness.

Charlotte Corday went to Paris from the provinces with the firm intention of killing Marat and thereby (she hoped) ending the Reign of Terror. She kept sending Marat requests for an appointment. He did not answer. She persevered and finally gained entry to his apartment. Marat, hearing a woman's voice, allowed her to be brought into him. Because of an illness, he had to keep his body under water, so he was in the bath when she killed him, with a dinner knife bought the previous day. Charlotte Corday was tried for murder; when asked what she had to say in her defense she replied, "Nothing, except that I have succeeded." Composedly, she met her death by guillotine. She looked forward, she had said, to happiness with Brutus in the Elysian fields.

What is strikingly similar in the stories of Charlotte Corday, the biblical Jael and Nora Astorga is their pride in what they have done and their insistence that they be given credit for their daring. All three also play on the fact that they seem harmless to their enemies. Nora Astorga and Jael used female "hospitality" to entrap. Having played on notions of what woman is like to disarm her enemy the revolutionary heroine involved in murder defies our notions of what a woman is. She uses stereotypes of female behavior to succeed and in succeeding overthrows the stereotypes.

Despite one's moral repugnance at any murder, the woman who murders for a cause demands respect in a way that Delilah, for example, that sneaky seductress, does not. The revolutionary murderess puts her life and her soul on the line. She fascinates because of her daring and aggressiveness. At some level many women, I believe, look for such stereotype-defying heroines, even—perhaps especially—murderesses. That is how I would explain all the interest in Jean Harris. We wanted to see her as a heroine-murderess, but she kept slipping out of the role into something much smaller, and what is ultimately interesting about the Harris case is not Mrs. Harris but the public's response—its fascination.

A Freudian would say that we are fascinated with female assassins because they represent our deepest fears. I would amend that to say "men's deepest fears." Men—the more macho, the more innocent—go into sexual encounters assuming the harmless and passivity of their partners. Women are trained to be wary of them. An aggressive sexual partner is no more than most women expect. An aggressive—even murderously aggressive—female is no deep fear of most women. Men have much more to fear from aggressive women than women do.

As we also know from Freud, the things we fear most we tend to joke about the most. Perhaps this explains the extraordinary levity with which the American press has tended to treat the appointment of Nora Astorga. *Time* captioned its picture of her "experienced hostess" and ended an article on her appointment with a quotation from a United States diplomat: "There's a limit to how close I'd get to her." A *New York Times* editorial titled "Femme Fatale" compared her to Marlene Dietrich in several film roles and expressed regret that Josef von Sternberg was not around to direct her.

A woman warrior takes up an enemy general's offer to go to bed with him and helps kill him instead. To some people that's the stuff of which legends are made, to others jokes. I, for one, wonder if a male version of Nora Astorga—a former revolutionary terrorist appointed Ambassador to the United States—would be treated with such levity.

APRIL, 1984

SUSAN JACOBY

"In the awful years of the terror I spent seventeen months waiting in line outside the prison in Leningrad. One day somebody in the crowd identified me. Standing behind me was a woman, with lips blue from the cold, who had, of course, never heard me called by name before. When she emerged from the torpor common to us all, she asked me in a whisper (we all whispered there):

" 'Can you describe this?'

"And I said, 'I can.'

"Then something like a smile passed fleetingly over what had once been her face."

Those lines were written by the Russian poet Anna Akhmatova as an introduction to her poem "Requiem," a grim and beautiful lament for the victims of the Stalinist terror in her country. I recently recalled those lines—as one might recall a prayer—in the midst of an interminable, sodden argument over the question of whether there is a "special female sensibility" in literature.

The argument took place at a holiday dinner party filled with the sort of people who don't read books written before 1970. The usual dumb discussion about female sensibility produced an unusually dumb comment from a professor of something-or-other (I hope for the sake of his students that it wasn't history or literature) at Columbia. Women, the professor intoned, have not produced writers who act as "witnesses to history"—no Aleksandr Solzhenitsyns, for example. Oh, professor, I thought, did you pick the wrong country to prove your point.

. . .

There is no law that says genius must be fairly distributed by sex or race or religion or height. As luck would have it, Russian poetic genius in the first half of the twentieth century was parceled out to two women and two men: Anna Akhmatova and Marina Tsvetayeva, Osip Mandelstam and Boris Pasternak. Of the four, only Akhmatova and Pasternak lived through what has come to be known as "the great terror"; only they survived to encompass the whole story in their art.

Also by terrible chance, this poetic constellation helped produce another great woman writer (or writer who happens to be a woman, take your pick)—Nadezhda Mandelstam, whose husband died somewhere en route to a prison camp in 1938. (Osip Mandelstam's fate was sealed when he wrote a poem describing Stalin as a "murderer and peasant-slayer.") Mrs. Mandelstam, often one step ahead of the secret police, traversed the length and breadth of Russia, preserving her husband's verse in her head lest his manuscripts be destroyed.

Then, when she was already in her sixties, Nadezhda Mandelstam began writing two extraordinary books (published in English under the titles *Hope Against Hope* and *Hope Abandoned*) that resurrected her husband, the culture that produced him and an entire world of humane and humanistic values that buckled under the weight of sustained totalitarianism. To understand what went on in the camps, you read Solzhenitsyn. To understand what went on in the imprisoned nation outside the camps, you read Akhmatova's poetry and Nadezhda Mandelstam's prose. The two women were fast friends who lived through the same appalling events.

These are the writers I began reading when I lived and worked as a journalist in Moscow in the late 1960's. I was more powerfully drawn to the Russian women than I had ever been to women writers in my own language; I now think the unfamiliar culture made it possible for me to approach writers of my own sex without relegating them to the second-rate categories of "lady writer" or "authoress" or "poetess"—categories I had absorbed in my impressionable youth from men like the professor at the dinner party.

Russians freed me from the musty notion that "manners" and domesticity are the province of women and great external events the province of men writers. There are fear and death and starvation—the stuff of domestic and public trauma—in both Solzhenitsyn and Nadezha Mandelstam. The angles of vision differ but both writers are "witnesses to history."

In *Hope Abandoned*, Mrs. Mandelstam (who always refers to her husband as "M.") describes his visit to a Soviet clinic for a physical checkup at some point in the 1920's. He was passed on to a psychiatrist, whose diagnosis "was that M. had the illusion of being a poet and of writing verse, though in fact he was only a minor employee who did not even hold a post of any responsibility and harbored all kinds of grudges, speaking badly, for instance, about writers' organizations. . . . M.'s delusion was, moreover, a very deep one: It was impossible to convince him that he was not a poet. The psychiatrist advised me not to succumb myself to this psychosis . . . and in the future to cut short all my husband's talk about writing verse."

The incident tells us as much about the course of the young Soviet state as it does about the Mandelstams' hounded lives. Mrs. Mandelstam—the writer, the woman—remembers everything. When *Hope Abandoned* was published here in 1974, a feminist writer criticized it on grounds that the author "seemed too preoccupied with her husband." How ironic that a feminist should suggest, as any garden-variety male chauvinist might, that the inescapable vantage point of a brilliant woman whose brilliant husband was murdered somehow disqualified Mrs. Mandelstam as a writer of universal vision. I prefer the interpretation of the Russian émigré poet Joseph Brodsky, who has described Nadezhda Mandelstam's evocation of her husband as "reminiscent of the creation from a rib—with the sexes reversed."

. . .

Anna Akhmatova's poetry (some of it is available in English transla-
tion) has the same quality of "bearing witness" that permeates her
friend's prose. The poetry written around the time of the purges has
a tone that is both elegiac and reportorial. "At dawn they came and
took you away" begins one of the stanzas in "Requiem."

"At dawn they came and took you away/You were the corpse,
I walked behind." That line refers to the arrest of her husband. Her
son, Lev Gumilev, was arrested three times while Stalin was alive and
was finally released from a labor camp in 1956. The poet writes about
all of this. What is "domestic" and what is "public" in the sufferings
of a woman, a mother, a child, a country? How do they divide into
"male" and "female" subjects?

Of course there is a female sensibility. Of course there is a male
sensibility. In a great writer of either sex, those sensibilities yield universal truths. I suspect that all of the dull dinner-party arguments on
this point stem from the fact that we read too few great writers and
too much junk. In another famous poem, Akhmatova lamented that
her life has been wrenched from its normal course by the horrors of
the age in which she lived. The verse concludes:

> But if I could step outside myself
>   and contemplate the person that I am,
> I should know at last what envy is.

Was it a man or a woman who wrote those lines?

JANUARY, 1978

The Married State

MARY KAY BLAKELY

Aweek after the journalist Sally Quinn got married, a young
woman who worked in the same building as Miss Quinn
asked her whether she, too, should marry the man she was
living with. Miss Quinn replied: "I wanted to say 'yes, yes, yes,' because I was so happy with my own decision. But then I remembered
from long, long ago in college when I was thinking about marrying a
man I didn't love. I asked my best friend how you could tell if you
were in love. She told me if I were in love I wouldn't need to ask that
question.

"So I told this young woman that she shouldn't get married because she had to ask the question," Miss Quinn said, offering the
young woman about as much useful information as the mothers who
tell their questioning daughters, "You'll know when the right one
comes along." One way or another, women have been telling each
other, "If you want to get married, don't ask questions."

In a recent story in *Ms.* magazine about "over thirty" marriages,
several of America's most successful women smile out from behind
gossamer white veils, wearing happily-ever-after expressions on their
faces. What I hoped would be a rational discussion of marriage turned
out to be a blushing illustration that even feminists can lose their
marbles on the subject of love.

I'm not worried about these women—they are capable and competent and will undoubtedly recover their lost marbles. They are in
love, and who could begrudge anyone the exuberant, expansive feelings
that accompany being in love?

What I am worried about, though, is that impressionable young
women who read these accounts will forget that these cheerful evalua-

tions of marriage come from the perspective of a bride, someone just barely into life on the other side of the vows. Asking a bride for her opinion about marriage is like asking a baby how childhood is going so far. The response is bound to be romantic—a lot of charming chatter but not much intelligible communication.

Young women eager for good news about marriage should remember that while a bride may be quite eloquent on the subject of love, she knows almost nothing about marriage yet. It can take years for a woman to fully discern the differences between "love," the intoxicating passion, and "marriage," the institution designed to capture it.

Marriage is the process that transforms a "bride" into a "wife," and the changes can be dramatic. In an article entitled "No One Has a Corner on Depression, but Housewives Are Working on It," the writer Gabrielle Burton says, "A man loves a woman so much, he asks her to marry—to change her name, quit her job, have and raise his babies, be home when he gets there, move where his job is. You can hardly imagine what he might ask if he didn't love her." And a woman loves a man so much, there is a powerful need to please, to accommodate even when his expectations don't coincide with her own. Such is the generous nature of love.

Brides are so happy they haven't noticed yet that the institution of marriage is designed to hold only one and a half persons. They don't immediately comprehend the multiple implications behind Norman Mailer's suggestion that the whole question of liberation boils down to one: "Who will do the dishes?" The same one who does the dishes also gets to be the half person.

In the case of "nontraditional" marriages, it can take a woman even longer to comprehend that she is the half person. Many intelligent couples like to believe they can balance the equation to an even three-quarters apiece. With a few liberating amendments—she gets to keep her job, maybe even her name, he helps with the dishes—they hope to even things out. So subtle is the shift from "bride" to "wife" that a woman convinced of her independence can miss it altogether.

I would certainly have remained oblivious to the myriad assumptions hidden in the institution of marriage had it not been for a woman named Agnes who rudely interrupted my bliss only six months after I became a bride.

I ran into Agnes at Hemingway's Moveable Feast, our neighborhood delicatessen in Chicago. We were returning from the bike paths along the lakefront, tennis sweaters draped cavalierly over our shoulders, looking like a couple who had just passed the screen test for an Erich Segal movie. We stopped at Hemingway's to find a treat to bring home. Newlyweds are fond of treats. After some deliberation, I selected a high-quality brand of butter-pecan ice cream and handed it to the man who was carrying our money in his wallet.

He looked at the price, something that had not occurred to me. He handed it back, explaining that $1.95 was exorbitant for any ice cream, and besides, he didn't like butter-pecan. I gave it back to him, because what was $1.95 between friends and besides, he didn't have to eat any. We stood there for some time, passing the pint back and forth, straining for patience, he refusing to indulge an irresponsible purchase, I insisting it was none of his business. His patience was melting with the ice cream when he delivered his final opinion: There was no way he was going to pay $1.95 for a pint of ice cream just because it said on the bottom of the carton "Hand packed by Agnes." He was starting to hate Agnes.

We rode home in stony silence. Only six months before I had been the kind of self-actualized woman who could walk into just about any delicatessen and order whatever I wanted. Dimly, I realized that this sudden loss in opportunity had something to do with the vows I had taken. I didn't remember ever saying, "And I defer all ice cream judgments to you." That's when I first became aware that love is not only blind, it is also deaf. A woman in love can't possibly hear the varied assumptions packed between the promises and the vows. The "I do" that took approximately ten minutes to pronounce will be followed by ten incredulous years of asking, "I did?"

But I also knew that to challenge a husband's ice cream authority was to challenge the vast incomprehensible expectations built into the structure of marriage. To question an ice cream decision would lead irrevocably to questions about vacuuming. And children. And sexuality.

We thought we had a "nontraditional" marriage because we were largely unaware that the roles of "head of household" and "subservient spouse" had a pervasive influence on our own relationship. We didn't fully understand how much a husband's sense of entitlement and a wife's sense of duty affected our own decisions about economics and work and power.

The next day, on the way home from work, I stopped at Hemingway's and bought six pints of butter-pecan ice cream, all hand packed by Agnes. I had to get rid of the status of half wife, and it was the first step to becoming an unwife. My success as an unwife depended largely on the cooperation of an unhusband, and I knew that undoing our unspoken vows could well result in an unmarriage. For better or worse, I packed our small freezer full of butter-pecan ice cream.

The young woman who asks whether she should get married is not really interested in hearing about the laborious journey from "bride" to "wife" to "unwife." The story would bore her, since she's in love and love is impatient with long explanations.

I would tell her about Agnes, who packs a lot of information about the institution of marriage between the pecans and the sweet cream. I would tell her simply, go ask Agnes.

APRIL, 1981

MOLLY HASKELL

There are couples who match, and couples who clash. The former are the ones who look more like brother and sister than husband and wife. They marry and have matching children and at Christmas send photographs of themselves that look like pictures from an L. L. Bean catalogue. When you see them you know that somewhere marriage is still a safe harbor, and king-size beds are still sending forth good, solid, gold-pedigreed citizens into a world that is, a little sadly, no longer theirs for the taking.

And then there are the couples who don't match. My husband and I could never be taken for brother and sister. Andrew is Greek-American, the quintessential urban ethnic: rumpled, swarthy, explosive, chocolate brown patches under chocolate brown eyes giving him the look of a doleful gangster. I am a pale-faced Southern WASP, repressed, poised on the outside, churning on the inside, not as bland as I look. We are—outwardly at least—a study in contrasts.

Perhaps if we had children sitting in front of us on a Christmas card, our tensions would appear to melt into congruities. Characteristics held in unalterable opposition between the two of us would mingle and merge and then, divided up four ways, give our ménage the look of historical necessity.

Gore Vidal once wrote approvingly of the exoticism of mixed marriages. In the spirit of the peacock lecturing the chickens, he denounced as boring the habit of marrying one's own kind, and reproducing predictable, ethnically pure versions of oneself. Easy to say from the sidelines. Speaking from within an "interesting" marriage to which I am wholly committed, I should nevertheless argue that there are some good solid reasons for like marrying like and staying within the tribe. One strays from its preserves at one's peril.

For one thing, the sense of ancestral continuity is much stronger in a homogeneous relationship than in a heterogeneous one. One feels the weight of it at intratribal weddings, where past generations gather to lead the young couple to its historical future. By contrast, a mixed-marriage ceremony often resembles the accidental rendezvous of two seagulls on a lifebuoy, riding out a storm.

My mother and my aunt went to Greece one summer, on a tour that took them up into the hills, and off the beaten path. In every little village, they reported on their return, they saw women pulling great heavy carts to market while the men sat around the tavernas drinking ouzo. But of course, I said, that's what's wrong with our marriage. Andrew comes from a culture where the women do all the work, and I come from one where the men do all the work, and we're both sitting around waiting for someone to do the work.

Lorelei Lee experienced a similar epiphany in Anita Loos's *Gentlemen Prefer Blondes* when she came upon that same unequal division of labor "in the central of Europe."

The barriers of tribal custom can be awesome. For example:

The Cocktail Hour. This ritual is claimed by WASPs the world over, but Southern WASPs have brought it to its austere apogee: the consuming of Scotch or bourbon (and occasionally an arriviste vodka) over a two-hour period that is the acclaimed highlight of the day, rendering dinner, and almost everything else in life, an anticlimax. It is easier to lead a camel through the eye of a needle than to initiate an urban ethnic into this hallmark of gracious living. Converting them to alcohol is not the problem, it's the what and how: They insist on choosing drinks they like the taste of, then gulping them down like soft drinks. Our courtship sustained some awkward moments when waiters would place my two-fisted highball in front of Andrew and his fruity-frothy concoction in front of me. Our compromise: vermouth-cassis.

Carving and Driving. What the bar mitzvah is to the Jewish boy and the toga ceremony was to the young Roman, carving and driving are to Southern American manhood. These accomplishments are virtually second nature and, like swimming, can't be taught after a certain age. Andrew can just barely wield a steering wheel, but the carving knife is beyond him. Compromise: We go to Andrew's mother's for Thanksgiving dinner. By subway.

Food. Ethnic food, the nuttier and grainier the better, is my passion. Not Andrew's. He is the only person I know whose eyes light up at the liquid diet dinner in a hospital. The orange Jell-O, milk custard, pineapple "ice" and "fruit" drink take him back to his youth as a Greek boy growing up as an American. His idea of "playing around" when I'm out of town is to load up on Wonder Bread, Miracle Whip and that globular red salt known as domestic caviar. Our compromise: We have what I want except when I go to the hospital; then I give Andrew my tray.

Wedding. Our Episcopalian wedding and reception must have come as a shock to Andrew's kith and kin. I've always felt guilty about the extraordinarily lavish wedding presents his relatives sent, no doubt anticipating the customary ethnic four-course feed, only to find themselves, after the world's shortest wedding ceremony, with two hours of heavy booze and light hors d'oeuvres and an evening to kill.

We have other friends whose marriages seem even more ano-malous than ours. M. and J. are not just Jew and WASP: He is a conservative Republican Jew from Great Neck, L.I., and she is a flaming liberal from the Middle West. He deliberately goads her with inflammatory remarks, and she never loses her heartfelt capacity for outrage. Their antagonisms, continually fresh and funny, feed the adrenaline of their love.

Why, with all the turmoil and uncertainty in the world, have we asked for more in choosing mates who would echo, rather than provide an escape from, the storm?

"Fixity of tradition, of custom, of language is perhaps a prerequisite to complete harmony in life and mind," wrote Santayana. Diversity in these matters, said he of the multifaceted background, would turn one into a restless philosopher. But for those of us who come from unified traditions, perhaps it's the philosopher in us that drives us to seek out diversity, even confusion. Having come from a culture in which everyone holds in their feelings in the interest of social equilibrium, I must have yearned for an explosive element in my life. Andrew, on the other hand, brought up on Mediterranean excess and effusion, retreated to an emotionally cooler place.

The risk in all of this is that you may discover you can't adapt to so radical a cultural change. But then, a certain taste for risk, and adventure, is what brought most of us restless types to New York in the first place. We didn't want to wake up every morning knowing precisely who we were and where we fit. Our own identities were evolving, floating free. Having made the initial break, we chose partners who would consolidate it—chose rupture as a way of life, marriage as the beginning of an existential drama rather than the happy ending of a romantic fantasy.

In choosing a life mate of a very different background, I and others like me were probably, without quite knowing it at the time, exempting this person, and ourselves, from the traditional roles associated with the institution of marriage, and demanding something else. In a great many "hybrid" couples, the man is the nurturing "mother"-like figure to a spirited but insecure woman. The woman's movement would never have got off the ground without such husbands—secure enough in their own identities and vocations to extend themselves, emotionally and intellectually, to women.

Still, the success—or failure—of these seemingly odd couples depends to a great extent on the success of both partners in establishing their viable independence. A modicum of "success" is assumed in advance, but at the first sign of weakness or failure the difference in background can become more exasperating than exotic. Then, the sense of isolation can be frightening. You're on a high wire without a safety net. You've burned your bridges, forfeited the automatic warmth and protection of the tribe.

There's pain in the uprooting, but being without that person is unimaginable. For better or worse, you are each other's homeland.

FEBRUARY, 1982

MARY-LOU WEISMAN

Whenever two or more married couples gather together to socialize, it's not just a party, it's a masquerade. One-upmanship becomes a duet, as both husband and wife conspire, he behind his masks, she behind hers, to present in the best possible light the *third* persona they have brought to the party, their marriage. The introduction of this glittering entity is a challenge to the others, a kind of throwing down of the conjugal gauntlet. By the time all that's left of the brie is the rind, the living room rug will be strewn with gloves. What follows, and in such good humor that it is often called "having fun," is in fact a competition for "best couple."

The competition begins the moment the requisite bottle of wine passes from guest to host. Best-husband-contender No. 1 helps best-wife-contender No. 1 out of her coat and, in so doing, plants a tiny kiss on her ear lobe. The gauntlet has been thrown. All over the room wives struggle to remember the last time their husbands planted a kiss on their ear lobes, and they cannot.

Contending couple No. 2 have just returned from a vacation in the Caribbean where they celebrated their twentieth anniversary. The sun shone brightly upon them every day. They went scuba diving. They took a course together before they left. You should, too. Before you go next time.

They discovered a fabulous restaurant on the French side of the island that hardly any tourists know about. Really romantic. It was a second honeymoon. No, really, it was. On the way over, they persuaded the captain of the cruise ship to marry them—a wonderful way to celebrate a twentieth anniversary, don't you think?

All over the room husbands and wives recall nonstop, $250-a-day,

American-plan rain, the ignominy of having to snorkel with minnows while couples who *do* things together, like take courses, cavorted with schools of purple fish in deep coral reefs. They didn't even know the island *had* a French side, or what it was they did to celebrate their twentieth anniversaries. They cannot remember. The brilliance of the other couple's presentation of happiness blinds them to their own. They can only remember that they did not get remarried.

Contending couple No. 3 cannot wait to get home. She pops canapés into his waiting mouth. He pats her bottom suggestively. She whispers hoarsely, "It it too early to leave yet?" He whispers back, "Soon."

All over the room, couples whose sex lives are commercially interrupted by Bernadette Castro and Sy Syms die a little as they imagine couple No. 3 in passionate disarray ten minutes from now in the driveway.

The winner of the best-marriage competition will be declared later that evening in the privacy of each couple's bedroom, when the votes are tallied. While she climbs out of her panty hose and he hangs up his tie, they will talk about the other couples at the party and who seemed to be the happiest. They may not talk about it directly, but talk they will. "Sounds like The Twos had a terrific vacation." Or, "Did you notice The Ones? It's nice the way he kissed her ear." Or, "Maybe we should take a course." The sign of a particularly successful party is when each couple votes another couple happiest, and all couples receive one vote.

The Saturday-night masquerade, heady in the enactment, carries with it as its price a heavy aftermath of self-doubt, sometimes called Sunday.

It is the sickening green sense that everybody is having a better marriage than you are. It is the same fantasy that tempts people to believe that everybody else's Thanksgiving dinner was catered by Norman Rockwell, and that only you have a father who can't carve, a mother who can't cook, a divorced sister, a daughter who decided to spend Thanksgiving with her boyfriend's family, an uncle who won't shut up about his EST sessions and no dog Spot. It is the same ultimately self-abusing urge that makes people cling to the fantasy— against all contrary evidence—that other people who are thin eat as much as they want. Only you have to diet.

Why do we put ourselves through this perpetual torture? Why this endless game of "Keep It Up," passing our marriages overhead like volleyballs bounced from finger tips to finger tips, while our arms ache? Why doesn't somebody call for a time out?

Sometimes I think that couples have a peculiarly mutual flair for theater, a perception of husband and wife as dramatic roles, a keen sense of romantic comedy and a genuine desire to make beautiful music together. Should one or another forget the lines, there is even a mutual proclivity to fake it.

At other times, I suspect biology. I become convinced that we carry this sadomasochistic behavior in our genes, stamped on our chromosomes. There's nothing we can do about it. Peacocks preen, apes pound their chests and couples too must strut their stuff. Maybe it has survival value for the species.

And sometimes I think our couple behavior is economically determined. It seems we are so essentially a capitalistic society that we can't even refrain from trying to sell one another our marriages, or at least we can't resist advertising them. We are after all a highly competitive society. We compete at work, at school, in sports and on television game shows. All of these are but pale imitations of the competitions that are played on Saturday nights on a field of hors d'oeuvres.

Somewhere, mercifully, in the deepest and most sane recesses of their minds, everybody at the party knows that since they were putting their best marriage forward, it is likely that everybody else was doing the same.

But can they be perfectly sure? There is always the awful possibility, however slight, that at least one of the marriages at the party was so naturally, so dazzlingly ideal that it dared to come unmasked.

There is also the possibility, statistically a lot more likely, that one of the couples at the party will be divorced within the week.

With a little luck, it'll turn out to be the couple who couldn't keep their hands off one another.

NOVEMBER, 1983

JUNE P. WILSON

oes a man's retirement have to be exile and house arrest?
Exile because the office in which the retiree had worked
much of his life told him in so many words to shove off,
Buster. Oh sure, they threw the obligatory party, but it had been clear
for months that the replacement couldn't wait to move into his office.
His phone rang less and lunches were fewer. Most painful perhaps was
the loss of his expense account, that lovely lolly that had for so long
allowed him to live beyond his means.

And all of it so precipitous too, with no time for acclimatization.
(This phenomenon seems to apply less to professional men—doctors,
lawyers and the like—who often practice until dangerously close to
senility. And too few women have retired from executive positions as
yet to constitute a valid sample.)

The house arrest was especially disturbing to his wife. Few
women view the daytime presence of a man in the home with anything but dismay. Haven't women always looked forward to Monday
while husband and children groaned? For years she had had the place
to herself; now she must share it with a caged and wounded beast who
wants cosseting.

The wife had been warned by survivors of other retirements: "If you
get through the first year, you may be all right for the long pull."
"Like marriage?" she had asked. "No, no. The drama is no longer in
the bedroom and nursery; now it's in the study and kitchen."

Taking this admonition to heart, she had asked her husband—
innocently at first—what he planned to do when he retired. Oh, he'd
find lots to do, he said, and changed the subject. A year later, move
apprehensive this time, she asked again. He said rather sharply that it

was his business and she was not to worry. She stopped asking and did start to worry.

Looking around at their retired friends, she wondered why men seemed to be ill-prepared for life after sixty-five. Her husband, like most men of his upbringing, professional standing and financial ease, had few distractions: a little golf, tennis or gardening, some cursory reading, an occasional play or movie. Somewhere down the line he had probably been shamed into sitting on the board of a philanthropy, but the commitment was shallow.

To "celebrate" his retirement she had bought him a nice English eighteenth-century desk; he had purchased a filing cabinet, an electric typewriter and one thousand sheets and envelopes printed with his home address. On D-Day Plus One, a man appeared at the door with four large cartons containing the contents of his office. They were placed in his study.

Her husband picked his way around the cartons and pre-empted the phone for two hours. He went to his club for lunch and returned at 4, disgruntled.

"Why do they keep asking me what I'm doing now?" he wondered.

"They assume that everybody wants to tap my vast pool of experience."

"Men usually say they've never been busier," she said.

"I know," he said. "They lie."

When three days had passed, she asked him when he planned to deal with the cartons. "In due course," he replied. On the seventh day, she delivered an ultimatum. Tight-lipped, he stuffed the contents into the file cabinet, unexamined.

It soon became evident that order would be a persistent bone of contention; like most couples they held dissimilar views on the subject. An adolescent's anarchy had long reigned in his bedroom closet and bureau; it now spread to his study.

Was it because he'd always had a secretary to keep order, while nameless people vacuumed his office, cleaned the men's room and cooked his lunches? For men like her husband, little had changed for generations. Their women meanwhile had been hit by two revolutions: the disappearance of live-in help during World War II and the women's movement, which was propelling them away from the household arts.

The drama, as foretold, soon shifted to the kitchen. He loved food; he liked to market and walked hours in the quest of exotic foods. True, in his search for the perfect olive oil, he tended to forget the milk and paper towels. And then he would dump the shopping bags on the kitchen table and vanish. It was months before he would face up to the dirt in a head of lettuce or the sand retention of spinach. She grieved over his casual view of where kitchen utensils belonged.

Was she being horrid? Yes, certainly. It was his house as much as hers (more, since he had paid for it), and she was making him feel like an interloper.

His role in the house had been exemplary when they were younger: He had given the 2 and 6 A.M. bottles to the pitiful babies, changed their unpleasant diapers, read them *The Secret Garden* and *Ivanhoe* when they got older, stayed home and gardened with them when other men deserted the family for the golf course, swelled with pride over their small triumphs, ached for their setbacks.

When retirement forced him back into the home, she had hoped that he would revert to his former helpfulness. But decades of conditioning had taken their toll—on both sides. The greater part of running the house, and the social, cultural and travel plans and their execution still fell to her. "A man doesn't invite people to dinner," he would say.

Some ingrained attitudes can't be changed, but after seven years both have become more resilient. Good health has been a factor, even as its maintenance eats up an ever larger part of the day: corrective exercises for backs, preventive treatments for teeth and the decoding of medical forms—all of it giving rise to dark thoughts such as "Is this body really worth preserving?"

The territorial battles have abated. A kind of androgyny has set in. The hormonal shifts of menopause had been the first step. He began to move into her world, she into his, even as they learned to create more breathing space between them.

Together they share a forty-five-year accumulation of experiences, memories and jokes, few of them bad. Then, too, they share the great globe itself, which waits outside their front door every morning. He will ponder the news; she will write a letter to the editor.

In his entry to his fiftieth class reunion, he summed it up with typical diplomacy: "My wife is the activist; I supply the wisdom."

JUNE, 1983

ANN P. HARRIS

When I hesitantly confided to a close friend that, after a difficult divorce and hard-won adjustment to single life, I was, to my surprise, considering remarriage, she hardly responded with the misty-eyed smile and heartfelt embrace I had expected. Instead she told me the story of a woman just my age in her office who had remarried and set off on her wedding trip, only to return three days later with a husband who had chest pains, was in a hospital recovering from a heart attack and would probably never be able to work again.

The second friend I told asked if I was sure this wasn't a rebound romance. The question puzzled me greatly because I had been separated for three and a half years and had gone out with several men other than the one in question.

My mother, I felt sure, would be overjoyed at the news, especially since she expressed approval of her future son-in-law two years before I considered him in that role.

She *was* overjoyed, so overjoyed that she paused to say how lovely it all was before she went on with her story about how her rent bill had gotten mixed up with the rent bill of the people downstairs and of how fortunate a mix-up it had been since she and the people downstairs were now fast friends.

After that it dawned on me that not all the world loves a middle-aged lover. The idea of finding romance in one's autumn years may appeal in the abstract, but when you confront family and friends with a concrete instance they often feel somewhat uneasy.

Curious as to the reasons for this, I was delighted to discover an article in a medical journal in which a psychiatrist discussed the remarriage of people with grown children. This event is unsettling, he said, because it flouts established attitudes toward the cycles of human life. Traditionally, love, marriage and child-rearing make up one cycle, to be followed, at least in the case of one spouse, by a cycle of loss and mourning. Remarriage, even if the spouse has been lost by divorce rather than death, disrupts the established patterns. Indeed, the author put it more sternly. Remarriage, he said, can be seen as a distortion, a violation, a misapprehension of the cyclical destiny of human existence.

That was more than I had bargained for. Did my friends, I wondered, truly see me as distorting the cycle of human existence? Even as I considered this theory my everyday experience seemed to point in a different direction. I felt that some of my women friends— and my accomplished, independent daughters—had been so pleased to see me adjust to single life, to find satisfaction in working hard, living alone, traveling alone, going out with men but not being dependent on male attention, that my decision to remarry seemed a capitulation to petty, conventional standards. Whereas I had been a shining example of the older woman making it on her own, now I was going to spoil it all by marrying and settling down just like everyone else.

I found myself avoiding, to some degree, talking about my coming marriage with the children. Here again expert opinion was less than reassuring. It seems that the advent of a new spouse may set grown children to worrying about such things as the management and division of family resources and the problem of generational succession— in other words, who will get what when the time comes.

Did my children have such concerns? Was that why I was afraid to express joy at what was in fact a joyful prospect?

This unspoken fear persisted through several frantic weeks, during which I talked with caterers, bought a dress, ordered invitations and picked out a cake, all on my lunch hour. It was still with me as my fiancé and I planned a wedding trip that would involve air travel. How, I wondered, could we arrange things so that if one or both of us was killed en route, our children would receive the inheritances they would have received if we hadn't been married?

Again, my experience seemed not to confirm professional theory. I found myself unable to concentrate on the problem of generational succession and I could not conceive of it as a burning issue in my children's minds since they do not seem to worry about money from one week to the next, let alone from generation to generation.

No, my real fear was different, and it finally revealed itself as I prepared an itinerary with addresses, telephone numbers and dates of arrival and departure. My real fear was that one of the children would write us a letter that began, "Dear Mom and Mr. Harris."

Since unexpected business demands obligated us to cancel the trip, my worry was wasted, but it was not totally unfounded. People who remarry do tend to have some unrealistic expectations and some quite justified fears that those expectations will not be met.

Many grown children do not easily accept a step-parent, even to the extent of calling this person Bob or Sue instead of Mr. or Mrs. Smith. A surface acceptance may be exactly that. Genuine love and acceptance take time, and when you remarry in later life you wonder if there will ever be enough time for these people whom you love to learn to love one another.

Similarly, friends who have supported you through a divorce and seen you steer smoothly into single life may find it hard to accept you as a member of a new marital partnership. They remember the relationship they had with you and your former spouse, their sadness when the marriage ended, the difficulty they may have had separating the two of you in their own lives and remaining on good terms with you both, the fear they may have felt that what had happened to you could happen to them. All those memories are stirred up anew when you are about to become an overage bride.

In some women I talked with I detected another unspoken fear: If a new marriage offers such interesting possibilities, might their husbands be considering these possibilities for themselves? Even more unsettling, might they be considering such possibilities for *themselves*?

If you decide, willy-nilly, to disrupt the generational cycle, there are forces working for you as well as against you. Anyone who has coped with travel arrangements, dinner parties and tax returns as a free agent knows that in matters such as these our society favors couples over singles. There is also widespread acceptance of the desire of middle-aged divorced people to prove that they can follow a failure with a success.

None of the experts I consulted offered a set of objective criteria on which to judge whether a particular remarriage—yours, for example —is in fact a success. But on an informal basis I would say that you can probably consider that you are making progress when your children stop greeting your new husband with a hearty handshake, your mother remembers not to call him by her former son-in-law's name and you— who have had your own remembering and forgetting to do—can contemplate wearing the diamond you received at age twenty-two. After all, isn't it simply a very pretty rock?

JUNE, 1984

Being Alone

JENNIFER ALLEN

B aby, it's chilly outside. It's chilly in here, too: one of the shaft windows in my railroad apartment is flapping open and shut, letting in pizza-scented breezes off Third Avenue. Yesterday, the latch that keeps the window shut dropped out of the soggy old wood that held it and got swallowed by the shaft. The same thing happens every winter: one raw evening in January I came home to find that a miniature dune of snow had collected on the table next to the window.

I don't mind the drafts so much in the spring; I welcome them in summer, when the air in this old building gets sweltry, thick as soup, and wet towels turn sour-smelling before they can dry. Winters are the worst. In winter, I muffle myself in my busted-window outfit: two sweaters, scarf, a blanket over the works. You're not too agile in a get-up like this—I know how babies feel stuck in snowsuits that set their arms at right angles to their bodies—but I don't get around to mending the window, not for a week at least. That's because I'm hardly here at all, except for pit stops: I drop off the dry cleaning here, sleep here when I'm not at my boyfriend's, but I try not to spend time here.

People I know in New York fall into two camps in the matter of apartment living: those who like to be home, and those who hate it. The ones who like it are often married or living seriously with someone. They have avocado pits sprouting in jelly glasses on their windowsills and invite friends over for dinner. The ones who hate it are mostly unattached and on the young side and are rarely home. "What's there to go home to?" we pout. A can of tuna, an uppity reminder from Con Ed to pay last month's bill, lonesome captivity.

·   ·   ·

I saw a play last fall that had no words and only one set. Here is the plot: a woman returns to her apartment after work, makes herself a supper of soup and two pieces of buttered toast, eats, washes the dishes, watches television and changes into her nightgown. Then she swallows a handful of pills and lies down on her sofa bed to die. I thought the play made perfect sense, in a way. Solo domesticity can spook a person.

For many of us home-haters, then, home becomes the foe, the mate we wish to be rid of whose very existence is a guilty-making reproach. We punish our apartments by making them unappetizing places to be in—no pictures on the walls, not enough lamps, a lumpy armchair—by neglecting them. This gets us off the hook, after a fashion: who could expect us to spend any time in such an unappealing place? It's easier to skedaddle, to stay out. I have a friend—she's beautiful, always elegantly dressed and accessorized—who is at home even less than I am. I think her busy nightlife has to do, at least in part, with her stove. She says the outside of her stove is so greasy that she gets stuck to it sometimes. No wonder she stays out.

Where are we, while our curtains are turning gray with soot? For one thing, we go to all of the parties we're invited to, bad or good. We're easy to spot at any gathering: we're the ones at the refreshment table, going at the hors d'oeuvres as if they were dinner, which they are. We also stay one drink longer than we should, so that we're forever ending up in soulful conversations with people whose phone numbers we find a week later, scribbled on a cocktail napkin and stuffed in a coat pocket.

But most days there are no parties; we have to fend for ourselves. As pockets of time go, 5 until 8 in the evening is the cruelest. Other people are putting old Supremes albums on their stereos, doing little shimmies to "Baby Love" as they shake the salad dressing. "Look, honey," wives are saying to husbands in kitchens where shiny copper-bottomed pots hang on the walls like huge new pennies, "I found the most beautiful chops." (A while ago, before I knew better, I had an affair with a married man. He'd separated from his wife, kept quirky hours, liked sitting in nightclubs stroking my cheek. Dusk killed the fling, I think. He could not bear that time of day without someone to go home to, buckled under the strain, began stealing back to his wife's apartment to pass those hours. He had been moved back in altogether for a week before I noticed.)

Home avoiders swallow hard and wrestle with entertaining themselves while daytime dies. Melancholia squats on its haunches right over the shoulder, ready to spring: it is possible, while waiting for a green light at 7 o'clock on a November night, to suddenly believe that the boy you dated in college and dumped was really your life's true love. Avoid, during these hours, extremes both tender and coarse: pretty toddlers who make eyes at you on the bus, Times Square, skaters at Rockefeller Center, any Chock Full o'Nuts. Stay away from harshly lit mirrors. Also from other single people in groups: for example, I take special care to keep clear of Greg's Deli at 91st and Third, which is two blocks from my apartment and across the street from a high-rise housing complex whose renters are all twenty-seven, unmarried, and enrolled in bank training programs. Every night the checkout line at Greg's stretches the length of the store; on it stand handsome young men and women, holding identical evening provisions: a gallon bottle of Tab, a pot pie, two bottles of Heineken, oatmeal cookies that come wrapped in packages of three.

Sometimes you can bulldoze your way through those hours, just squash them into submission. Work's the best weapon. It's easy to stay busy at an office, licking envelopes, making Xeroxes, wielding the tape dispenser and stapler, writing plucky memos that begin "Thought the enclosed might interest you." My home-hating friends have other methods: one hits the Idle Hour book and magazine store in the Village, where customers are allowed to riffle through every magazine in the place if they want to, for as long as they like. Another goes underwater for an hour every day. Fifty brisk laps in a health club pool, she finds, is as good a way as any of getting through the hard time.

But occasionally, in spite of all the precautions, purposefulness slips away with the last light. I find myself in peculiar places. I'm sitting in a discount store at Seventh Avenue and 16th Street trying on shoes, something I usually have no patience for. There's a pair I like pretty well, but they're too expensive and a little too pointy for my unslender feet. I brush off my misgivings, listen to the teen-age salesperson when she tells me I will make a "really cute" impression in these shoes, decide that I must buy them right this minute. Feeling naughty and excited, like a porky girl about to devour a box of doughnuts, I write a check so fast that I start to scribble the name of the store on the line where I'm supposed to write my signature. There. Now I have a token, proof: money has been spent, therefore I exist. My spirits won't go flat for hours, not until I get home and look at the shoes in the mirror and see that I look only moderately cute at best.

The rest of the evening is easier. Bless friends, boyfriends: one of them is usually available for the 7:50 show at the Regency or a cheap dinner out. When they aren't, I grit my teeth and go home, or I call an older, married couple I know. They are always home at night; they always tell me to come over for dinner right away. When I get there, Nancy gives me a pair of her husband's wool socks to pad around in. I set the table while she makes spaghetti and her husband goes on, at some length, about his day in the world of broadcasting. After dinner we line up on the living room couch and watch the news, and the husband snaps mildly at us for talking during the big stories. It's very pleasant.

If it gets late, I sleep over, in the bedroom their daughter has vacated for her own apartment. It's a snug, child-size room, with a short, skinny bed. I have to lie sideways and bend my knees to fit in it, but I'm happy to. In the morning I tiptoe out before they wake up, trudge to my apartment for a change of clothes. Next year, I tell myself as I head up Third Avenue, I'm settling down.

MAY, 1982

ANN P. HARRIS

When my husband and I separated after one of the longer-running marriages of modern times, I knew that I would face a lot of problems. I am happy to report, however, that it is possible not only to survive these problems but also to enjoy them.

For instance, take the problem of depression. A total negative, you might say. But did you ever wake up one morning and want to rush into the shower, rush out to work, rush to Bloomingdale's on your lunch hour, call your psychiatrist and thank him, invite eight people for dinner and sign up for a Spanish immersion class that very day? Did you ever get up and realize that for the first time in three months you hadn't thought of taking warm milk, herbal tea, a snort of sherry or a pill the night before?

The fact is, you can't really appreciate subclinical mania until you've been depressed. If you've never had the post-separation blues, you've never had the exhilarating feeling of having licked them either, and believe me, it's sensational for the ego.

Then there's the problem of going alone to a party. Your first impulse is to say you're busy, then you slap your wrist and accept. The day before, you're sure you're getting the flu. When you're dressed, you wonder why you ever thought you could wear black, and the shoes that fit in the store are making a blister on your heel. This is just as well, because adjusting your shoes gives you something to do after you've just met two dozen people who are all talking to one another and none of them is talking to you.

You do one of two things. You say forget it, and after a decent interval of wandering around with a drink in one hand and a miniature quiche in the other, you leave. Not a bad declaration of independence, as independence goes. Or else you screw up your courage and speak to one or another of the two dozen people, who, for a wonder, turns out to be interesting to talk to and, even greater wonder, interested in talking to you. It doesn't matter if this person is male or female, or how long you talk, or how many such people you find to talk to. The marvelous thing is that you never once ask yourself who your husband is talking to and why he doesn't come over and rescue you from this boring lady, or boring gentleman, and why the two of you can't leave quietly and go to the movies.

When you're alone, *you* can leave quietly and go to the movies.

Another good thing about going to parties alone: No one assumes that an adequate conversational opener is to ask you what your husband does.

Many formerly married people find eating alone a problem, but I secretly love it. I love the mystery of it. Will there be frankfurters in the refrigerator or not? If not, will there be eggs? Did I or didn't I eat the doggy bag of Chinese gourmet food that I was kindly allowed to take home by my date, the Chinese gourmet? And whatever the meal of the evening proves to be, will I eat it at 6:30 or at 11? I never really know when the mood will strike me to take apart an old tweed skirt and completely rework it (a four-hour job that is usually followed by my throwing out the skirt), but since the mood generally strikes when I get home from work, dinner may necessarily be delayed. And who, I ask myself, would willingly wait four hours for dinner while someone alters a skirt, except the owner of the skirt?

Breakfast alone isn't bad either. You have it when you get up, not when he does. You have it in bed if you want to. And if you spend too long over coffee and the paper, you can leave the bed unmade. This can happen when you're married, too, but then it's usually he who has left the bed unmade and you who have neglected to make it. There's a subtle but significant difference when you're the one who does both.

The problem of what to say at awkward conversational moments crops up so often that the quick riposte will soon become second nature. For example, what to say to bare acquaintances who assure you that you will be happier in your new life ("How would you know?"). How to reply to old friends who intimate that taking a full-time job can put too much strain on a marriage ("I always felt that Jim had every right to his career.")

A very common problem in the conversational area arises from the fact that married women customarily talk about "our" first apartment, "our" trip to Italy and what "we did in the summer of sixty-eight." Separation will offer what may prove to be a perpetually exciting challenge to your memory, your sense of identity and your presence of mind: the challenge of saying "I" when you are thinking "we."

When you're alone, you face the practical problem of bills. Pay them. If your absent husband offers to pay them for you, you should refuse. Let's face it, a midlife marital split is unreal: You're unreal, he's unreal, it's unreal. What's needed is reality, and the way to get it is to write out your own checks to the landlord, the telephone company and Consolidated Edison. After a little prodding, it will eventually dawn on these people that if you can write real checks you must be a real person, and they will begin not only to accept your money but to send you bills—bills made out in *your name.*

That's reality, and it's heaven.

Perhaps the most significant problem you face when your marriage breaks up is income tax. In my former household, we used to eat in the kitchen from January through April, because the dining-room table was full of mysterious papers that couldn't be touched. Some of these papers were my checkbook stubs, containing unexplained entries about which I would be interrogated at inconvenient moments.

There really were no convenient moments for these questions, since it is never convenient to admit that you deposited $15.67 in your account last October and you have no idea why.

Now, I litter the table with my own checkbook stubs and W-2

and 1099 forms and charitable contribution receipts. I read with fascination Schedules A, B, C, D, E and SE. I go over the instructions in Form 1040 line by line and marvel at the fact that at the end of ten days or so I am going to come out with a figure for line 37. I look fondly at this little book, remembering that it was responsible for one of the most joyous moments of my life, when my accountant and I had a difference of opinion as to my tax status and I turned out to be right.

Not all women feel as I do about income tax. I have a friend who was so upset by all of this that she made a play for her accountant. Personally, I wrote a thank-you note to the I.R.S.

While you are dealing with the problems of non-marriage, it is tempting to think that the solution is remarriage. It isn't. That prospect will bring with it a new and different set of problems.

If, however, you should find yourself faced with these problems, enjoy them. You've earned them.

JUNE, 1984

LINDA BIRD FRANCKE

One of the things I achieved in my thirty-ninth year was the incomprehensible luxury of regaining not only my own bedroom but my own bed as well. It was startling how much the regaining of lost nocturnal turf meant to me.

For more years than I comfortably cared to remember, I had shared both bedroom and bed with more people than I also comfortably cared to remember. Whether bedroom coupling was caused by lack of space, a dearth of funds or the marital premise that twin beds are the first sign of a failing marriage and that separate bedrooms signal the drafting of a separation agreement, I had lain beside someone else's snores for a score and fifteen years.

As a little girl, my first roommate was my older sister, who perversely and persistently shined a flashlight on the ceiling over my side of the room, then slowly lowered her hand over the beam until the giant claw tore at the fine edge of my control. Then, for three years there was a merciful period when she went off to boarding school and I claimed the bedroom as my own, having the unembarrassed space to chat myself to sleep every night, pretending on alternate evenings that I was Nancy Drew solving every conceivable mystery on Larkspur Lane, or Heidi nestled in a bed of fresh hay, waiting for Peter the Goatherd to bring me my morning mug of frothy goat's milk.

But then it came my turn to start the boarding school/college cycle, and in the next five years I escalated into one, two and finally three roommates. My private chats with myself were replaced by counting the breaths of my adenoidal sleepmates and trying hard not to listen to the radios several of them played all night under their pillows, the discovery of which by the pumpkin-breasted housemother would have meant instant expulsion from the school and possibly death.

It didn't get any better after we were daisy-chained into the greater world. And after an overshared apartment with four friends, and three years of trying to sort out laundry, bills and lamb chops, I was desperate. Marriage, I thought. That will do it. Then I'll finally have my own place. But I had overlooked one thing. The husband gets to live there, too. So not only did I lose the fantasy of my own bedroom at the altar, I irretrievably lost my own bed as well. Amid piles of wedding-present queen-sized sheets from Porthault and color-coordinated towels with my new initials on them (for I had lost my own name as well), I embarked on the next fifteen years of shared bedroom life.

Now, for those of the togetherness school, a warm body to snuggle up against on a cold night or when the occasional terrors strike is one of the elixirs of married life. But the operative word is "occasional." Though some very pleasant things do occur in bed or on the living-room floor, there is no compelling reason to spin that pleasure into eight hours of shared sleep. And it was that every-night sharing that caused me to start couch-hopping around our New York apartment, sleeping one night in the living room, another in the dining room, and even several, inexplicably comfortable, on the bathroom floor. I was not avoiding my husband, who is a lovely man, but searching for some long-lost pocket of privacy where the scientific principle of cause and effect concerned only me.

If I woke up freezing cold, it was not because someone else had wrestled the quilt onto his side or kicked out the plug on the electric blanket. In the bitter nights of winter, I could climb into the feathers wearing ski socks and various layers of the morning's clothes without hearing justified snickers of incredulity. It was a joy to find some time and space that was not reactive, and though it occasionally puzzled my husband, my children saw nothing strange in my emerging from the dining room in the morning with my blanket over my shoulder.

Exploring cautiously with other women my new discovery of

sleeping alone, I soon found that after their initial reluctance to admit to such marital blasphemy, they too found solace in those nights when their husbands were away traveling or in the summer city while the women tended to the country rentals.

"I go to bed with some trashy novel and a bag of Doritos," admitted one such friend in East Hampton, "and I practically wag my tail with the pleasure of it. Then Sam comes on the weekend and he says, 'Ugh, how can you read that trash, and you know I can't sleep with the light on, and what are all these crumbs in the bed?' He's right, of course, but those nights are worth anything." Another friend thinks her marriage has been saved by the fact that her husband now spends week nights in the city and returns to Connecticut on the weekends.

"When we all lived in New York he'd come home, drink a couple of martinis to relax, then get into bed with cheese and crackers and watch television," the now weekend wife said. "Of course he'd fall asleep and I'd end up crumbing his chest into the 'silent butler' just like I was cleaning up during a cocktail party. This way of life is better."

Though I hesitate to pull the mattress pad out from under the marriage counselor industry, which professes that sleeping together is staying together, I can't believe more relationships wouldn't survive if bedroom sharing were an elective rather than the required course. As children we dreamed of gaining the life stage of having our own rooms and our own things and we all wrote angry cardboard signs which read PRIVAT—KEPE OUT AND THIS MEANS U! So where is it written that having successfully attained adulthood, we no longer have that same need for privacy?

But now, during an experimental year of country living during which my husband joins me on weekends, that traditional barrier has been broken. I now sink into my own bed in my own bedroom each week night, making a little guilt-free nest in the comfortable clutter of clean laundry, and half-read books and newspapers while shooing away the dog, who believes strongly in nightly togetherness. I read late or not at all, watch 3 A.M. television or turn off the light at 8:30. Solo sleeping is an eight-hour holiday of private indulgence that leaves me slightly more willing to serve the family and worldly good in the morning. And besides, I'm told on long-term authority that I was the one who did the snoring anyway.

SEPTEMBER, 1977

ANEES JUNG

The black Plymouth that drove us to school had dark draperies. Seated in the back seat, we felt suspended like spring dolls in a magic box. We were five little girls. We emerged every morning from a house in Hyderabad that in many ways was like a citadel. It had high white walls, courtyards that were never without flowers and stone terraces from where we saw the stars, the moon and a world that seemed to extend farther and farther. It was a house enclosed but not shut. The girls had their garden, their games, their books and each other. And then there were all the other women—the relatives who came carrying the color and flavor of the old city; the bangle-sellers, the folk singers, the nannies. They grew up supporting each other, the way women do when they are pushed into a circle where their strength becomes their survival.

Father, the only familiar male figure, embodied the ideal. He exhibited courage to look into the future, nourished the tenuous link between the outside and the inside, and helped create balances that spelled harmony within the family. He lent the outer dimension; the women provided the energy that surged within; both gave the house its light, its life, its warmth and radiance.

Almost hidden but tightly packed within each of the girls was a vast sense of wonder that, within such citadels, tends to acquire poetic proportions. The outside always beckoned.

At times I pulled at the dark draperies and tried to peer out. The ayah—who combined the qualities of a matron, a guardian and, to a lesser degree, a servant—rebuked me. No one was to see us, she warned gravely, for we were little treasures to be claimed in time by those who had earned the right to do so.

. . .

Twenty years have passed. I have still not been claimed. The old ayah, I have learned, died some years ago, probably of a broken heart. Her little treasures, unguarded, have scattered, have been pushed into worlds where Plymouths with dark draperies do not exist. I have graduated from the magic box into the hurly-burly of a newspaper office. I no longer peer at landscapes. They have begun to peer at me as I pass among them every morning seated in a taxicab driven by a hefty Sikh, who speaks a robust language I pretend to understand.

The doorman at the office gate is slouched on his bench; other men loll around in the courtyard. Though they are technically my colleagues, I do not know their names or the quality of their lives. They have a vague sense of who I am: My arrival is noticed; they turn around and stare. Few have the courtesy to nod a greeting, a gesture that should naturally come to people when they work together. They do not realize that to stare at a person, more particularly a woman, is rude. But then they probably do not see me as a woman, a creature whose place is ideally her home. I represent for them that new species of women who have brazenly crossed the Lakshman Rekha—the mythical line that was not to be crossed even by the gods.

My face tightens. I hear my footsteps as I march in. I become a "memsahib," a symbol those men have come to recognize and respect.

For seven years I spent my sun-filled days in a newspaper office. And each morning I did not fail to note an uneasy feeling of discomfort buried deep within me. Recently I gave up journalism and took to the corporate life. My days are frenetic, crowded, laminated with a veneer of national purpose and social commitment. My nights have not changed. I am torn between the two, for they no longer connect or bind. The chair I sit in during the day is taller than the one I last occupied. So is my office. But not my world. In fact it has shrunk; it encircles one kind of people, one way of doing things. It feels as if I have entered a cloister, patterned on ancient, inflexible, often repetitive rules. It is well guarded to lend one a sense of physical security.

My cloister is curtained by cane through which the world is visible.

I leave it as the sun wanes and return home—to a servant, to the fuzz of a white dog and a Jat village beyond my balcony.

In the village there are no cloisters. The walls are more like garden fences, tentatively raised with uneven stones. The houses are shelters of brick and mud with roofs of grass, not fortified to guard people or separate them from nature. Their fragility connotes impermanence. Yet the lives lived in them are rooted, whole, integrated. The village lives in its open spaces. People share them naturally with animals. When the rains come ropes become swings, pots become drums and there is song and children's laughter. The season brings relief from the long, hot sun. Nights are filled with the cry of peacocks, the chipped sounds of crickets. I lie awake trying to separate one sound from another. They do not intrude, only accentuate the stillness.

And so the years move, the seasons change. I move with them, seeking my peace, my alternatives. Would I have been happier without these years? Perhaps not. For they have been large years, although the road I have traveled has not been mapped; it emerged on its own. And the road that lies ahead is not clearer; the landmarks emerge only on arrival. People tell me I have "arrived," but I do not know what it means. For I never really planned a career—just grew into it. Hence I make my norms as I go along. They cannot be shared with others as they are strictly mine. I have yet to find a face that suits a working woman and a graph that determines the patterns of her life. I continue to live an experience for which I have not yet found a name.

I am a Moslem woman, from Hyderabad, a city whose name conjures images of fragile women weeping behind veils. How then can I be a working woman, live alone, be "modern"?

I live alone, but not by choice. Secretly I long for courtyards filled with the laughter of children, for stone terraces where one slept and heard others breathe. Living alone narrows one's concerns, reveals the inadequacy of joys that are not shared. Even freedom without sharing become abstract and unreal.

For me it has always been others who have helped open windows, tear veils. I carry the essence of these people in my life—in the way I live, work, seek to be happy. My world speaks more of them, less of what I naturally inherited.

All that remains of Hyderabad in my apartment is a threadbare Bokhara rug, my mother's unused silver mirror and an old wooden frame that for years has preserved yellowed pictures of little girls dressed in lace and brocade, with large round heads and wide, wondrous eyes. Childhood walls have fallen away. Flowers are no longer the pride of courtyards. Nor are little girls. I am one from among them.

MAY, 1984

SUE HUBBELL

Yesterday afternoon I was lying on a mechanic's creeper underneath my half-ton 1954 Chevy pickup truck with a grease gun across my chest. The public radio station that I can get in the Ozarks of southern Missouri was kindly filling the barn with Bach's Third Orchestral Suite in D Major. But I wasn't listening very closely. I was thinking about farming.

It's comfortable lying on the creeper, with its padded headrest, out there in the cool of the barn, and under the truck is as good a place as any to listen to Bach, but I hadn't crept under there to do so or even to think about farming, for that matter. My truck has twenty grease points, and they have to be tended often in a vehicle that old. While greasing them I noticed that I had been careless with the right rear shock absorber. Not only was it missing, but the bracket that held it in place had been ripped loose too. I drive over rough, rocky roads and through bumpy pastures in my work, and I was trying to think where I might have lost the shock absorber. I put the grease gun down in trying to recall where I had driven the truck since I greased it the last time, for I knew that the shock absorber was in place then. But, with the brain half listening to Bach, I had shifted to thinking about farming, which is what I do to make a living.

Every year the Department of Agriculture mails me a farm census form to fill out. One year I forgot to return it and the department began sending me nagging, reproachful letters indicating that the picture of American agriculture would not be complete without my finished form. American agriculture has enough problems as it is, and I do not want to add to the burden, so now I fill out the form promptly and return it. The information that I have to offer is meager, and I wonder what the computer makes of it.

The Department of Agriculture wants to know how many acres of wheat I plant, how many pigs I fatten, how I market my corn, how many hands I employ and the age of my tractor and plow. It has that sort of picture of what a farm should be.

Instead, I have to report that I have 18 million bee souls living in 300 hives. I have to acknowledge that my pasture grows Queen Anne's lace, black-eyed Susans and daisies. That I work alone on these 90 acres. That I am female, yes, and 50 years old. There is no place on the form to explain about the honey house full of machinery that extracts and processes the honey that I harvest from the bees, so the department believes that my only farm machinery is the three-quarter-ton '82 truck that I use to haul honey to market and the '54 Chevy that I was lying under. My crop for the past year cannot be measured in heads or bushels, so on the line marked "Other" I write that it was 33,000 pounds of honey. There is a proper line for chickens on the form, so I gratefully write in that I have three dozen laying hens and one mean rooster and that I sell eggs at the local feed store, but I don't think even that is quite what the government has in mind.

There is not enough space on the form to explain that, at the price of one gallon of honey each year, I rent from other farmers enough land to put out my beehives in groups of 10 or 15. My bees cover 1,000 square miles I do not own in their foraging flights, going from flower to flower, for which I pay no rent, stealing nectar but pollinating the plants in return. It is an unruly, benign kind of agriculture, and making a living by it has such a wild, anarchistic, raffish appeal that it unsuits me for virtually any other.

There is no way to explain it on the form, so the Department of Agriculture will never know that although my pasture may grow only daisies, it is beautiful, particularly on a moonlight night, which is one of the main reasons I am a farmer. I would like to tell how I sit in the living room of my cabin in winter twilight and watch deer browsing in the pasture beyond the barn. I would like to describe how it looks here on my 90 acres when the dogwood and redbud bloom start together in the springtime. And about the pretty, rocky, fern-lined creek that runs along my southern boundary. I walk down there a lot because it is different at all seasons of the year and there is a lot to keep track of, but there is no space on the Federal form for any information of that sort.

Owning the 90 acres and making a good enough living from them to allow me to live here is a heady thing, though I sometimes spend a bad few hours around 2 A.M. tossing and turning and worrying about how cheap import honey is eroding the domestic market, about the effect of the Federal price supports on my sales and about how I'll ever be able to meet the interest payment on my crop loan. But that is the price of being a farmer and entrepreneur, and I'd rather pay that price than work for someone else.

Fifteen years ago I was a wimpish librarian at Brown University, and I could have greased the sports car that I drove to work and performed some of the mechanical work on it, but it never occurred to me to do so. Instead I was at the mercy of experts who kept the objects necessary to my life in good order. I didn't understand much about how those objects worked, and I often felt helpless and irritated because of that lack of understanding.

Now, since beekeeping is not the kind of farming that makes a person rich, I have had to learn rather a lot about doing things for myself. For instance, heating my cabin with electricity or gas is beyond my means, so I have a wood stove and cut firewood from my lot out beyond the pasture. The job, I have discovered, is a pleasant one. I cut my supply in July, an hour or two each morning while the woods are cool and misty and fragrant.

Mechanical work, such as changing the truck's oil and greasing it, is not so pleasant. Bits of caked mud and old grease fall into my eyes while I am doing it, but the old truck serves me well and I like to treat it courteously in return. One day last winter, when it was so cold that my fingers wouldn't hold the grease gun, I had Clyde, down at the

gasoline station, grease it for me, and I noticed, with unspeakable smugness, that I do a better job than he does. And I like being on intimate
enough terms with my truck to discover that the shock absorber is missing and that I can replace it, that the tail pipe needs a new strap that I
can fashion or that the bolts holding body and frame together have
shaken loose on the rough roads and that I should tighten them before
damage is done. I wouldn't know those things unless I spent a certain
number of hours staring up at the underside of the truck while greasing it.

That was how I got to thinking about farming yesterday. Becoming a farmer—Type: Other; Land Owned: 90 acres; Status: Single;
Sex: Female; Age: 50—has forced a competence upon me that I would
never have had under other circumstances. And that, I realize as I lie
on the creeper under my Chevy, has made me outrageously happy.

Of course the Bach helps. There's nothing like Bach to grease a
truck by.

JULY, 1984

Having Children . . .
and Raising Them

JOYCE MAYNARD

I have been spending my evenings, this past week, watching Olympic skaters spin around the ice. In my dreams, and any time I find myself on a smooth frozen pond with no one watching, I am Tiffany Chin. I hum myself a sound track, rely heavily on hand gestures rather than triple jumps and camels. Because the truth is, I'm not much of a skater, even when I'm not, as I am now, nine months pregnant with thirty extra pounds and a sore back.

For the first eight and a half months of this third pregnancy of mine, I have been carrying on my life pretty much as usual. It's the two children with us already who demand the attention I once gave to childbirth manuals and nursery decoration. Also, I tell myself I know all about babies, and having them. When people inquire how I am, I tend to register surprise at the question and then say, "How about you?" I have tended almost to forget that around March 1 a baby is going to be born here.

But there comes a point in a pregnancy—and it's here—when the body and the mind get pretty much overtaken, and every inch is occupied territory. Three times in the past six years I've reached that point in the middle of a New Hampshire winter—my son and daughter's birthdays coinciding with the full moons of one February and another March. And now here I sit once more, staring out a window at nothing but mud and snow, putting off taking the ten steps between my chair and the door, where our dog is scratching to be let out, because the task just seems too tiring. I've spent the last twenty minutes drawing mustaches on the models in the annual *Sports Illustrated* bathing suit issue. I might as well belong to a separate species from those flat-bellied, golden-skinned women in their silver bikinis.

· · ·

It's an odd state to be in, this period just before the birth of a baby. The mind empties. I see my true self slipping away, being replaced by a person who behaves, not like me, but like full-term pregnant women everywhere. Unexplainable tears. A ravenous appetite for salt one night and sweet the next. A need—as real as an artist's for paint or a keyboard—to wax the floors and repaint the kitchen. I want to hold not only babies, kittens, puppies, but also a nearly full-grown Irish setter. "That letter you wrote had the word 'tiny' in places," a friend tells me.

So I bake cookies and stare for half an hour into the tropical fish tank, watching a cobra-skin guppy circle a plastic model of a scuba diver who endlessly raises and lowers a piece of plastic buried treasure. I fold laundry and sort old baby clothes, bury my face in the little T-shirts, remembering the one who wore them last. And I read him the story of *Babar and His Children*—the chronicle of the triple birth to his wife, Queen Celeste, of baby elephants named Pom, Flora and Alexander, and try to explain an illustration that shows Babar watering a flower and seeing in its center the image of a baby elephant. Of Babar poised over his royal stationery to write proclamations and producing a drawing of a baby elephant. I know the feeling.

The strange part is what follows. That as the full-term pregnant woman sits, face to the sun, in a calm tidal pool, staring out to a sea with not a whitecap in sight, suddenly—she never knows when—there comes a tidal wave. I have known plenty of women to dread the birth, and afterward to curse the agony they went through. For myself, I look forward to the event with the anticipation of a passionate surfer. More accurately, with the anticipation of one who never could surf, or ski, or stay on a skateboard even. The last one chosen for every school field-hockey and basketball team she ever played on. Before I had children I always wondered whether their births would be, for me, like the ultimate in my gym class failures. And discovered, instead (no particular skill evident here, except maybe concentration), that I'd finally found my sport.

My son was two days overdue the night a call came from Canada to tell me that my father, in a Victoria hospital with pneumonia, was not likely to live through to morning. Not much to be done about it: he couldn't have heard me if I tried speaking to him, and I wouldn't have known what to say anyway. I put down the receiver and told my husband, who had been watching the Boston Celtics play Los Angeles. Then I felt the sickest I have ever been in my life, and my legs began to shake so badly that I lay down on the bed and he lay across my shins to steady me. We had seen a baby of ours born, on that same bed, four years before, and still I thought this was death my body was registering, not birth. Just to be safe we called the midwife—forty-five-minute drive from us—suggesting that she come over. But things happened very fast then and five minutes later I heard a sound in the room coming from my mouth, but almost unrecognizable—a sound that I have heard only one other time in my life, when I pushed our daughter out into the world. Steve felt for the cord around the baby's neck and guided him as he corkscrewed out our ten-pound boy.

The next morning, when our daughter came downstairs to find the top of her brother's head sticking out from under the covers of our bed, where he slept between us, what she said was, "My dream came true." And the thing that always strikes me with amazement is how, in a house where there had been three people a few hours earlier, there were now four, although no one had come in the door.

I think of my children's births—carry them around with me— every day of my life. Sometimes it will be just a fleeting image: my friend Stephanie coming into the room, the day our daughter was born, with a bagful of oranges I'd asked her to bring over, seeing them spill out in all directions on the bed. My husband holding out a towel he'd warmed on our wood stove to wrap around a baby who would be born before the towel had time to cool off again. Audrey's thick tuft of black hair that I saw and touched before I even knew the sex of the still unborn person it belonged to. Her hands on her cheeks, like some vaudeville chorus girl pantomiming surprise, as she shot out. The feeling of a newborn baby's skin. Eyes wide open, looking at light for the first time.

. . .

One more thing I want to say: if I had been unable to have babies my-self, I would have grieved over never having known what it's like to carry a baby, to feel movement from inside my own body, and most of all I would have missed, terribly, watching my child born. But the world is full of adoptive parents, and people who had their babies before the return of natural childbirth, and the acceptance of fathers in the delivery room, and though I often hear those men and women speak with regret over having missed out on their children's births, they didn't miss out on their children. And I will never know what it's like to ride on a bobsled or execute a triple toe loop in Sarajevo. I love riding the wave of childbirth—love even how hard it is, and when the moment comes that I know I've done it for the last time, I'll mourn. But giving birth is an experience and parenthood is a state of being; the one passes, the other never ends.

FEBRUARY, 1984

MARY KAY BLAKELY

The young boy thrives in the limelight of family attention and affection. Three of his most steadfast cheerleaders—three familial fans—are gathered around the kitchen table for a supper celebration.

He's seven today. The age of reason.

His head bobs up and down in the waves of his intemperate glee. Instinctively, I survey the landscape of his head, searching around the crown for the familiar cowlick that sends the hair in all directions.

The nurse is holding a mirror between the stirrups. "See! Can you see it! The head's crowning!" I see the swirling mass of hair, spinning strands, drawing me deeply into the mirror, into the rushed beginnings, the unstoppable contractions, the contradictions of motherhood. I know that spot. The mental snapshot I took seven years ago at 4:15 A.M., that most kissed place on the crown of his head.

We clear the dishes and he breaks open the box of birthday candles, counting the waxy spirals to the magic number. "Know what 5 plus 2 is, Mom? Same as 3 plus 4!" He smiles at me with new-math wisdom.

How can he be seven? We're both still getting used to the bonds of motherhood, still jockeying for position in the me and he of it. The job of my longest tenure, mothering—the state of semi-surprise, semi-delight, semi-confusion. When can I expect to be accustomed to motherhood if not after seven years?

The smile spreads over the tiny acreage of his freckled cheeks, a smile contagious up to his brow, a smile deliberately intended to charm the susceptible mother at the table. It works. It works just fine.

I pass the picture of him on the breakfront every day, returning the chuckle I read on his face. It's a private joke between us, the ka-leidoscopic pleasure of knowing each other.

He pokes the candles through the thick chocolate frosting on the top of the cake. There's a calculated clumsiness in his actions—he has to pause after each one to lick his fingers. Seven delicious executions of candle planting.

The personality is permanently formed in childhood. All things shaped and molded—by SEVEN? Little psyches firmly in place? Before he can read the Bhagavad Gita? Before he can argue the Constitution? Before he can comprehend what Simone de Beauvoir meant? Before he has fallen in love/gone to war/left home? No. More shaping and molding to come. Much more. Outside my influence.

The cake is placed on the table for the opening ceremony, its iced surface now a relief map of fingerprints, with a small population of teetering candles, the intoxicating symbols of a developing life.

This is the boy the man will come from. Will I like—no, will I love—the man the way I love this boy? The forthcoming man. A vague fear of him. The maleness that threatens to separate us.

I have yet to face the understandable panic in my friend's last letter, the sentence jumping off the page like a banner headline: "No. 1 son sprouted pubic hair this summer!" She, caught between her class-action anger at men and her wild devotion to her two young sons. "How do I talk to him now? How will I know when to knock on his door?" The mother and young man exchange places of power, in accordance with custom, in recognition of the status of "man." Is detachment inevitable?

His dad places a modest pile of presents in front of him, still wrapped in the brown bags they were brought home in. This boy, the son of two working parents, doesn't know that children usually cele-brate their birthdays with homemade cakes shaped like giraffes and presents of primary colors and complicated bows. This boy knows only parcel-post brown and cellophane tape.

In twenty years, in his group-therapy sessions, what will his "unhappy childhood" stories be? He asked for a cap gun. Nobody got him a cap gun. Nobody would. "Vous travaillez pour l'armée, Madame?"—"You are working for the army, Madame?" a Frenchwoman asked the poet Adrienne Rich, learning that she was the mother of three sons. There are things he wanted, he will tell the therapist, that we didn't give him. A gun. What else?

His face reflects the disciplined excitement of an experienced gift-getter, holding the mirth back behind the dike of the wrapping paper. I memorize him with a gulping, hungry, mother gaze: the distractingly tweakable cheek, the huggable head, the body so perfect. The boy, increasingly, commands a private space around him, a space that even needy mothers may not trespass. No tweaks on the cheek without his permission now, as he claims more territory for himself.

The regret and the pride, the teeter-totter of relentless motherhood. What will the man-child do with his independence? Will he become "such a man as our daughters, born and unborn, will be pleased to live among," like the poet Audre Lorde describes, the kind of man who understands that "women do not exist to do his feeling for him"? Or will he be an exasperating man, one who wears women out with expectations and resistance? Will this man-child have an invitation to the promised land of women's affections and respect?

Finally, the wrappers give way under his insistent probing and his laugh rolls out uncaged from the strain of young impatience. The prize at the bottom of the Cracker Jack box is a large spaceship—clearly a boy toy, clearly the gift of parents aiming to please. Clearly a compromise—he'll defend it, no doubt, with imaginary cap guns and unloaded index fingers.

This, the age of reason. I want a truce called in the battle of the sexes, the possibility of reasonableness on the threshold of his manhood. I met a young man of such reasonableness, a rare young man in a class I taught once. He seemed to absorb the meaning of the women students without needing to translate their native language into his own image, without retreating from their anger, without defensiveness. In his jour-

nal he likened the class discussions to a campfire circle of intimate friends. He felt privileged to be in their confidence. He "wanted to please them," he wrote, because he "enjoyed the company of the women." He thought they were marvelous, these women who were becoming his friends, in their rawness, in their realness, their rowdiness. This young man, I thought when I read his journal, has a very good chance of learning to love women.

We lit the candles on the cake, the boy's face a flashcube of happiness. Looking at him, capturing the candid range of expressions, there are no amendments I wish to make to the boy of seven, so magnificent are his raw materials. I want to light more candles for him without extinguishing any of these.

I wish I could wrap up the formula for him, to become a man "our daughters would be pleased to live among." A man who would "enjoy the company of the women." A man who would earn the privilege of their respect. I wish I could give him the Promised Land for his birthday, an invaluable gift for a man-child arriving at the age of reason.

He was pleased with himself when he blew out the candles. And then we sang him a song.

MARCH, 1981

JOAN GELMAN

They just gave out the Mother of the Year awards again, and I didn't win. You could have fooled me. You could have even fooled my sons. It's easy. I've been doing it for twenty-four years. Take Sundays when they were real little. The mother's helper was off and so was the husband I had divorced after a three-year marriage—an act that certified my insanity in a suburban community where you only divorced a man if he was a mass murderer, and then only if he had been kicked out of the country club. (The stampede to the divorce courts that followed later recertified me as a pioneer.)

He got the Dodge and I got two kids in diapers (180 a week). Sundays were too long. I decided to make them shorter. Around 4 P.M. —sometimes even 3:30—I would pull down the shades, start yawning and snuggle the kids into their cribs. If I could get past Josh, I was home free.

"Time for nighty-night, angel," I would croon. "Wasn't that a good dinner?"

"What dinner?"

"Don't you remember? You had tomato juice, lamp chops, french fries and chocolate ice cream. Wasn't that good? Aren't you full?" (Always use imagery).

"Uh, huh, thanks, Mom," my trusting little boy would reply vaguely and go off to sleep. Six-month-old Gregg needed no further proof. It his brother was sleeping, it had to be nighttime.

Some people would call this child abuse. I call it preventive medicine. Obviously I was way ahead of my time. Ask any health nut now and she'll tell you the best thing you can do for your body is to fast on Sundays. Listen, pioneers are pioneers.

Anyway, fasting was safer in our house. I'm not the world's greatest cook. Friends who enjoy my pizza heated in its own box will disagree, but I got there slowly and I wasn't always perfect.

One problem is I have no imagination when it comes to meals, so we always had the same thing. For the first ten years Josh ate hamburgers and Gregg ate bologna. In spite of what my mother said, they *did* learn to eat other foods. Later, Gregg ate hamburgers and Josh ate bologna.

My creative talents were really tested the day Gregg came home from second grade saying his teacher wanted all the mothers to send in their favorite recipes for a class cookbook. That's when I had my first full-blown anxiety attack. The next one hit when John asked me to make him a costume for the school play.

Hold it, I thought. Don't panic. What about your spaghetti recipe?

Sure enough, a few months later, *Second Grade Cookbook* arrived in the mail. And whose recipe turned up on the first page?

MRS. GELMAN'S SPAGHETTI

Into 6 quarts of rapidly boiling water to which 2 tablespoons of salt have been added place the macaroni product and boil for 10 to 12 minutes, according to desired tenderness, stirring occasionally. Drain and place on platter. Add sauce.

Gregg was proud. I was proud. That is until my friend Rita ("Mrs. Tannenbaum's Chicken Cacciatore") call me in a rage.

"How could you do that to Gregg?"

"Do what?" I asked. "Mine made the first page, didn't it? Gregg's a star."

But the glory was short-lived. One night I found an opened box of Rice-a-Roni behind the peanut butter. An amazing find, as I didn't stock up on a lot of delicacies; a side dish in our house heralded Thanksgiving.

Following the instructions, I emptied the pack into a saucepan, stirred and waited for it to happen. After an hour nothing had happened. Josh finally figured out someone had taken the rice out of the box and the thing I was waiting to puff up was the flavoring.

After that we ordered out. I told the kids that takeout food was bad for them, so they never wanted anything else.

They never got anything else when we moved to New York. We found the perfect apartment. Junior high was two subways away, but Bun & Burger and McDonald's were just around the corner.

I gave them money for dinner. Gregg thought the man behind the counter at Bun & Burger was his father because he ate with him every night. (Give them continuity.) I didn't argue. I think you can get away with a few off-white lies.

Years ago, the kids and I grew attached to the same man and I suddenly found myself engaged. Just as suddenly I changed my mind and broke the news. "Don't unwrap any more wedding presents, kids. We're not going to marry Paul."

"How come?"

"I found out he doesn't like to ski. How can we go skiing Christmas?"

Worse than a mass murderer. Looks of relief flooded those little faces. They were doing fine without a father, but only Joan Crawford would ask them to give up skiing.

In the country tell your kids they're old enough to get themselves to the dentist, the orthodontist, the allergist, religious school, the drug store, the market, Little League or the emergency room and they'll be the first to agree—as you pick them up in your car every day after school. Mass transportation in the suburbs means car pool. And as long as they don't drive you don't work full time.

In Manhattan it's another ball game: *you're* up at bat. I found myself working until midnight as a television news writer. They found themselves buying Ajax.

"Didn't you feel guilty?" you ask.

Yes, the night I stayed home and cooked.

I don't know a kid who feels sorry his mom's not home to make sure he doesn't watch porn on cable TV. Anyway, I think kids should be heard and not seen. It's good for their self-esteem. Call home from work and your son proudly tells you he's outsmarted yet another mini-mugger on the way home from school and you can sound thrilled. Hard to do in person.

Can you imagine if your only contact with your folks in high school had been on the phone? No pained expressions about how rotten you look? It's like growing up on the radio. No one ever sees your hair.

Supermoms know self-esteem is where it's at. That's why, when Josh was a baby, I used to ask him: "Why do I love you?"

He would answer, "Because I'm Josh."

Finally, when Gregg was old enough, I tried it on him. "Gregg, why do I love you?"

Without missing a beat, he said, "Because I'm Josh."

I knew I had the award sewn up when he burst out laughing. The Mother's Day committee has probably been calling me for years, but I wasn't home.

JULY, 1983

DEIRDRE LEVINSON

He was already fifteen months old when we adopted him. Even now, seven years later, I still miss those first months of his life, but the agency told us the babies were in such bad shape that we'd be best advised to put in for one who, having survived his first year, wouldn't be likely to die on us. They said we couldn't afford to be losing another child, could we? Then they sent a social worker to look us over at home, and she urged us to start right away Vietnamizing the household. I saw in a vision herds of water buffalo in concert with hordes of United States conscripts milling sluggishly around our apartment. Go find where to hire such recherché supplies. Turn to the Yellow Pages, let your fingers do the walking.

It was just as well, as it turned out, that we didn't work overtime Vietnamizing the household, because it wasn't a Vietnamese that we got after all. What we did get was a Cambodian—one of sixty starvelings airlifted, under heavy fire, from the orphanage in Phnom Penh and flown one wintry day early in 1975 to Montreal, where we hastened breathlessly to claim him.

The airport was thick with prospective parents. Never, the agency representative averred, addressing us briefly together, never in all her experience of babies for adoption had she encountered a batch so beautiful. Every blessed one of them a dazzler, she said.

I scanned the procession of ill-favored scraps, each more hideous than the last, as one by one, amid flashing press cameras, they were passed down the ramp to their enraptured, evidently purblind new parents. I reminded myself sharply that looks weren't what counted; beauty is but a flower; man looketh on the outward countenance, but the Lord looketh on the heart. But when our name was called, I saw at first glance, the moment I clapped eyes on him bundled up in a red blanket, that this one—running sores, running nose, lusterless hair, rotting baby teeth regardless—was not only far and away the pick of that bunch, he was a spectacular beauty by any criterion, the medical one excepted. "Beautiful?" snorted the pediatrician we rushed him to—a black colossus, disgustedly scrutinizing our scantling couched commodiously in the palm of his hand—"Then find me some beautiful flesh on his bottom to give him a shot."

We named him Malachi, after the last of the Hebrew prophets, and sent out near and far to all friends and relations—including, advisedly, those of our kin who didn't hold with our adopting, let alone an Oriental, a goy baby at all—our announcement of his adoption, inscribed with the words of his namesake: "Have we not all one father? Hath not one God created us?" Notwithstanding which, as soon as he was strong enough, we had him ritually circumcised, thus making him officially as Jewish as any Jew on this earth.

Malachi himself, meanwhile, was concerned with even more bedrock matters. Though fully of walking age when we got him, he was too weak to crawl, let alone walk. But that was all that was weak about him. He knew right from scratch what he wanted, which was a family —father, mother, sibling rival and all—and he set out at once singlemindedly to establish his claim, sounding the charge against our five-year-old Miranda, contesting, matchstick arms in full flail, brown nose thrust between us, her right to the merest kiss in his presence.

"I wouldn't mind so much," Miranda observed with extravagant candor the day he fell sick, "if this one died." But this one was not about to die: he had come incubating chicken pox, which he proceeded to share with his sister. They shared that, shared a room, were obliged, willy-nilly, to come to terms with sharing us, too. They developed a working relationship.

Until he could walk, she dragged him around with her by one leg. She plaited his long, by now thick and glossy black hair with pink ribbons, dressed him up in one of her old baby frocks and called him Debby. She rolled him up in a shawl, crooning lullabies, called him

Toby after her dead little brother, familiarized him with Toby's framed picture, acquainted him with the whole history of her loss. "Take his picture out," Malachi demanded once he had learned to talk, "and put mine in there."

Though he made himself one of us fast enough; and though he could even pass on occasion as ours by blood (as an interested passenger looking the four of us over on a Manhattan bus once observed, the girl was her father all over again, the boy the image of me); and though my own mother pronounced him conclusively in the matter of character far more my child than Miranda, bless her, with her refined little ways, he contrived at the same time to use his otherness to unfair advantage. "I'll go back to Cambodia," he would threaten when crossed, and when we said we'd just follow him there if he did, "You can't," he would parry triumphantly, "you don't know where it is."

It wasn't until he started nursery school that he learned that being what he called "adocted" wasn't all beer and skittles. One summer afternoon at going-home time I found him waiting for me on the steps there, the disconsolate subject of the speculations of three Lilliputian companions. He wasn't—they called me to witness—really mine, was he? I wasn't his real mother, was I? Rising magnificently to their challenge, fronting each midget in turn, I picked them off one by one. "Did *your* parents search the wide world for you? Did *yours* for you? And how many steps farther than the hospital did *yours* go to get you? Not two steps, not one. Whereas *we* searched the wide world to get this boy."

That, he and I agreed as we stalked off down the street together, should settle their hash once and for all. But there was more to it than that. "You wanted to get me?" he took to asking unprefaced, sitting at the kitchen table, staring hard at the wall. Or in the elevator, apparently addressing the push button, "You wanted to get me?" Then at last point-blank, "You wanted a brown boy, Dad? Ma, you wanted a boy like me?"

A boy *like* him? Search the four corners of this earth for his like, where breathes the half-American, half-English-Jewish Cambodian boy of his age who can match his speed in the 100-yard dash, who can play the recorder so melodiously, throw a fishing line as dexterously, make friends as firmly, belch as resoundingly as our boy can? Show us the boy with an eye as sharp as his for finding money in the street. We should all have such a son. One time he found twenty dollars in a lump on the sidewalk. He has asked me to make special mention of that.

From time to time he resolves to save up his trouvailles to finance a family trip to Cambodia. There the four of us will gaze our fill at the marvelous temples he knows so well from the picture book. He will acquaint us there with his people. We will sit by the Tonle Sap, the Great Lake, watching him, foremost among his fisher compatriots, land prize after prize catch of fish.

NOVEMBER, 1982

MAGGIE SCARF

I was in stage Alpha, the "gateway to sleep," when my daughter S. called to say that life had no meaning. "But Daddy's already sent in your tuition," I protested; a mistake, I had thrown away a high card. For S.'s voice, which had been thick and hoarse with existential sorrow, became brisk and businesslike at once. "He sent in *last* semester's tuition," she said, in the sort of voice that has documents to support it. "But that was long ago, this one's not due for at least a few more weeks."

"Hang on, he's sleeping. I'll get this in the other room."

The house, outside the circle of warmth under the bed quilts, was arctic. I half-ran, half-stumbled down the darkened stairway, and picked up the phone in the kitchen pantry. It was like pulling my finger out of a sea-dike: a flood of complaint surged in, whirled around my head. Her studies were endless and purposeless. Many of the things she was being forced to do had no intrinsic interest to her. Her friends? None of them cared about her—she was enmeshed in a web of false and unsatisfying relationships; and the fact was, she wanted out.

"But what about Wendy and Nancy?" I asked. She'd been so fond of her roommates, last year. She had thought that they cared about her, S. answered darkly, but now she no longer thought so. She must leave school at once. Nothing she was doing seemed to have any importance—including a recent A she'd received in a very difficult test in psychology. "Weren't you pleased about that?" I put in hopefully. No, she hadn't even studied for the test, so what did the A signify?

Her present life, in a word, had no point. She'd only gone to college, in the first place, because *we* had seemed to think it so important. But now it was time for her to start making her own decisions: we must allow her to be herself. She needed her independence and autonomy. Therefore, she was coming home.

. . .

"You're coming home because you need your independence?" I asked, speaking the words slowly. S. must have heard the wonder in my voice.

"Not to *stay* there," she added rapidly; she had other plans entirely. She would, after several weeks, go on to Cambridge, Mass., where she would get a job doing research for a professor at Harvard.

"Which professor?" I inquired nervously.

"Oh, I don't know. But it doesn't have to be Harvard; it can be somebody at M.I.T. What I mean is, just some kind of a job as somebody's research assistant. You know."

I didn't. "But you're just a sophomore. And I doubt you'd be prepared—I mean, in terms of the training you'd need. And besides, where on earth are you thinking you'd live?" The "gateway to sleep," as the high whine of hysteria in my voice informed me, had probably just shut down for the night.

"I don't know," answered S., her voice slightly cool, as if she'd been insulted by this objective, practical stance. "I guess I'll find myself some sort of an apartment." I reminded her that real estate in Cambridge is exorbitantly high. "It's different for kids," retorted S. stonily. "There are all kinds of funny, cheap places that someone my age can live."

I can't say that I heard her words so much as I experienced them physiologically. A biological mechanism, deep within me, had now thrummed into activity: Fight-or-Flight is the name of this bodywide reaction; it is the motor of anxiety and terror. "I am not happy," stated S. accusingly, "and I am coming home." The sudden gonging of the clock—12 midnight—made me think I'd stumbled into a role in an Ingmar Bergman movie. It was crucial, I felt, to keep her talking.

S. didn't seem inclined to stop. We moved into one of those deep and probing conversations that can only occur in the dark eye of the night when emotions ride at fever pitch—and telephone rates do not. We talked about life, and its meaning; about love, death and the courses S. was taking this semester; about women and about men. Most of all, though—in terms of total air time—we talked about the boy that she'd just broken up with. He'd applied for medical school and chances were that he would be admitted.

We relived their entire relationship, moment by moment. "Happiness," I told S., dredging up a quote from Viktor Frankl, "cannot be pursued; it must ensue." She didn't answer.

"What that means," I went on, after a silence, "is that happiness is a byproduct of other things that are happening in a person's life." To chase after it directly, I added, was often to lower one's chances of actually attaining it. S. observed, her voice doubtful, that she understood what I meant but that she couldn't buy into it.

Why not?

"Well, that would be buying into passivity."

She had a point, I suppose.

It was just after 1 A.M. when we parted, and S. acknowledged that she did feel much better. It was now the early hours of Wednesday morning, and she was coming home to seek her independence on Thursday. There was nothing to be done in the meanwhile—except, perhaps, get some sleep.

It wasn't till dawn, though, when all expectations had been surrendered, that I finally lapsed into unconsciousness. It didn't last long. At 7:30, a scant few hours later, I wakened to a muddled sense of grief. What was that taste of clay in my mouth—and why did I feel as though I'd just undergone major surgery? What was I doing on the sofa, wrapped in my husband's winter jacket? And why was he standing there, with a confused expression on his face?

A hesitant thought, in one area of my brain, went off to investigate in another. And it came back, almost instantaneously, with the full file folder on the night's occurrences: I groaned aloud. S. would be buying her ticket today, and journeying forth to find her autonomy tomorrow. I explained what had happened to my husband, and had the satisfaction of hearing him groan, too.

I was in stage Delta, the deepest phase of slumber, when S. called to say she'd changed her mind. It was very early—close to dawn on

Thursday morning—and hers was a dawn kind of voice. It was the voice of the R.A.F. pilot, about to take off on a mission: clipped, determined and yet rich with underlying tremolo. She and Wendy and Nancy had had a long bull session which had lasted for most of the night—I cringed—and they had helped her to an important realization: "If I'm not happy at school, I probably won't be happy at home, either." She was going to stay where she was, face up to the difficulties, and do her best to work them through in a mature fashion.

It had been somewhat shortsighted of me, she added sternly, to agree that she could come home. It would certainly have been a regressive thing for her to do. I hesitated, thought about this charge, took the accusation under advisement.

Suppose I *had* refused her? That would have been a Parental Felony—"Total Rejection." This is a serious crime which can, on conviction, bring a sentence of years of alienation—with the perpetrators picking up most of the victim's bills throughout. But "Maternal Overprotectiveness" is merely a trivial misdemeanor. I entered a plea of guilty to the lesser charge, and the case was settled.

S. had, she told me, another matter to discuss. What was it? Well, the zipper on her ski parka was broken: did I think it could be fixed or would the whole parka have to be replaced? Readers, you who have been parents to an adolescent can alone comprehend this sequence: for never, at any other phase of the life cycle, does what is High Tragedy seem so indistinguishable from what is Low Farce.

DECEMBER, 1980

SUSAN JACOBY

Some years ago, while reading the morning paper, I heard a dull thud and looked out the window of my second-floor apartment to see the broken body of a teenager who had apparently jumped from a higher floor. Then, a few moments later, came an equally terrible sight and sound: a balding, bathrobe-clad man, howling with the anguish of a trapped animal. "Why?" he asked the police officer over and over. "Why couldn't I stop him?" The man was the boy's father.

I had somehow managed to forget this scene until I listened to John and Jo Ann Hinckley, the parents of John W. Hinckley, Jr., in their recent television interview with Barbara Walters. The Hinckleys apparently agreed to the interview because they have been deeply disturbed at the hostile public reaction to their son's acquittal by reason of insanity for all the crimes committed in the course of his attempt to assassinate President Reagan.

Many of Miss Walters's questions focused on the insanity issue, but the most compelling portions of the interview were concerned with the Hinckleys' pained, obvious attempt to assess their responsibility as parents for the disastrous course of their son's life. You could almost hear them posing the same question as the distraught father outside my window: Why? Why didn't we know what was going on in our son's mind? Why weren't we able to help? *Where did we go wrong?*

I suspect the Hinckleys did go wrong on a number of counts, but I doubt that they went any further wrong than millions of other parents who have watched troubled children emerge into perfectly ordinary, productive adult lives, complete with jobs, mortgages, children of their own and garden-variety neuroses. And I am not at all certain that John

Hinckley, Jr., would have turned into a normal adult even if his parents had recognized the awful depths of his rage and somehow managed to do everything "right."

With each passing year I become more impressed not by the malleability but by the intractability of certain elements in the human psyche—especially those traits, frequently labeled character, that are connected with the exercise of moral choice. I suspect that these aspects of character are much less susceptible to parental influence than most twentieth-century child-rearing experts would have us believe. This is not to say that parents exert no influence for good or ill but simply that —with the obvious exception of extreme, relentless physical or emotional abuse, or both—there are limits to the ability of parents to determine their children's destinies.

On the witness stand during the trial, Mr. Hinckley wept and blamed himself for his son's acts. Advised by a psychiatrist who obviously saw young Hinckley not as a potential psychotic but as an immature ne'er-do-well, Mr. Hinckley turned down his son's request to come home (after he had followed his usual pattern of quitting a job and disappearing). The assassination attempt took place several weeks later.

"In looking back on that," Mr. Hinckley testified, "I'm sure that was the greatest mistake of my life. I am the cause of John's tragedy. We forced him out at a time when he just couldn't cope. I wish to God that I could trade places with him right now."

The day after this painful testimony a number of prominent psychiatrists jumped into print with statements that were sharply critical of Hinckley's "abandonment" of his son and of the doctor who had advocated taking a "tough line." The gist of their opinions was that no parent should ever tell a disturbed child to fend for himself—even if the "child" is twenty-six years old—and that both the Hinckleys and their psychiatrist should have known better.

These observations were, I suspect, attributable partly to professional embarrassment that one of their accredited colleagues was involved in the fiasco. But I also felt that the critical comments betrayed a gross insensitivity to the all-too-human inadequacies of a parent who was neither a mind reader nor a soothsayer, just an ordinary father who saw his son not as a dangerously disturbed man but as a rebellious boy.

As Jo Ann and John Hinckley described their lives in the interview with Miss Walters, they had always regarded their family as perfectly ordinary—"about as typical and middle class as you could get." It was unquestionably a family run along old-fashioned patriarchal lines more common a generation ago than in recent years. Mrs. Hinckley was inclined to treat her son more gently than Mr. Hinckley was, although she was as disturbed as her husband by his lack of friends, poor performance in school, and inability to finish college or hold down a job.

Although Mrs. Hinckley tended to believe that her son needed a bigger dose of tender loving care, she felt obliged to go along with her husband in order to "present a united front." In their home presenting a united front meant that she stifled her doubts about the shape-up-or-ship-out posture favored by both Mr. Hinckley and the psychiatrist.

In listening to Mrs. Hinckley, I felt a combination of sorrow and anger at the subservient posture she was describing. But there is no way to tell whether a bigger dose of tenderness and understanding would have been any more effective in penetrating their son's violent fantasy world than Mr. Hinckley's stance was.

Moreover, I could also sympathize with Mr. Hinckley, a hard-working self-made man with a son who proved unable to assume any of the responsibilities of adult life. "Every father wants his son to become independent," he said, visibly fighting back tears. I feel for Mr. Hinckley because I also place a great deal of importance on hard work in order to reach the upper limit of one's potential.

My parents brought me up that way, and although I had a number of serious disagreements with them over the years, I always accepted that part of their value system. Today I am sure I would be devastated to have a child who rejected the work ethic. I hope I would be perceptive enough to recognize the difference between teenage rebellion and destructive inner demons—but that distinction is not easy to make when an intelligent child wishes to conceal evidence of emotional pathology.

In any event, both the Hinckleys have been shaken to the core by the nightmare that only became real to them when their son pulled the trigger outside the Washington Hilton Hotel. Mr. Hinckley, who described himself as "a man who never cried until two years ago," declared that he has "drifted a long way from the view I had that everything is black and white."

One thing has not changed, both parents said: They have always loved their son and they always will. Mr. Hinckley, who is a wealthy man, could have paid for a first-rate lawyer without exposing himself and his wife to the anguish of their courtroom appearances, to the psychological second-guessing following the testimony and to the hostility that some people will surely express in response to their defense of the insanity plea in the interview with Miss Walters. Instead, they are continuing to do the best they can on behalf of a son whose behavior re-remains a psychological and a moral mystery.

MAY, 1983

Person to Person

LYNNE SHARON SCHWARTZ

He always sat in the back row, as far away as he could get: long skinny body and long face, thin curly hair, dark mustache. Sometimes his bony shoulders were hunched as he peered down at his notebook lying open on that bizarre prehensile arm that grows out of college classroom chairs. Or else he leaned way back, the lopsided chair balanced on two legs and propped against the rear wall, his chest appearing slightly concave beneath his white shirt, and one narrow leg, in jeans, elegantly stretched out to rest on a nearby empty chair.

Casual but tense, rather like a male fashion model. Volatile beneath the calm: someone you would not want to meet on a dark street. His face was severely impassive in a way that suggested arrogance and scorn.

He must have been about twenty-seven years old, an extremely thin young man—ascetic, stripped down to the essentials. His body looked so brittle and so electrically charged that I almost expected crackling noises when he moved, but in fact he slipped in and out silently, in the wink of an eye. His whole lanky, scrutinizing demeanor was intimidating. He would have no patience with anything phony, I imagined; would not suffer fools gladly.

About every fourth or fifth class he was absent, common enough for evening-session students, who had jobs, families, grown-up lives and responsibilities. I was a trifle relieved at his absences—I could relax— yet I missed him, too. His presence made a definite and compelling statement, but in an unintelligible language. I couldn't interpret him as readily as I could the books on the reading list.

I was hired in the spring of 1970. It was wartime. Students were enraged. When I went for my interview at Hunter College I had to walk past pickets into a building where black flags hung from the windows. I would use the Socratic method, I earnestly told the interviewer, since I believed in the students' innate intelligence. To myself, I vowed I would win their confidence. After all, I was scarcely older than they were and I shared their mood of protest. I would wear jeans to show I was one of them, and even though I had passed thirty and was married and had two children, I would prove that I could be trusted. I was prepared—even eager—for youthful, strident, moral indignation.

Far from strident, he was totally silent, never speaking in class discussions, and I was reluctant to call on him. Since he had a Spanish name, I wondered whether he might have trouble with English. Bureaucratic chaos was the order of the day, with the City University enacting in microcosm the confusion in the nation at large; it was not unusual for barely literate or barely English-speaking students to wind up in an Introduction to Literature class. His silence and his blank arrogant look could simply mean bewilderment. I ought to find out, but I waited.

His first paper was a shocker. I was surprised to receive it at all—I had him pegged as the sullen type who would give up at the first difficult assignment, then complain that college was irrelevant. On the contrary, the paper, formidably intelligent, jarred my view of the fitness of things. It didn't seem possible—no, it didn't seem *right*—that a person so sullen and mute should be so eloquent. Someone must have helped him. The truth would come out in impromptu class papers, and then I would confront him. I bided my time.

After the first exam he tossed his blue book onto my desk, not meeting my eyes, and, wary and feline, glided away, withdrawing into his body as if attempting a disappearing act. The topic he had chosen was the meaning of "the horror" in Joseph Conrad's *Heart of Darkness*, the novella we had spent the first few sessions on.

He compared it to Faulkner's *Intruder in the Dust*. He wrote at length about racial hatred and war and their connection in the dark, unspeakable places in the soul from which both spring, without sentimentality but with a sort of matter-of-fact, old knowledge. He knew

Faulkner better than I did; I had to go back and skim *Intruder in the Dust* to understand his exam. I do know that I had never before sat transfixed in disbelief over a student paper.

The next day I called him over after class and asked if he was aware that he had an extraordinary mind. He said, yes, he was. Close up, there was nothing arrogant about him. A bit awkward and shy, yet gracious, with something antique and courtly in his manner.

Why did he never speak in class, I asked.

He didn't like to speak in front of people. His voice and his eye turned evasive, like an adolescent's, as he told me this. Couldn't, in fact. Couldn't speak.

What do you mean, I said. You're not a kid. You have a lot to say. You write like this and you sit in class like a statue? What's it all about?

He was in the war, he said, and he finally looked at my face and spoke like the adult that he was. He was lost for a long time in the jungles of Vietnam, he explained patiently, as if I might not know what Vietnam was, or what a jungle was, or what it was to be lost. And after that, he said, he couldn't. He just found it hard to be with people. To speak to people.

But you're so smart. You could do so much.

I know. He shrugged: a flesh-and-blood version of the rueful, devil-may-care, movie war-hero shrug. Can't be helped.

Anything can be helped, I insisted.

No, he insisted back, quietly. Not after that jungle.

Hunter had a counseling service, free. Go, I pleaded.

He had already gone. They keep asking me questions about my childhood, he said, my relationship with my parents, my toilet training. He grinned quickly, turning it on and off. But it doesn't help. It's none of that. It's from when I was lost in that jungle.

You must work, I said. Don't you have to talk to people when you work?

No, he was a meter man.

A what?

He went around checking on cars, to see if they had overstayed their time at the parking meters.

You can't do that forever, I said. With your brains!

Well, at least he didn't have to talk to people, he said sweetly. For now. Maybe later on he would get braver.

And what would he do if I called on him in class? If I made him talk?

Oh no, don't do that, he said, and flashed the wry grin again. If you did that I'd probably run out of the room.

I never called on him because I didn't want to risk seeing him run out of the room. But at least we stopped being afraid of each other. He gave up his blank look, and occasionally I would glance at his face, to see if I was still making sense or drifting off into some seductive, academic cloud of words.

I thought of him a lot this summer after I saw young men lined up at post offices to register for military service. I thought of him also when I heard Ronald Reagan and John Anderson, on television, solemnly pledge themselves to the defense of this country's shores. No candidate has yet pledged himself to the defense of this country's young men, to "taking every measure necessary" to "insure" that their genius does not turn mute and their very lives become the spoils of war.

OCTOBER, 1980

FAYE MOSKOWITZ

Now that I have reached fifty, I find myself, more and more, stepping outside myself to see what is becoming of me. As my body thickens and my face seems to thumb its nose at the kindness of cosmetics, I select from the trick-or-treat bag of memory a feature here, a character trait there. I notice that I place my thumb on my chin, my fingers on my temple when I listen, just the way my father did, twist my Bobeh Stollman's skinny brown hair into a knot at the back of my head. Some matches are obvious, but it has taken me years to realize that one of the women I have been becoming all along is an incarnation of the Pushke Lady.

Winter Sunday mornings in Detroit, my father and I would walk to the Warsaw Bakery on 12th Street to buy bagels. After cold that bit like an ax blade, runny noses, ice squeaking beneath our galoshes, we would stand inside the cinnamon-scented steam box until the fog on our glasses cleared enough for us to make the familiar choices from freshly laden bins and boxes piled high with crusty rolls and sugary cakes. No matter how early we came, the Pushke Lady was there before us, sitting in a chair safely out of the draft, shaking her canister under our noses. Jewish National Fund, Pioneer Women, Hadassah, milk for Jewish orphans, trees for Palestine—thanks to the Pushke Lady, no Jew would have to slather cream cheese on his bagel with a guilty conscience.

During the Depression, when we moved to a little town not far from Detroit, spring brought the tramps, pale and spindly, looking like plants do when they have had to reach too far to find the sun. Coming home from school, I would often spot a man at the back door looking for odd jobs, slouch hat or cotton cap held in both hands over his chest, hungry, and my mother would feed him: cold potatoes, bread, coffee; we had little enough ourselves. Drying her hands on a dish towel just inside the screen door, she would listen to the story as though she had not heard one like it many times before.

Miraculously, she always had a dollar or two put away from what my father gave her. Her "knippl," she called it, and more than once I saw her fish out a dime or a quarter from the old Droste's cocoa box where she kept it to send on his way a tramp whose story had particularly touched her heart. Afterward she would tell me, as though making excuses, "It's a mitzvah to feed the poor."

Our house was a regular stop for pious men in need of a kosher meal who might find themselves without time enough to reach Detroit or Chicago before sundown of a Friday night. "You're doing a mitzvah," my mother would say when I grumbled about giving up my bed to a stranger. What has become of them, those grizzled men in long, black coats, poring over yellowed prayer books by the light of our living room window on Shabbos mornings so long ago? My mother would believe they were in heaven now, saying prayers for all of us.

I reached adolescence just before the creation of the Jewish State, and although my family still felt, then, that Jews should wait for the Messiah to carry them back to Israel, they did not put on sack cloth when I joined the Labor Zionist Movement. Certainly I was doing what I had been brought up to do when I stood on a street corner holding a canister, vying with the newsboys for their customers' change. This time a new cause benefited, but the Pushke Lady's spirit hovered above me, crowing over every coin.

As a young-married, locked into a small suburban community by babies and a lack of transportation, I met my fellow prisoners by collecting door-to-door for the Torch Drive, the name given to the United Way Campaign in Michigan. In kitchen after kitchen, twin to my own, I drank coffee, shared recipes and surprising intimacies with barely post-adolescent women like myself. Almost always, I came away with a few dollars in my envelope to justify my visit and the sense that I had performed a mitzvah to justify my life.

The children grew, and I collected: Dollars for Democrats, March of Dimes on Roosevelt's birthday, Unicef on Halloween. Later, the Pushke Lady syndrome became more complicated. When my oldest daughter was sixteen, I took her with me to the Alabama state capital to meet the Freedom Marchers who had walked from Selma to Montgomery. We both still remember the voice of the Rev. Dr. Martin Luther King, Jr., floating over our heads in the electric air and the long, sober train ride back with blinds drawn and lights out for fear of snipers. I didn't tell my daughter the trip was a mitzvah or even that it was part of *her* pushke training, but she knows it now.

Living in Washington during the sixties, we made our home a way station for peace marchers. The spaghetti pot bubbled, and the sleeping bags came out at the drop of a bull horn. We offered Band-Aids for blistered feet and legal aid for those arrested, and telephoned more than one hysterical parent to report a son or daughter in good hands. I have met people, perfect strangers, who accurately describe the inside of our house and tell me they were drop-ins for this march or that. *They* may not realize they stand at the head of a symbolic queue that began for me with an old man who carried a prayer book in his satchel—but I do.

Fund raising is computerized now; we're not quick to let strangers into our homes, and no one seems to be marching very much, but the Pushke Lady in me still believes the "knippl" makes a difference. The world grows larger and more complex, yet hunger and pain have not lost their simplicity or directness. Besides, the way things are, I need to store up all the mitzvahs I can get.

OCTOBER, 1981

MAXINE HONG KINGSTON

I just opened an envelope in the mail to find a mimeograph sheet smelling like a school test and announcing the twentieth-year high school reunion. No Host Cocktail Party. Buffet Dinner. Family Picnic, Dancing. In August. Class of '58. Edison High. Stockton. The lurches in my stomach feel like doubt about the strength to stay grown up.

I had not gone to the tenth-year reunion; the friends I really wanted to see, I was seeing. But I've been having dreams about the people in high school, and sit up with an urge to talk to them, find out how they turned out. "Did you grow up?" There are emotions connected with those people that I don't feel for friends I've made since.

"When I think of you, I remember the hateful look you gave me on the day we signed yearbooks. That face pops into my mind a few times a year for twenty years. Why did you look at me that way?" I'd like to be able to say that at the No Host Cocktail. And to someone else, "I remember you winking at me across the physics lab."

I dreamed that the girl who never talked in all the years of school spoke to me: "Your house has moles living in it." Then my cat said, "I am a cat and not a car. Quit driving me around." High school is a component of the American subconscious.

Another reason I hadn't gone to the tenth was an item in the registration form: "List your publications." (The reunion committee must be the kids who grew up to be personnel officers at universities.) To make a list, it takes more than an article and one poem. Cutthroat competitors in that class. With no snooty questions asked, maybe the people with interesting jail records would come. We were not the class to be jailed for our politics or white-collar crimes but for burglary, armed robbery and crimes of passion. "Reunions are planned by the people who were popular. They want the chance to put us down again," says a friend (Punahou Academy '68), preparing for her tenth.

But surely I am not going to show up this year just because I have a "list." And there is more to the questionnaire: "What's the greatest happiness you've had in the last twenty years?" "What do you regret the most?" it asks. I'm going to write across the paper, "These questions are too hard. Can I come anyway?" No, you can't write, "None of your business." It is their business; these are the special people that formed your growing up.

I have a friend (Roosevelt High '62) who refused to go to his tenth because he had to check "married," "separated," "divorced" or "single." He could not bear to mark "divorced." Family Picnic.

But another divorced friend's reunion (Roosevelt '57) was so much fun that the class decided to have another one the very next weekend—without the spouses, a come-without-the-spouse party. And my brother (Edison '60) and sister-in-law (Edison '62) went to her class reunion, where they had an Old Flames Dance; you asked a Secret Love to dance. Working out the regrets, people went home with other people's spouses. Fifteen divorces and remarriages by summer's end.

At my husband Earll's (Bishop O'Dowd '56) reunion, there was an uncomfortableness whether to call the married priests Father or Mister or what.

What if you can't explain yourself over the dance music? Twenty years of transcendence blown away at the No Host Cocktail. Cocktails —another skill I haven't learned, like the dude in the old cowboy movies who ordered milk or lemonade or sarsaparilla. They'll have disco dancing. Never been to a disco either. Not cool after all these years.

There will be a calling to account. That's why it's hard to go. A judgment by one's real peers. We're going to judge whether The Most Likely to Succeed succeeded.

In high school we did not choose our friends. I ended up with certain people, and then wondered why we went together. If she's the pretty one, then I must be the homely one. (When I asked my sister, Edison '59, she told me, "Well, when I think of the way you look in the halls, I picture you with your slip hanging." Not well groomed.) We were incomplete, and made complementary friendships, like Don Quixote and Sancho Panza. Or more like the Cisco Kid and Pancho. Friendships among equals is a possibility I have found as an adult.

No, my motive for going would not be because of my "list." I was writing in high school. Writing did not protect me then, and it won't start protecting me now. I came from a school—no, it's not the school—it's the times; we are of a time when people don't read.

There's a race thing too. Suddenly the colored girls would walk up, and my colored girlfriend would talk and move differently. Well, they're athletes, I thought; they go to the same parties. Some years, the only place I ever considered sitting for lunch was the Chinese table. But there were more of us than places at that table. Hurry and get there early, or go late when somebody may have finished and left. Not eat. Who will eat with whom at the Buffet Dinner?

I notice that the chairman of the reunion went to Chinese school, too; maybe seeing her name, the Chinese-Americans will come. I will have people to eat with—unless they're mad at me for having written about them. I keep claiming our mutual material. They will have recognized themselves in the writing, and not like me for it. That people don't read is only my own wishful thinking.

And Earll says he may have to work in August and may not be able to escort me. Alone at the Dance. Again.

One day a popular girl, who had her own car, stamped her foot and shouted to a friend who was walking home with me. "Come here!" she ordered. "We go home with one another." To be seen going home alone was bad. They drove off. "I remember you shouting her away from me," I could say at the reunion, not, I swear, to accuse so much as to get the facts straight. Nobody came out and said that there were groups. I don't even know whether the friendships had a name; they were not called groups or crowds or gangs or cliques or anything. ("Clicks," the kids today say.) "Were there groups?" I could ask at last. "Which one was I in?"

My son, who is a freshman (Class of '81), says he can't make friends outside his group. "My old friends feel iced out, and then they ice me out."

What a test of character the reunion would be. I'm not worried about looks. I and every woman of my age know that we look physically better at thirty-eight than eighteen. I'll have objective proof of the superiority of older women when I see the women who are eighteen in my dreams.

John Gregory Dunne (Portsmouth Priory '50) said to his wife, Joan Didion (McClatchy High '52), "It is your obligation as an American writer to go to your high school reunion." And she went. She said she dreamed about the people for a long time afterward.

I have improved: I don't wear slips anymore; I got tired of hanging around with homely people. It would be nice to go to a reunion where we look at one another and know without explanations how much we all grew in twenty years of living. And know that we ended up at thirty-eight the way we did partly because of one another, psyches and memories intertwining, companions in time for a while, lucky to meet again. I wouldn't miss such a get-together for anything.

JUNE, 1978

TOVA REICH

"So why are we killing each other?" I put it to my neighbor. Two ordinary women chatting on a front porch, a squirming baby riding the hip of each, the odd number of three children apiece, the wives of doctors—what could be murderous in the hearts of two such women except perhaps the instinct to strangle any bully who is cruel to one of their own?

And now, here was her father-in-law visiting; in countless ways he reminded me of mine, as I had just told her, and that's what prompted my anguished question. In and out of his son's house he shuffled, her husband's father, his hands clasped behind his back, a gray woolen vest under his suit jacket, a hat on his head, with nothing much to do, just like my father-in-law when he visited our alien domain; two men in their seventies, her father-in-law and mine, diffident men, taking pains not to get in the way, foreigners with exotic American grandchildren. She and I had more in common than we dared acknowledge, including a ripeness for enmity, among the most intimate bonds of all.

She was talking about her first-born, her prince of princes, who played intensely with mine, heir apparent of the bordering state. "I would have sworn he didn't know a thing," she said of her son, "until yesterday." Yesterday she had overheard the boys settle a dispute which, from the sounds of it, must have sprung up weeks ago. "O.K., you smeared us in sixty-seven," hers recapped, "but seventy-three was a draw, right?"

They were friends, our sons. They split a cherry Popsicle down the middle, each boy sucked extravagantly at his half, their lips were dyed identically. But there were also days when they positioned themselves on opposite sides of an imaginary line: "Get off my property!" they shrieked, and they brandished their sticks.

Once, when my phone was out of order, I asked to use theirs. In his downy Arabic accent, her father-in-law said of course, certainly, please, come in, and he escorted me to what I needed with the familiar cordiality of the Old World Jews who had populated my childhood. As I carried out my business, my eyes rested on the silver-framed portrait of King Hussein. "Yeah, I knew that guy when I was a kid," her son tossed out to me, referring to the Hashemite monarch. The child was born in Amman, Jordan, six years ago; he has the red hair and fair skin of his American mother, and though his grandfather now made his home in Syria, I made my peace with the conclusion that they were Jordanian.

It is ironic that they, so Arab, and we, so Jewish, should now reside side-by-side in the demilitarized zone of Chevy Chase, Md., the fence dividing us toppled and rotting, a beaten path through the ivy joining the two houses. We were wary at first, as she admitted more readily than I, but in time we came to trust each other.

And why not? There is an undeniable kinship between us. When we open our door to let you in, we open it wide; when we cut a cake, we slice you a big piece; when you mention our children, we feel utterly at your mercy. Her husband is like the men I have always known. At a party, he does not take the plate he has filled at the buffet and eat off his lap, as Americans do. He finds a little table, he dines; when a utensil is missing, he looks around reflexively for the nearest woman, a mother's darling boy, just like a husband, then he resigns himself to modern realities and rises to serve himself.

And when my darling boy fell in the street, he, my Jordanian neighbor, was the first to run out, and the treatment he provided was exactly what his colleague, my husband, would have given in similar circumstances; an ice pack, a solemn examination of the bump, followed by direct intervention—a kiss where it hurts.

So when she called to say that her husband had suffered a probable heart attack, I was afflicted exactly as if it had been a relative. She had to go to the hospital immediately. Would I help out with the children? Oh, there was no limit to what I would do if only she would let me; feed the children, read to them, tell them stories, put them to bed, hold them, especially the three-year-old, whose sense of the disruption was acute.

The next day this little girl and her big brother embraced suddenly, right in my yard, clinging to each other for a long time. Later, the boy rode his bike in circles at the intersection, sobbing loudly, and I was allowed to comfort him. But with time, all of us absorbed even the shock of so energetic a man being struck and chastened; the change was incorporated into the domestic routine. Family arrived to get the household back on its feet, and every morning my neighbor drove to the hospital to spend the day at her husband's side as he slowly recovered.

Before she left on one of those mornings, we again stood on the porch, babies astride our hips. Naturally, we talked about the event. It had been a blow, not only to the body, but to the spirit; it's no accident that the metaphorical home of the spirit is the heart.

"Have you told his father yet?" I asked her. Not yet, she said; her husband planned to call his father soon to report that he was not feeling well. "That's exactly how we used to do it," I approved. "We never spilled all the bad news at once." I told her again how emphatically I had recognized her father-in-law. "What does he do in Damascus?" I wanted to know. "In Damascus he's a poet." She gazed at me like someone about to plunge. "Before that he was a lawyer," she continued. "Then, in 1948, they lost everything. They're Palestinian, as you know. They lost everything. It's a fact. We might as well face it."

Her father-in-law would be informed bit by bit. His sorrow could never be contained in the package of a poem. All that day I was drawn toward their house, looking for a way to help, but I was no longer needed.

JULY, 1979

BARBARA LAZEAR ASCHER

Whenever I see a bag lady, I see myself slipping past the edge of time and space into an abandoned doorway. "We are all bag ladies in our souls," says a friend who has certainly had her successes. She tells me of riding a bus recently when a bag lady climbed on, heaving herself and her possessions through the door and up the steps. Some sense of pride or purpose, or both, pushed her past the seats reserved for the handicapped and elderly, down the aisle to the back where one long, overheated seat served as an inspection table for the contents of her bags.

The men continued to read their papers. "But the women became very tense, as if she were sending a current through them," my friend recounted. "We sat up straighter, drew our knees together and clutched at whatever was in our laps. When she got up to leave, there wasn't a woman on that bus who didn't turn to watch her safely down the steps, and gaze after her until she was no longer in sight. But she left behind a scent of vulnerability."

It is a fearful scent of our own. Not Proust's madeleines, but it sets off our imaginings. We can see ourselves rummaging through trash cans, reaching for a tin can because it will make a perfect cup, rejoicing in rags because they warm the feet. Even women with regular jobs can imagine this. Even those with five-piece place settings for twelve.

The other day as I was walking up Third Avenue, I was startled by the rushed breath of a cough sweeping my ankle. It came from a mouth set among rags, sucking the last smoke from a used cigarette. Her head was propped against the doorway, her feet within inches of a man who stood reading the menu in Parma's window. If she had had a sense of whimsy, she could have stuck her bare, nailess toe into the cuff of his pinstripe pants.

His nostrils flared for a moment, took in the smell, but failed to identify it as urine mixed with four layers of clothing mixed with twice-eaten food mixed with oozing sores. A veritable stew of womanhood. The scent of our own dependencies.

We know that, like meteors, all that keeps us in orbit and shining —away from that doorway, those garbage piles—is our faith in gravity. In choosing love as the star to which we attach the heart's invisible threads, we shoot through the atmosphere, cling as we spin through the galaxy and hold on for dear life because we know that stars have quirks. Why, just the other day one that had lost its grip fell through the roof of a house in Wethersfield, Conn.

I've known other stars to fall into black holes in space. Sucked in, crushed and extinguished. Of course there was no escape. Nothing ever gets out of a black hole. And there is no help for it. No cosmologist can go in with forceps and yank out a star.

So we dig our toes into earth for a gritty hold. We collect antiques and achievements to plant ourselves in place. But we fall for love, we hope for eternity, and we see the evanescence of things, knowing that where we wish for monuments there are only mists.

If all goes well, our children grow and leave us. According to national statistics, the men we love will die before us or suddenly find commitment not to their liking. The more we open our hearts, which seems to be the way with women, the more vulnerable we are if cast adrift. What we gather about us can be carried in bags. What we hold dear is easily mobilized.

No job can stay us. No wealth can shield us from the fear that someday we will be left alone, shot forth from our magnetic field. We see our hearts bend with the burden of bags, move with rhythm but without purpose, gather in the castoffs of strangers' lives because we have lost faith in our own.

Is this why Helen Frankenthaler paints big? Why Judith Jamison perfects her leaps? Why Rosalyn Tureck spins and spins and spins

Bach fugues, preludes and fantasies? To weave herself into the fabric of his immortality? Is this why Lady Bird Johnson roots herself to the earth with wildflowers, and the astronaut Dr. Sally K. Ride offers herself up to space? Is this why I went to law school?

Perhaps.

Certainly centuries of legal principle should hold me in place. (I even studied Talmudic law, just in case.) And certainly my heart would come to rest in an office with a river view and a secretary outside the door.

"Making it," having it all," securing our futures have been motivated in no small way by our identification with the bag lady. Our accomplishments, titles and pension plans were to protect us from the future we saw out of the corners of our eyes as we stalked the streets or rode the buses.

But in crowded theaters and on quiet walks we whisper of our fear, "We are held in place by wrapped rags and shopping carts."

When I decided to leave the practice of law, a concerned and careerless friend with grown children and an overworked husband called to register her distress: "If you become too involved with your husband and children there will be nothing left of you in the end. What about your autonomy?" She might as well have asked, "What about the bag lady?" We both knew that was what she meant.

I did not tell her that no number of oil and gas deals or exciting victories in the New York Court of Appeals had banished the woman hovering above me like a Chagall clock. Walking home late at night with a heavy briefcase in my hand, I had often fallen into step with a bag lady pushing her cart. I felt that I was walking with my future.

I understand my friend's concern. She assumed, as many of us have, that careers guarantee an end to dependency and vulnerability, which, in fact, are matters of the heart shying away from the brain's reaches like toads scurrying beneath leaves. They are the consequences of need and caring and kindness and generosity and tenderness—those things which are a woman's soul first and last, no matter how much power and prestige are pressed on top.

On Madison Avenue between 75th and 88th streets you can see a bag lady who travels with a cat. How she lassooed it and why it complied is a mystery. But I can guess why she captured and tethered it to her cart. That cat sits on top of her trash as its crowning glory, the ultimate find, a beating heart.

I imagine that in her dreams she forgets which is the self and which is the cat. He gives her a vision of herself as sleek and bound in fur. She gives him her scraps. Outside Parma they eat fettuccine Alfredo caught in discarded mussel shells.

Such is love.

FEBRUARY, 1983

PHYLLIS THEROUX

Reality has recently come to my attention. It has always been there in a rather offhanded sort of way, but it resembled a quilt that oftentimes slipped from my lap while my mind raced ahead thinking about what the whole thing would look like once it was finished. That is the way it is with idealists, whose beady eyes tend to focus upon the distant cloud as opposed to the oncoming bus, and probably we would all be better off living in the country, where clouds predominate.

It has become necessary, however, to pay some close attention to certain downtown realities that have nothing to do with clouds whatsoever, unless one is referring to thunderheads. But see how easily the idealist lifts the real to a symbolic level, given half a chance? The facts are that there came a time when I realized that I didn't have a grasp of certain facts at all. Like what kind of life insurance was in my portfolio, the tax-deductibility of a second telephone, and was I, or was I not responsible for filing an estimated return on my income which fluctuates as wildly as my heartbeat did when I contemplated all these totally non-cosmic questions.

But these questions had to be answered, and one morning I picked up my telephone, with the same fear that one anticipates a blind date. I wouldn't wish the experience upon my worst enemy (although some of my best friends could profit from it). It is a terrifying thing to confront the ragged edge of one's temperament, the Jungian fourth corner that resists trimming off in the worst way, but the only thing worse is refusing to trim it off at all.

The first call was to an automobile insurance company. It was sheer luck that connected me with a sweet, compassionate agent who called me by my first name and took me carefully over the rocks that could smash me promptly, if I didn't act fast.

"Now, you'll want a comprehensive collision clause," she intoned softly, "and there's the question of bodily liability that we'll discuss just as soon as I check to see whether this particular policy covers you adequately for medical expenses. And I'm wondering," she added thoughtfully, "whether you want to take advantage of our out-of-work salary provision, in the event that you should be permanently incapacitated from earning a living?"

Needless to say, I was mentally in the hospital already, having driven my car straight up a telephone pole from sheer anxiety. But the agent sensed the panic and like a midwife who understood her patient's emotional state, she countered my nerves with a string of soothing remarks. "Just one step at a time, honey, one step at a time, you're doing fine." By the end of the conversation, I was awash in gratitude, told the agent that she was a remarkable human being, and I would consider it an honor to take her to lunch. Also, my car was insured.

It was several days more, however, before I could bring myself to make the next call to my insurance agent. Life is a lot more complicated than automobiles, and the conversation promised to be a far more wide-ranging discussion. But midway through the call, which had its depressing moments ("You mean you've never filed Social Security?" "Sorry, you're loaned out on that policy."), I switched into a totally unexpected frame of mind and could hardly keep from laughing. It centered upon my health insurance. I was quite sure that were I to have a medical examination, the doctor would turn his face to the wall and announce that I was post-terminal.

"Health insurance?" repeated my agent, "No problem. I've got a terrific policy right here with Prudential, better than most government coverage, and no examination is necessary. I'll file today if you want—get you covered by Monday."

I do not actually know my insurance agent, but he has always existed somewhere out there, like a shoe factory that it was never necessary to visit as long as there were outlets in town, but I conceived of an instant love for him. The calm voice, the ready answer, the absolute grasp of the sticky codicils of life that I needed to get through it—a warm feeling went right through me. From this new vantage point of rocking in the bosom of Abraham, I heard myself saying, "Jerry, I am fighting off a tremendous temptation to ask you out for a date." "Fine," he chuckled. "I'll be free after the weekend."

And so it went. Call after call after call. I expected computers and tape recorders; I found human beings at the end of the telephone. Even at the telephone company. Where I had some very complicated problems to unravel and fully expected the spirit of Harold Geneen to prevail on every level, it got friendlier the higher up I went.

But it should be inserted here that while the process (by no means completed yet) was essentially positive, a little reality goes a long way. And although it pays to be brave and eye-on-the-eight-ball, there are limits. Idealists, unfortunately, tend to think that limits are merely in the eye of the beholder, and one must simply keep wading through the waters and never lose sight of Jerusalem.

That is right, but that is wrong. There are times when Jerusalem collapses behind a film of tears and resembles nothing so much as a circus tent with its poles kicked loose. Suddenly, the chaos one is attempting to deal with comes fluttering around the candle, like so many moths bent upon gutting the flame. And since one can only spend so many waking hours protecting that flame, and it is difficult, in any event, to stretch 360 degrees around it, the flame goes out. Hello, darkness, my old friend, my eye! In this closet of pitch-black uncertainty, the uninsured nature of life reasserts itself with a vengeance. And it looks overwhelming.

Reality has taught me several things recently. That it must be dealt with, although its bark is worse than its bite, unless you simply dangle your arm carelessly out the car window and let any old tree whack it off in passing. But the deeper lesson is that there are times when reality doesn't merely *look* overwhelming, it *is* overwhelming, and while this is difficult for an idealist to admit, that fact must be faced. *How* is the next question.

There are those of us who know how to snatch a stick and give reality the proper beating it deserves. Others are very handy with the old Scarlett O'Hara "I'll think about that tomorrow" approach. But when the rock and the hard place are struggling to make contact, and a human being is caught in the middle, only a fool asks for anything short of deliverance.

It is a difficult thing to admit that one is, in the long run, incapable of the long run. But ironically, that is the admission reality seems to want of us. And then, as the eyes clear and one's vision restores itself, lo and behold Jerusalem reconstructs. It was always there. But sometimes it simply goes underground for a while, in order to allow us a little time to focus upon the intricacies of the Keogh Plan. Actually, I haven't looked into the Keogh Plan yet, but it's on my mind, which is extraordinary in itself, given the other things that I would rather be thinking about.

SEPTEMBER, 1977

Women at Work

BETTY ROLLIN

knew, when I got out of college in the late fifties, that it would be tough out there. And when I landed, seat first, in journalism, I could tell right away I was not in a place where competitive games were played for fun. So I knew I'd have to work hard. But I never expected to care about work so much. I never expected the *Sturm und Drang*. Nor, when they came, the thrills and chills. Thrills and chills and *Sturm und Drang*, I had always thought, were what you felt over men, not over jobs. Yet, there I was, keening under a fluorescent light in the midtown offices of some magazine over an assemblage of words, getting myself so strung out before 5 in those early days that often I had no energy left for whatever romantic life I had hoped to pursue after 5.

As I got older I calmed down. I learned to have lunch. I learned to keep my mind from wandering toward where my lead sentence had gone wrong while moving slowly on a dance floor with a potential husband (as were all men in the fifties who were not your father or your brother). Eventually, and I do mean eventually, one of the good ones stopped being potential. But even as a bride I continued to get all worked up about work and I still do.

For the most part, it's nice to feel that way. I love going out on a story with, say, a television crew and hearing my heart thump when an interview goes well. I love caring that much and I love that I've continued to care.

But there's an ingredient in the caring that I don't love, one which I assumed would have left me by now and hasn't: fear. Fear, that is, of screwing up. Of not coming through. After all these years fear—and sometimes terror—continues to rise like steam with the onset of each new assignment, whether it's on camera or on paper. Not until a task is done do I ever believe it *can* be done and, past experience notwithstanding, I usually believe it can't. Which is to say I usually believe *I* can't.

I think I'm not the only victim of chronic self-doubt. I think it's a common—female—affliction. Particularly among women who are as charged up about work as I am—and yes, to a much lesser degree among the younger ones. I know all about the theory that says men are as scared as we are and they just repress it. Well, O.K., then maybe repression works. Because when I look around the workplace I see an awful lot of men who are less competent than they think they are and as many women for whom the opposite is true: women who are far more competent than they know and, if they keep it up, more than they or anyone else will ever know.

Of course, at the start of a career a feeling of insecurity is appropriate. It shows you know what you don't know. Why, when you're wet behind the ears, *should* you feel you know what you're doing? I lost my own professional virginity in 1963 at *McCall's*. (I wish it had been *The Paris Review* or even *Life*, but one doesn't plan these things for the telling afterward.) I had gone to *McCall's* because my best friend from Sarah Lawrence's mother's best friend's best friend was the managing editor, and once inside her office I managed to con her into giving me an assignment to write an article. I didn't know how to write an article, but I figured I'd worry about that later.

I was right. I worried about that later. And I remember the morning the worry peaked. I had spent about ten weeks—the entire summer—researching the piece. That would have been reasonable had it been about the Cuban missile crisis, but the subject was actresses who did TV commercials. I had interviewed every woman in New York who had ever washed anything, wiped anything, served anything or put anything on her face, on her body or into her mouth in front of a television camera. I had amassed sixty pages of notes, and now it was Labor Day (1963), the deadline would strike in ten days and I had to start writing.

When I awoke that morning I hit the floor running. I washed my face, brushed my teeth, got a pot of coffee going, tightened the sash on my bathrobe; snapped my typewriter out of its case, placed it on the kitchen table, retrieved my notes from the floor where they were stacked in manila folders, unwrapped a pack of bond paper, put the top sheet in the typewriter, looked at it, put my head on the keys, wrapped my arms around its base and cried.

Had I known then how many times during the next two decades I'd have the same I'm-over-my-head-and-this-time-they're-going-to-catch-me feeling, I might have become a receptionist in a carpeted law office and married the first partner in a three-piece suit who asked me. But I didn't know. I thought, if I get through this, it'll be over.

And after two weeks, six drafts and some loss of body weight, it *was* over.

Until the next time.

And the next.

And the next, and so on until today. O.K., so now that I'm a big girl I don't cry anymore, but often I still *feel* like crying.

Why don't men?

I put the question to a (young) male producer I work with at ABC News who, by the way, is as competent as he thinks he is.

"When you're on a story," I asked him, "do you ever think it's not going to work out?"

"Sure," he said merrily. "All the time!"

"Do you worry about it?"

"Sometimes," he said, not sounding sure.

"When it doesn't work out, do you usually figure it's your fault?"

"No," he said, sounding sure.

"Suppose it *is* your fault. Does it make you feel terrible?"

"Nah," he said.

"Why not?"

He looked at me. "Aren't I entitled to make a mistake once in a while?"

. . .

Sure. And so am I. But I don't feel entitled. And it seems to me a lot of women don't feel entitled. And I know why. It's because they let us in and we feel we have to be perfect. Never mind how many women are out there working. The workplace is still, for the most part, owned and run by men, and we're there because they've allowed us to be there —sometimes because they *had* to—and we know it and they know it and they know we know it. So we better be good. And some of us *are* good. But it's hard to be good when you're constantly nervous that you're not. On top of which, trepidation is, I think, still considered becoming to a woman. It is not to a man. A man is supposed to be confident and sure. So as long as he doesn't buckle under the pressure to be sure, he is.

I see two pluses in all of this. One is if you think you don't know much, and admit it, you may wind up learning more than the next bloke, who thinks he knows it all. The other is when you're afraid of not coming through and you *do*, it's that much more of a kick. Whenever I see myself on television and my words sound less than inane and my hair isn't in one or both eyes, I am relieved to a point of near euphoria. Each time a piece of writing is accepted for publication, I feel like having my own parade. Which is to say I have, on these occasions, a *very* nice time, a much nicer time, I'll bet, than the one I'd have were I that little bundle of self-confidence I know I'll never be.

AUGUST, 1982

PATRICIA O'TOOLE

F ew of the women I know seem to have financial means of the sort economists call *capital*—material wealth, in any form, to be used for the production of more wealth.

Unaware of the size of the earnings gap between male and female executives, I have been assuming the worst about those women whenever they complain about their personal money troubles. Self-indulgent, I would think, looking at their Cartier watches and Ferragamo shoes. Careless. By depleting themselves in the 100-yard dash, acquiring the clothes and the trappings that declare their success, they have nothing left for the marathon.

One could argue persuasively that the dress-to-excess style is expected of executive women, that unless they turn themselves out like visiting royalty, they will be looked down upon or, worse, ignored. (Watching the rumpled gray flannel, droopy socks and stained neckties that board commuter trains in affluent New York City suburbs like Darien and Noroton, I have sometimes thought that true equality of the sexes will not exist until women are allowed to show up at the office in the same sartorial chaos as men.)

Wardrobe issues aside, most female executives are genuinely distressed by their lack of capital. Seeing the distress, I have often attributed it not to the lack of capital but to my catchall explanation for every problem related to women and money: Women suffer from fear of finance. Convinced they would make horrendous mistakes if they tried to invest, they deal with their money in a way that assures they will never have to make investment decisions. They spend it.

Because I often write on personal finance, women sometimes ask me what to do. I explain that every investment expert I have ever interviewed gives the same counsel: Define your goals and draw up a plan to achieve them.

Then the women ask how to do that without a sum large enough to attract a good adviser. "Accumulate it," I would say with the boundless self-assurance Providence reserves for fools. "Every month be as conscientious about paying yourself as you are about paying Bendel's and Bloomingdale's. That's what men do."

This sort of insufferable certainty deserves a comeuppance, and I just got it. Researching an article on the value of an M.B.A. degree, I discovered something that everyone, myself included, seems to have overlooked: The reward that women get for rising as high as they can in corporations is an increase in the gap between their earnings and the earnings of men at the top.

For years equal-rights activists pointed out that women earned only 59 cents for every dollar earned by men. So it was cheering to read that the gap is closing; women are up to 63 cents. But top executive women, despite their fat-sounding salaries, earn only 37 cents—yes, 37 cents—for every dollar earned by top male executives.

The numbers come from Heidrick & Struggles, Inc., the executive search concern based in Chicago. A survey of ranking women at 1,300 of the country's largest corporations uncovers the fact that the majority of them earn $50,000 a year or less. Another Heidrick & Struggles survey of top management (a category that is 99 percent male) at large corporations discloses that they earn $134,500 a year. I stared in disbelief when my calculator said that $50,000 is to $134,500 as 37 cents is to $1.

Like a child who wants to believe in Santa Claus despite mounting evidence against his existence, I came up with "reasons" for the discrepancy. It must be a case of apples and oranges. And, in fact, Heidrick & Struggles confirmed that it does not make perfect sense to compare the two studies. About half the female executives surveyed were corporate secretaries or assistant corporate secretaries, many of whom earn less than $30,000 a year. The survey of senior managers was restricted to vice presidents and above. What we have here, then, are surveys of women who are mostly junior officers and of senior officers who are mostly men. It is hardly surprising that the seniors earn more.

But these numbers raise more issues than they settle. Why, for example, are senior officers almost exclusively male? Why, in scouring 1,300 corporate annual reports for names of female officers, could Heidrick & Struggles turn up only 497 of them? And why do half of these hold relatively powerless low-paying jobs?

Those questions beg for answers, but until we have them all we know is this: Top female executives earn in the neighborhood of $50,000 a year and have been locked out of the club in which top male executives earn $134,500.

Wrestling with these numbers, calling all over the country in what turned out to be a vain search for more exact comparisons of male and female executives' pay, I remembered Disraeli's observation that there are three kinds of lies: lies, damned lies and statistics.

Perhaps the problem was one of history. The numbers must be showing the tatters of an age when women *were* grossly discriminated against. Many of the women now at the top are in their late fifties and early sixties; they are women who tasted opportunity when the men of their era went off to fight World War II. As products of less enlightened, less egalitarian times, they just have not gotten the rewards that have gone to their male counterparts.

Things must be changing, I thought, especially now that so many women are getting M.B.A.'s. Young men and women will enter the business world on equal footing with equal seriousness about their careers, so from here on there will probably be little or no difference in their pay.

A Stanford University study indicates this hope is unfounded. Released last fall, it shows that in 1978, five years out of the university's Graduate School of Business, men were earning an average of $38,000 a year, women $30,000. The Stanford women had started out earning

94 cents on the male dollar, but in five years they had managed to slip to 79 cents. Given a little more time, they too could be earning 37 cents.

The disparity between the pay of male and female executives is especially vexing because it involves the largest, wealthiest, most visible corporations—the ones that boast the loudest about their commitments to affirmative action and equal opportunity.

What will these corporations do about the 37 cents? Defend themselves, no doubt, with arguments that women executives have "preferred" lower-paying jobs, in departments like public relations and personnel. (Interestingly, now that personnel has grown enormously expensive because of complicated fringe-benefits programs and endless government regulations, there are indications that more and more female personnel directors will find themselves working for highly paid "human resources" vice presidents, most of them men.)

When the defense rests, the question will still remain: What will corporations do about the 37 cents?

It would be a good question to ask at an annual shareholders' meeting. But since women executives have so little investment capital compared to their male colleagues, precious few of them own the shares that would entitle them to go to the meetings and ask.

MAY, 1981

GAIL SHEEHY

One Saturday in August of 1968, Carolyn Reed was cutting up green beans for her employer's dinner party, which was why she couldn't be in Washington for the great civil rights march. That night, serving guests who could talk of nothing but the march, Mrs. Reed paused with interest at the elbow of a doctor who had saved her husband's life.

"What do they want?" the doctor was saying. With that peculiar lapse of the rich who assume serving people are simply moving shadows without ears, he took a helping from Mrs. Reed's platter and answered his own question: "What they need is an education."

"Excuse me," Mrs. Reed said, dumping every bean on her platter into the doctor's lap. "If I had an education, I would know how to serve green beans."

Today, Carolyn Reed is leading the movement to upgrade household work. Named last June to head the National Committee on Household Employment, she demonstrates by example that a woman who was born illegitimate, adopted informally by the black kinship network in the South, educated perfunctorily before she ran away at the age of sixteen, and who became a household worker for the next twenty years, can stop—halfway through her life—dare to say no, and find in herself the presence to be a leader.

But beyond her personal example is her issue—probably one of the pivotal factors in making it possible for a woman to become a leader. And while Carolyn Reed plans to give about five years to the cause of professionalizing household work, her eventual goal is something else.

The dirty little secret is: She wants to go back to being a household worker.

. . .

By the time Ella Council appeared at my door to apply for the job of household manager, I had all but given up. We had limped through the lean years, when the greatest portion of my salary still wasn't enough to motivate my surrogate at home to walk down four flights and buy milk instead of sloshing the baby's cereal with Tropicana. In hope of finding someone who wasn't outright hostile to the job, we had tried the Filipino connection, the Argentine connection—anybody but an American—and now, sent by a household employment agency, here was a woman born in North Carolina.

"Miss Council, you look like a lovely person," I said right off the bat. "Let's save each other a lot of grief, and not pretend this is a time in America when either one of us can feel comfortable about a black woman working in a white woman's home."

"I like your smile," Miss Council said.

Over the last seven years I have watched Ella Council tame the temperamental players and master the hundreds of eccentric moving parts that make up a home. She is the extended mother to my child, the urban guerrilla who can always find cheap meat or charm the super to fix the leaks, the Jewish mother who leaves me homemade chicken soup for a weekend alone with my typewriter.

The dirty little secret is: I could not manage without her.

Behind just about every successful woman I know with a public as well as a private life there is another woman. The dirty little secret is, all but one of the female leaders has household help—including Carolyn Reed.

"I can't be Superwoman either," she discovered, shortly after her appointment as the one-woman band leading a national organization with 10,000 members and 45 affiliates around the country. So Carolyn Reed hired herself a household technician (the term she prefers) at $35 for what is supposed to be a six-hour day. Mrs. Reed may not come home until midnight—but her Mrs. Pope refuses to leave until she arrives. "You go right on to bed, honey," Mrs. Pope will say, "I'll stay to tuck you in."

Now Carolyn Reed knows what it is to have a case of the guilties as an employer.

Why all the secrecy and guilt?

Because both parties to this private compact usually carry some residue of shame—the employee because the antecedents in slavery are still too close; the employer because either she doesn't earn enough to pay the woman she employs a decent living or she earns enough to buy $100 shoes but keeps a senile vacuum cleaner that thinks it's a blow dryer.

Many professional women tell Mrs. Reed, "Oh, May and I are like family." May doesn't sit down and eat with them, of course, nor does May say much about what's bothering her—usually because she is afraid she can't articulate it or she doesn't want to hurt people's feelings.

"Household workers are very good at lying—to survive," says Carolyn Reed, "until one day they do the disappearing act." Anyone who has been through this knows it only happens on a morning when the youngest breaks the juice bottle, you have a speech to make in Boca Raton and the dog is in heat.

The theme running through all the complaints Mrs. Reed hears from household technicians is the lack of professionalism with which they are treated. Almost no one defines the job clearly, or pays them on time. Social Security is rarely deducted, preventing them from collecting retirement benefits. To upgrade their dismal income, Carolyn Reed proposes a household technicians' union, tax deductions for general household workers and degree programs in schools. But most important of all is to raise the consciousness of professional women who employ the technicians.

A fair offer by a woman who earns $45,000 a year, has two teenage children in New York, and wants a technician to do the cleaning, cooking and laundry five days a week, would be, says Mrs. Reed, "$200 a week plus a bonus of two weeks' salary at Christmas and two weeks off."

It is going to cost to bury the Superwoman myth. But if the concept of partnerships between women at home and women out in public life catches on, it makes contracts, incentive plans, bonuses and windfall profit-sharing sound eminently sensible. Half the household workers have already walked out on the job since 1960, leaving a little more than one million "Mays" to be fought over by the eighty million adult American women. What will it be like in the new decade, when 45 percent of women with children under the age of ten will be out working?

"They can get all the computers they want," as Mrs. Reed says. "Someone will still have to clean the computers."

Despite her warning to employees to beware the opening remark, "We want you to be part of the family," Carolyn Reed strongly approves of the personal relationship that inevitably develops. In fact, it was the emphasis on doing by her late and beloved employer that mobilized Mrs. Reed into going to meetings and eventually becoming a leader herself. The employer was Julia Clayburgh, mother of the actress Jill Clayburgh, for whom Mrs. Reed worked thirteen years, the last two nursing her during cancer and, near the end, visiting her in the hospital twice a day. On the evening of Mrs. Reed's birthday the hospital called to say that Mrs. Clayburgh refused to take any further food or medication. Mrs. Reed rushed up to find her employer's eyes shut still as stones.

"I'm dead," Mrs. Clayburgh said.

"You've always said that on my special occasion, you would do anything I asked you to do," Mrs. Reed reminded her.

"Oh, no," Mrs. Clayburgh quipped, "not another birthday."

It is hard to die on someone who brings you your sense of humor. Later that night Mrs. Clayburgh took nourishment.

Given the mostly ragged support systems with which we try to make do these days, such relationships are worth all the care and money that can be spared to cultivate them. More power to Carolyn Reed if she can upgrade the professional relationship to the point where it can permit a personal relationship, not as a dirty little secret, but in the spirit of shared human nourishment.

JANUARY, 1980

PERRI KLASS

I t had been a long and difficult night in the hospital. I had had only two hours of sleep, and toward morning a young patient had died of cancer. I was sitting in the nurses' coffee room, staring into space, when the intern, who had had no sleep at all and who had been responsible for everything on the ward, came in and found me.

"Are you O.K.?" he asked, and I promptly burst into tears.

And then I lied. I told the intern that I was crying for the young woman who had died, whose parents were sitting by her bed, dazed and saddened by the ending of a long and terrible ordeal. I said I was crying for the patient and for her parents, but I knew that in large part I was crying for myself. I was crying because I hadn't slept much, and because I had a long day in front of me in which I would be put on the spot and have my ignorance revealed again and again, a day throughout which I would feel tired and sick and heavy-headed and inadequate. And also, of course, because a young woman had died. It was embarrassing enough to be crying in front of the intern; the least I could do was pretend my motives were purely sympathetic and altruistic, rather than substantially mixed with self-pity.

The prospect of crying in the hospital haunts many women I met, medical students like me, and interns as well. It seems to hover on the edge of our minds as something we are likely to do, something we must not do because it will confirm all the most clichéd objections to women as doctors. Crying will compromise our professionalism as well as our strength. Actually, before I started my clinical clerkship in the hospital, it never occurred to me to think of myself as someone who cried in public.

But it turned out that I cried frequently and helplessly in the hospital. My very first week there, I discovered that there was one particular room I could not enter on morning rounds without tears starting to slide down my face. The rooms were decorated with large prints of Impressionist paintings, and that particular room had a Mary Cassatt painting, a woman holding a child. I had suddenly found myself working over a hundred hours a week, spending every third night in the hospital, and I missed my baby badly. I simply could not look at that painting.

I cried for the patients. I cried after a man talked to me for fifteen minutes about what a vigorous, lively, intelligent person his wife had been before her stroke, and then took my hand, called me "doctor," and begged me to hold out some hope that she would be that way again.

I cried because I forgot to do things. I cried because I didn't know how to do things. I cried because I did things, only to find out they were unnecessary. In fact, looking back on those first couple of weeks in the hospital, it seems to me I was always ducking into bathrooms to sniffle into paper towels and splash cold water on my face. I cried, but I took great care not to be seen at it.

I have come to realize that I was not the only one crying. A friend told me about crying because a patient was dying and she could do nothing to help and everyone kept saying it was a "fascinating case." An intern told me about crying because one night when she was swamped she asked a more senior doctor for help, only to be told off the next day because asking for help was a confession of weakness. Perhaps we cry because we are in a harsh environment that offers us little comfort, and in which we frequently find ourselves unable to offer comfort to others.

I brought up the subject with a couple of male students. No, they said, of course they got upset, and frustrated and unhappy, but it hadn't gotten so bad they actually *cried*. This may simply reflect the much remarked-on truth that men are slower to tears than women in this society. It may also suggest that the hospital is still a male environment, the medical hierarchy created by generations of male doctors, and maybe it all seems a little more comfortable to male students. Or again, maybe they were lying, just too ashamed of those tearful moments in the bathroom and the weakness they implied.

I cried so easily last summer because some of my protection was stripped away. Working in the hospital, even as a student with very limited responsibility, I was constantly on the line. Did you do this? Why not? What would have been the right thing to have done? What are the possible consequences of what you didn't do? Precisely because I was a student, I was questioned regularly by any number of people, some of whom were under tremendous pressure themselves, and not inclined to make allowances for my greenness.

The steady tension, the fear of making a mistake and the mistakes that inevitably do get made can raise the emotional pitch much too high for comfort. In addition, I was sleep-deprived and deprived of any time for my family or friends, for anything that might have mitigated the intensity.

And finally, the hospital is a place where all sorts of emotions are visible. I saw people mourning and people screaming with pain, people crying with terror and people dying. It's hard to say exactly what effect it has, this everyday drama and melodrama, but perhaps it led me to exaggerate my emotional responses to the tiny dramas of my own life: Will I get three hours of sleep tonight or only two? Will I remember what I read last night about heart disease when they quiz me this morning?

It is easy to lose your sense of proportion in the hospital. In fact, it is hard to know what proportion means in a place where people are struggling for their lives, or living with tremendous pain. The medical student, like the intern, tries to maintain both balance and compassion on a schedule that allows for little rest and no relief. And frequently she runs the risk of being overwhelmed, by sorrow for others, by tired hopelessness about her own competence, or by helpless anger at doctors whose idea of teaching involves constant tests of strength and occasional humiliation.

I wish I had been telling the whole truth when I said I was crying for the patient who died that night. I can accept my own compassion much more easily than I can accept the mixture of disorientation, inadequacy and self-pity that was actually behind most of my crying in the hospital. And yet, I suppose, accepting those less than nobly sensitive motives is also a necessary step toward acknowledging my own human limitations. Those limitations, after all, even in this age of technological health care, are also in some sense the limitations of the medical profession, whether or not it cares to admit them.

SEPTEMBER, 1984

SYBIL ADELMAN

was one of the people who cried when *The Mary Tyler Moore Show* went off the air. Mary, Lou, Rhoda and the others were almost real and the stories often hit close to home. During that last episode—as Mary took her final look at the empty newsroom—I relived my own last day as Carl Reiner's secretary. In many ways Carl and I were Lou and Mary. Remember how she'd knock on his door when she had a problem? Well, I had a problem every ten minutes, only I never bothered to knock. For five years Carl listened to all my stories, not once confusing the boyfriend who'd never leave the right tip with the one who'd never leave his wife.

Mr. Grant had a bottle of Scotch in his desk; Carl had recipes. He and I both loved food: eating it, preparing it, talking about it. No script ever seemed to delight him so much as the list I'd typed of all the restaurants within twenty miles of the studio. He took lunch seriously and we always gave a lot of thought to where we'd eat. Carl taught me how to order in a Chinese restaurant: "Leave it up to them." He helped me get over my reluctance to eat sashimi: "Think of it as lox." He introduced me to raw clams: "Think of them as sashimi."

Visitors to Los Angeles are all dying to get onto a movie set. There I was getting paid for hanging around the set and laughing with the actors while Carl directed a show. And during those months when he was writing a script, I'd busy myself doing crossword puzzles and needlepoint.

If asked to describe my job, I'd have said, "Part heaven, part euphoria." I'm sure I'd still be Carl's secretary if the women's movement hadn't come along pointing a finger at me with the question, "What's a nice woman like you doing in a place like this?" I began to resent that the studio executives, those men who bought movies and sold Mercedes without shopping around, earned over ten times what I earned. What did they know that I didn't? *They* knew people would line up to see Barbra Streisand in a movie! I'd *waited* on those lines.

Carl, the first producer on his block to have his consciousness raised, was now referring to me as "my sec—my assistant." Some men were quick to embrace feminism, at least the part about splitting the check, but they were far less eager to share their executive power.

After considering my options—stay with Carl and hope the movement is a short-lived fad or make some changes—I decided to apply to graduate school. I had a B.A. in psychology from N.Y.U. and could easily imagine myself with the collected works of R. D. Laing, gazing out the office window while intoning to a client, "How do *you* feel about it?"

There was a new school in downtown L.A., across the street from the world-famous Tommy's Drive-In hamburgers. Since the school wasn't yet accredited or even advertising at the bus stops, I was sure I'd get accepted. Who else would be applying? The application was typically Californian: "What honorary societies were you in? Include all previous lives." The rejection letter said they were sorry; they'd filled their quota of Pisceans. Now I really felt lost.

Carl began producing a new situation comedy. I was surprised by the writers who dropped off their scripts at my desk, men with more Gucci shoes than talent. To me writers were Shakespeare, Chaucer, Kafka—not guys who looked like my Uncle Seymour. If they could earn good money writing for television, so could Uncle Seymour . . . and so could I!

Comedy is often written by teams, so I suggested to a friend that we try writing a script for *The Mary Tyler Moore Show*. What did we have to lose? Nights, while the overpaid established writers were writing off veal Oscar at Dan Tana's, we'd be writing our script at Ernie's Taco House.

. . .

We showed the finished script to Carl, who seemed sincere, although not enthusiastic, when he said, "If I were producing this series, I'd buy your script. The script is very good." When I asked him why his praise wasn't more spirited, he said, "I'm not producing Mary's show. I'm trying to produce a show for Dick Van Dyke and none of my pencils has a point." He pointed to the stubs on his desk. "I used to have pencils with points. Seems to me you used to sharpen them." Caring about nothing after the "Your script is very good," I handed Carl my ballpoint pen and went back to my desk to get an agent.

The agent I called liked our script and offered to represent us. We were his first female writers. He'd describe us as "Cute, fun to look at and they smell good." Maybe we sounded like his new seal act, but we were getting writing assignments.

One morning Carl called me into his office and confided that he'd been feeling uncomfortable. "How can I ask you to sharpen pencils when I know you're writing?"

"Don't be silly. Ask!" I said, leaving before he could be more direct. I started sharpening pencils like crazy. I updated the files. I took the dead people out of the Rolodex. There was no way I'd let myself be ousted from my warm, secure, familiar secretarial job. Oh sure, it was exciting to see my name on the screen and it was great getting those big checks. But I wanted to stay with Carl—to cling to his paternalism, to use his IBM Selectric typewriter.

Then one afternoon my partner called, "This is it."

"When?" I asked, my voice already shaking.

"Tomorrow."

"Tomorrow?" It would take me days just to get my needlepoint yarn together—years to adjust emotionally to being on my own.

"Her play is closing in two days so we're flying to New York tomorrow." We'd been hired to write a show for Jane Alexander and the producers wanted us to see her perform on Broadway.

"But what about Carl?"

"He can't go."

. . .

When I blurted out to Carl that I'd have to leave, he wrapped his arms around me and kept repeating, "This is great, chochke. Just great." But we both had tears in our eyes.

That was six years ago. I now know how to read a contract. I use phrases like "estimated taxes" and "deal breaker" and I can even keep my voice modulated when I have to ask a secretary to type something for me. But there are times when I'm alone at the typewriter, struggling with a scene, that I wish I'd hear Carl calling from the next room, "Chochke, where should we go to lunch?"

OCTOBER, 1979

A Sense of Place

MARY CANTWELL

I had passed the hotel often over the years and I'd been in it three times. The first time I was calling on a famous old man whose suite was a monument to horsehair upholstery and stained glass windows and who was giving a rather strange party. Or maybe the party wasn't really strange, only the guests. I remember a lot of women in late middle age with flyaway hair, crocheted sweaters stretched over breasts that had never known bras, and strings of amber beads. They all wore rump-sprung skirts.

The second time was a birthday party for a friend who was turning forty. The host and hostess were between apartments and, shipwrecked for two or three months, were making the best of it. They had draped crepe paper around the tiny dining area and across the peeling ceiling and managed to produce a roasted chicken and a lopsided cake out of an oven that never went above 350, but we were all depressed. Depressed because the guest of honor had reached an age unimaginable and undesirable to us then, and because the room was the kind that promises no exit.

The third time, I was interviewing an actress in town for a play. Her suite was presentable—"because the producer coughed up for a piano and some pictures"—but on leaving it one walked through scarred corridors to a street where old black men, and a few old white men, held sad travesties of cocktail parties. Cheap wine in paper cups and a brave bonhomie. I had a horror of that hotel.

One day though, I, too, moved into the place. I, too, was between apartments and tired of moving from sublet to sublet, tired of real estate ads that never panned out and of never being anywhere long enough to memorize the phone number. So we—my daughter and I, the dog and three cats—moved into that hotel because the rates were good, the room was big, and no one seemed to notice that there were six of us.

When my daughter came home from school the first night, she cried, despite the familiar typewriter and portable TV, despite the several pictures I'd saved from storage and the lamp I'd borrowed from a friend, the pots from Lamston's and the leaves I'd bought at the subway stop. But soon she smelled soup and saw the salad I was tossing—wonderfully fresh greens from the Korean market across the street—and settled in. Mama had done it again, the thing mothers are supposed to do. Mama had made a home.

It was a strange home. The rest of the hotel was a no-man's land. We avoided the kids with blood-streaked eyeballs who sometimes, too blurry to tell room 222 from 223 or 225, pounded on the door looking for Joe. Or Jean. Or Lisa. And a fix. There was one conversation with the tall man in the long raccoon coat who carried a cat on a leash. "No," I said. "I do not want a leather purse/joint/snort." When another man who claimed to live down the hall phoned to borrow a cigarette, I told him I didn't smoke. And when a short, spectacled boy who sat in the lobby every morning told my daughter he wanted to paint her, I checked up on him and found he'd been charged, but not convicted (the judge was dozing), of rape. Cherubic in his glasses and his baby paunch, he would stare at me as I headed for the elevator, knowing that I knew but didn't want to scare my child. "Nod to him as you go by," I said, "but no more."

One night a woman screamed and the neighbors across the courtyard yelled, "She's on the first floor, to the left," and I marched down, still the college monitor. "Just tell us what you want," I said, impatient, as she wailed about her lover who stood, limp as cooked asparagus, in the doorway of their room. There are many famous people who have lived, still live, still stop, at that hotel. But it was hell.

And not hell. Our room was—how else say it?—a clean, well-lighted place. It was a cold winter, but the radiators shuddered with heat, and in the fireplace the Dura-Flame logs from the delicatessen shook with flame. The water was always hot and dinner simmered on the stove (I couldn't trust the oven) and scented the room. We read— she, her schoolbooks; I, books borrowed from friends—and we watched *Masterpiece Theater*, and the dog and the cats nudged us in our sleep, jubilant because they were never more than five feet away from their owners.

Those whom I love, I love passionately. There is no moderation, no measure. I cannot bear loss, I mourn for years. The inclination is to keep, to hold, to enclose. That winter it was as if I were pregnant again, not only with my daughter, but with our pets, our few possessions. All were safe, under one very small roof, and I was the caretaker. There was no way they could be lost unless the fortress, which was myself, was broached. It wasn't; I stayed on guard.

We were in the hotel eight months. Spring came, and with it, opened windows that let in the sound of radios across the courtyard, family quarrels and the screech of cats. The subway sprouted daffodils and I brought them to the room, bringing with them the scent of all that was not in the room. Rain, soft air, things growing. We were restless. One cat, prowling, fell out the window. My daughter took to staying overnight with friends who had twin beds, proper meals and proper parents. I longed for invitations to dinner parties, and to buy dish towels for a kitchen of my own. The dog sniffed, ran, nostrils flared for more life than was lived on one short block on 23d Street. It was time to move, to give birth again.

We moved. Friends came one morning and helped us carry out the clothes, the pots and pans, the pets. Only the desk clerk said good-bye; we knew no one else. We have our own place now. The pets, lost in space, have not established their own territories yet and yowl. There are no boundaries; they are frightened. My daughter has a bed with a quilt and I have a phone number that is ours, and dish towels imported from France. But all those—the bed, the phone, the dish towels—are not as important as they were once. In fact, they are next to nothing now.

. . .

It is unsettling to lose one's dependence on things, to have put away one's passion for a painting, say, or a special cup. One is left with people, pets, and we all know how evanescent, being mortal, they are. I like our new home. It was a stable once, with high ceilings, and there are two prints of horses' hoofs in the concrete of my bedroom floor. But I know already that I will never again be as peaceful as I was in that hotel. Then there were no things, nothing to distract me from what was animal around me, and I would awake to hear my daughter, the dog and the cats breathing in the dark, listen a minute, and then sleep as if couched on zephyrs.

A few days ago I walked to the Pottery Barn for a door mat, eight jars for jam and two bags of sea salt. I am a householder again. Coming home I passed the hotel, our old Laundromat and the Korean market. The black and white men were passing cheap wine at the corner and newspapers rattled in the gutters. The wind was whipping up from the river and even Lamston's was almost empty. There's a scaffolding in front of the hotel—the bricks are falling—and the same fugitives are sitting in the lobby. "Dear God," I said to myself, remembering the five pairs of eyes that had fixed on me, depended on me, "how happy I was in this place."

FEBRUARY, 1980

PHYLLIS THEROUX

There was a time when what I knew I knew with great clarity. Then there was another time when what I didn't know poked its foot from behind the curtain and demanded to be integrated—all at once. I was on a train.

Behind was a lawn-cool campus filled with girls like me—enthusiastic innocents who meant well but weren't quite ready to do anything about it. Ahead was a young stockbroker, my first rendezvous with New York, and a letter home that I was chafing to write as soon as I had something to say. But in the middle lies the story. As the train bore down upon Grand Central it swept past a broad swath of Spanish Harlem and I was given my first involuntary look at the flip side of the mattress I had always bounced on with such certitude.

Bucket-jammed fire escapes hung off sweat-stained rooms. Angry women in curlers smoked inside. Children ran wildly through alleys spray-painted with obscenities. I saw nothing but junk, poverty and unsanctified pain. Worse, I realized that I had no idea how to "fix" it, and while I had often asked myself why I should be the one to suffer the indignity of second-hand clothes from rich cousins, suddenly that question reversed itself. Staring at the obscene filmstrip flying by the window, I wondered what I had done to merit a date at the Plaza Hotel. I was forced to utter, "Nothing." My hands began to perspire.

The first slip on a cosmic banana peel is very painful, primarily because it is so unexpected. But as I rubbed my hands up and down the sides of my coat, frantically sorted through the index cards in my mind for an answer, the card that kept appearing on top of the pile bore the face of my Uncle Ned. Uncle Ned was a cool, seersuckered gentleman with quiet eyes, a slow smile, and an existence free of the usual slubs that mar the fabric of most people's lives. His toast came upright on a silver rack, his *Wall Street Journal* was always folded in the requisite four sections for the commute downtown, and when asked, he had opinions about things—thoughtful, well-researched opinions that always hung together.

I was desperate for a thoughtful opinion before my head blew off and while I couldn't quite imagine the two making contact, I wondered what Uncle Ned would say if his eyes strayed from the *Journal* to confront the untidy sorrow of Spanish Harlem.

The train arrived at Grand Central before I could get the Uncle Ned of my mind to deliver up the integrating solution I needed and Spanish Harlem lodged itself in my mind as a symbol for everything I didn't understand, people I hadn't met, and ideas I was fearful of pursuing.

An hour later I was sucking on a swizzle stick discussing "Papal infallibility" with a stockbroker, outwardly unchanged. But the fact was that I had almost choked on my first thin slice of life. I was nineteen and a pretty wobbly pilgrim, but the pilgrimage had begun.

I am double that age today, and while I have yet to solve the "Spanish Harlem question," I don't think my Uncle Ned is any nearer to solving it than I am. In fact, some years back I realized that he wasn't even *trying* to solve it, whereas I have taken enough trains and bumped into enough different sorts of people so that I no longer view Spanish Harlem as a threat but as an opportunity—to expand, diversify, appreciate, even embrace.

This thought has been part of my luggage for some time now and it travels well. It certainly makes train rides more fun, turning the unexpected into something to celebrate and here we all are catching the curves together.

But the other afternoon, in a rather tired frame of mind, I took the train from New York to Southampton and quite unexpectedly stepped upon another cosmic banana peel, although this one didn't materialize until after I had descended from the train.

Southampton is the end of the line in more ways than one, and to be truthful I was looking forward to a little chilled consommé on a private beach. But I was also expecting to laugh at it a little, make my secret jokes about the "Uncle Neds" in their floppy expensive shirts sitting next to women who wore bathing suits that I didn't think they made anymore. And predictably all the material I needed was there—up to and including a gentleman who did nothing but "hold."

"What do you mean, 'hold'?" I asked the woman next to me.

"I mean," she said with a laugh, "that he has holdings, and he holds on to them for a living."

It was all good fun, until suddenly it wasn't. I felt sad. Looking at the tow-headed children, their pretty mothers, the lantern-jawed dowagers, the white-haired man staring out to sea was like looking through an old scrapbook, a pre–Spanish Harlem scrapbook, where everything was perfectly clear—like chilled consommé.

At the end of the afternoon, we would take our beach umbrellas away, sit on a white porch, have supper, and read our *Ellery Queens* until we were too tired to turn another page. It would be so calming and quiet, like the noise that stocks make when they are appreciating in a vault. And, of course, that is exactly what one's stocks must continue to do if one wants to partake of the privileged simplicity of Southampton. It was that illusion of simplicity that bowled me over, made me homesick.

That nostalgia did not devolve upon anyone's net worth but upon everyone's acceptance that there was one way of being, of doing, of looking, of speaking. And while I knew this was not true, I wished that it were.

Of course, I argued, Southampton isn't real life, but then again, these people on the beach are real, footprint-leaving people, aren't they? In other words, there's something to Southampton, just like there's something to Spanish Harlem. What's exhausting is trying to integrate one with the other.

Lying on the white sand under a beach umbrella I decided that nobody was asking me to do that, and as I tried to determine how many days it would take before I got bored, I was in no hurry to leave. For the time being I was content to "hold," which is the difference between nineteen and thirty-eight, I suppose.

AUGUST, 1977

JANE ADAMS

My spare room is rarely empty lately; friends move into and out of it for days, weeks, sometimes a month or more. I enter their lives in progress, as they do mine; we sit up late at night talking as they stop here on their way to somewhere else.

The room is generously windowed; through the leaded-glass panes the early sun streams in, making puddles of gold on the wide oak floorboards. There are clean linens on the bed, new books on the night table, flowers on the marble-topped commode. The view is grand: sharp-edged mountains, light glistening off the whitecaps. But the windows into their souls—these are the vistas that intrigue me.

David comes to my door one evening, rumpled and distraught. They have had, he says, the final disagreement, the last word, and in the morning he will make a plane, but tonight—tonight, is the spare room empty?

It is; Maggie has just left. She inhabited it for a month; she brought her own worn comforter, her radio that hummed plaintive love songs late into the night and a list of things she must do: divide the books and records, store the furniture, notify the realtor, lose ten pounds, call a lawyer. Anabell was here for three weeks in the spring. Long after she left I pictured her in Madrid or London or Rome, haunting the American Express office, waiting for the letter from Michael begging her to come home. My children missed her when she left; she made animal pancakes on weekend mornings, conjuring mythical creatures out of batter and oil. She never minded when they crept into her room, turning the television set down low so the noise wouldn't wake her.

There has always been a spare room in every house and apartment I have lived in since I left home. When I was a child, mine was the room from which I was banished when company came for the weekend. Sometimes I didn't mind very much; when Uncle Buddy came he would whistle me awake early and we'd go off to the bakery for sweet rolls and bagels before the others stirred. But often I minded quite a bit, and so I have always had a spare room.

I like it when friends come to live in my spare room for a time that has a beginning, a middle, and an end, all of which are determined, more or less, from the start. I like it that the careful and difficult pitting together of two different ways of being and doing, which bind or burden more permanent arrangements, is not part of ours; it is my space, after all, so those delicate questions of turf and territory rarely intrude.

I have lost count of the number of keys that the locksmith has copied for those who came here at the beginning of an adventure, or at its end; before Allan left for the sabbatical in Mexico, after Carol came back from the winter working at Wounded Knee, when Peggy sold the house in December and had to wait until spring for the sailboat she bought in its stead. They stopped here between jobs, between homes, between planes. But lately, they come more often between love.

George Washington must have slept here one night when he and Martha had a fight, remarks a long-married friend who helps me change the bed and freshen the room for the next in the seemingly endless stream of the temporarily uncoupled who come here to catch their breath and begin again.

Occasionally the postman comes to my door with a letter mailed to this house but not to me. The answering-service operator relays my daily messages and inquires tentatively after a new guest: Will he or she be there for long? Sometimes, and sometimes not; at times the doorbell rings at midnight and I answer it, then retreat to the privacy of my bedroom, knowing that in the morning I may find the extra key on the table, the hastily written note of apology, the spare room vacant again.

. . .

Friends are family you choose for yourself, particularly when you are a continent away from the one into which you were born. Years ago, in a time when "happily" was not as important as "ever after," I chose these friends and they me. We are, as the writer said, both caseload and caseworker to one another; that is a definition of friendship I treasure.

But sometimes my patience wears thin, though not as thin, it occasionally seems, as the ties that bound some of them together. I wonder at how quickly love seems to vanish, like a stone sinking into a pond, leaving only ripples that disappear from the surface in seconds. I marvel at the way my friends move in and out of liaisons, relationships, marriages. I am not surprised—I know the statistics of divorce as well as anyone—but I am dismayed. One never knows the texture and shape of any marriage except one's own, and mine ended years ago, so perhaps I am no judge. But it was not boredom or restlessness that finished it, as it admittedly does for so many of them; one counts one's own pain greatest, after all.

My parents arrived for a visit; this week, the spare room is theirs. They have been married for forty-five years—nearly half a century in which, certainly, some promises have not been kept, some needs not met, some dreams not fulfilled. Their was a great love affair; an elopement days after they met, a marriage kept secret for a year before the public ceremony that declared a commitment long since made privately. The romance went away after a time; in my mother's jewelry case are the cards signed "Your Secret Husband" and the dried, curled edges of the gardenias he used to give her. Are you happy? I ask as she unpacks her things, and she raises an eyebrow. Happy? she asks, Whoever said you're supposed to be happy?

Whoever, indeed. None of those friends who move in and out of my spare room was achingly, painfully unhappy; but each, distinct, might be happier with someone else. Not would be, not could be, not even should be . . . but might be. They are consumers of commitments; they abandon one for another, for a better, newer, bigger version. Nothing, they tell me, lasts forever, and I agree, sitting up with them late into the night.

But some things do, or should. My parents' marriage has been a noisy one, and not all the sounds were laughter, but it has endured and continues to endure. I want to bring my friends into this room with my parents and show them that some promises are for keeping, but of course I will not. I will change the linens again and put newer books on the table and fresher flowers on the commode, and the room will be there for them when they need it. Because that's what friends, and spare rooms, are for.

SEPTEMBER, 1980

NELL IRVIN PAINTER

Ghana is one of the best things that ever happened to me, even though it was a long time ago. My family and I lived there for two years in the mid-1960's. Ghanaians impressed me from the moment I stepped off the plane. For aside from a few travelers, everyone was black, an even, opaque, velvety black that I had never seen in the United States. The customs officials, families greeting passengers, taxi drivers, policemen, they were all intensely and beautifully black.

The people in the airport not only looked different from American Negroes, they also carried themselves differently. They stood with self-assurance and spoke without implied apology. Their dress seemed to announce that they were sure of themselves. They wore the bright colors and large prints that respectable American Negroes eschewed for fear of being conspicuous or seeming to reinforce unfortunate stereotypes. Ghanaian women wore long, two-piece dresses of a batiklike print that I learned was called wax print. The dresses were designed to flatter African figures and to take advantage of the prints, whether they were flowers or portraits of public figures.

Most of the men wore Western dress, white shirts with plain, dark ties and trousers. The contrast between dark skins and white shirts dramatically reinforced the blackness of skin and the whiteness of cloth. A few men wore traditional dress, a toga-wrapped cloth of either printed cotton or Kente cloth, made of several narrow hand-woven strips of blue, yellow, red, and white silk sewn together. Kente cloth, which is both beautiful and expensive, announced the wearer's national pride and his importance. Men wearing traditional dress showed off their calves and their sumptuously decorated sandals. In comparison, the American men travelers in their boxy suits seemed dowdy.

The city of Accra and the university at Legon presented me with a new spectrum of color. I squinted into an enormous, brilliant sky. All the buildings and walls presented complex patterns of textures and colors, for something grew on every surface—bushes, flowers or mold. The California Bay Area that I had left was a gray-blue place with mostly light-colored people. But now I moved in a world of bright contrasts. The dirt was red, the trees and grass blue-green, the buildings white with red-tiled roofs. Cerise bougainvillea climbed whitewashed walls and cascaded over fences. This colorful landscape and the very black people in white or brilliant clothes together altered my visual sense of everyday life.

Many Ghanaians invited us into their homes, chemistry professors, a carpenter, an herb doctor, and our landlord, among others. We ate in mansions more luxurious than anything we could ever afford and in bungalows so crowded that we winced. At every point on the scale of wealth, the people were Ghanaian, each one as black as the others.

As black Americans unaffiliated with the United States Embassy, we enjoyed several advantages. Nearly everyone regarded us as kindred, and they called us Afro-Americans, not American Negroes. Ghanaians disassociated us from their main grievances against the United States: imperialism and racial discrimination. Those who had studied in the United States or visited for any length of time included us in their nostalgia, if their memories were fond.

With our unstraightened hair in wax-print dresses, Mother and I looked enough like locals to pass, provided we kept our mouths shut. This silent assimilation made me something new. I felt inconspicuous and free. This is not to say that I felt like a Ghanaian. The better I came to know the various sorts of Ghanaian lives and customs, the more I realized how thoroughly American I was. Yet I never felt terribly foreign in Ghana. Knowing full well that I could never take part

in Ghanaian national life, I felt far less an outsider than I had sometimes felt in California. As a black person in a black country, I was very
much at home.

At first I found being a member of the racial majority disorient-
ing. I had grown up in Northern California as a member of one of
several racial minorities. In the 1940's and 1950's my family had encountered outright discrimination in housing and occasional difficulties in
getting decent service in restaurants. But by and large, racism didn't
present us with serious problems on a day-to-day basis. My parents
taught me about racial discrimination, however, and for as long as I
could remember, I felt connected to people of African descent in the
South, the West Indies and Africa. Any failure of mine, I was convinced, reflected badly on 400 million black people throughout the
world. My successes, of course, made them all proud. I bore my responsibilities without complaint, certain that my actions counted in the
world.

Growing up as I did with a strong Pan-African orientation, I took my
social and political bearings by race. How to decide which team to root
for? Favor the one with the black players, then later, the one with the
most black players. (This system doesn't work so well anymore.) Which
side of a political issue to support? See how it will affect black people
as a whole. Which movie to see? The one with a black character. Without my realizing it, my response to racism was a keen sense of race.

In Ghana, however, racial solidarity and the American way made
little sense. I realized this first in politics, mostly at the Star Hotel.
Ghanaian and Afro-American students and my friends and I spent
many tropical nights at the tables around the Star's outdoor dance floor,
drinking Ghanaian beer, smoking Ghanaian cigarettes and talking
politics. That is, my friends talked politics. All I could sort out was
colonialism, which was related to racism.

In the independent republic of Ghana, however, the issues were
not racial, but economic. Should the inefficient collective state farms

expand, although they were losing money hand-over-fist? Should the prosperous, private cocoa farms, which brought in most of the nation's hard currency, be nationalized? Should the government emphasize the development of agriculture or industry? When those who profited and those who suffered were all equally black, I couldn't figure the racial angle. But as economic questions superseded racial ones in my mind, I slowly discovered the politics of class.

Similar processes occurred in other areas of my life, as the racial thinking I had brought from the United States gave way. At the university, where geniuses, dumbbells and average students were black, I discovered the quality of ordinariness, which American race relations denied to blacks. In my studies of African history, I began to separate the politics of power from color. The outlines of human nature emerged.

Ordinary humanness affected me deeply as a woman. In the United States I was a woman, but always—outside the tight circle of family and close friends—a Negro woman. A Negro woman in the United States was not the same thing as just a woman, without a racial qualifier.

In Ghana, I became just a woman. I let down my burden of responsibility to the 400 million people of African descent, for I was surrounded by friends who were thinking seriously about the future and also having a good time. I had love affairs. I had my heart broken and broke hearts in my turn. I was free to enjoy myself and be something I have often missed intensely in the years since I came home—ordinary.

DECEMBER, 1981

GAIL GODWIN

I live in a village where the artists are buried separately from other people. On one side of the road is the main cemetery with its neat rows of headstones. On the other side, across the brook behind the framer's shop and up the grassy knoll, is what has come to be known as the Artists' Cemetery.

Sometimes I walk up, under the craggy aegis of Overlook Mountain—which presides over both cemeteries—and read the names and inscriptions on the gravestones. There are delicately carved animals on some; there are poems, many of them written by the people buried beneath them. Many of the stones are works of art themselves.

If I have any habitual meditation up here, it's the one that ponders that age-old question: How separate am I, as one who calls herself an artist, from the rest of my society?

How separate *ought* I to be?

"You didn't work again this year, either?" asks the tax accountant's receptionist, looking in vain for a W-2 form she can staple to the top of my records.

No, I did not commute through dark, icy mornings in order to ply my trade in somebody else's office space. I did not have to be there at a specific hour, not leave before a specific hour, or eat my lunch at the same time every day. For these blessings I am truly thankful.

On the other side of the ledger, however, I provided my own health insurance and my own retirement plan. No cost-of-living increase is built into my job, and I pay a hefty self-employment tax for my one-woman cottage industry.

I am a registered voter and take my vote seriously. I once did go out into a very dark and icy morning to vote against a man I knew was greedy and dishonest. He lost, and I felt powerful and magic.

As seminarians are said to argue endlessly over how many angels can dance on top of a pinhead, we apprentice-writers at the Iowa Workshop, back in the militant sixties, used to argue endlessly over whether we could do more good out at the barricades or at home in front of our typewriters.

I remember the day many of my colleagues spent picketing the building where a napalm manufacturer had come to recruit. I wanted to stay home and work on my novel. I squared things with myself by going down to the police station at the end of the day and bailing out two of my friends with my checkbook. I felt pretty good about having found this method to cover both bases at once: the political arena and the ivory tower.

Since then I have become an inveterate check writer for the debts I owe and the causes I believe in: disabled veterans, village rescue squad, National Public Radio, E.R.A. But the time has come when my checkbook doesn't always square it with my conscience anymore. I have to be on call to lock up my ivory tower for a day, or even a week, and drive somewhere in order to let my body be counted in the growing crowd that chooses the continuation of healthy human life over greed and technological hubris. If I don't show up at those barricades, I'm as good as saying I don't believe the power of megatons can cancel out— in one minute—all the millenniums worth of the power of art.

In one sense, my job requires frequent commuting. It requires me to go out into the world and soak up impressions, then come back home, recover from the confusion and excitement, and sort out those impressions. I can't take it *all* in, in any single trip or in all of them combined, or else I'd never get home again. "Do not live in an ivory tower," advised the novelist Salvador de Madariaga, "but always write in one."

If I don't go out enough, my fictional furniture dwindles, characters' conversations lag or sound old-fashioned; their surroundings become scarce in those surprises and strange turnings of which life is such an artist.

. . .

If I don't stay in enough, hoarding the attentive silences, I lose the calm inner space in which all the things I've seen outside have a chance to stick up their heads and place themselves where they ought to go in a story. "'It is only an afternoon'—'it is only an evening'—people say to me over and over again," wrote Dickens to someone, "but they don't know that it is impossible to command one's self to any stipulated and set disposal of five minutes—or that the mere consciousness of an engagement will sometimes worry a whole day."

I'm always aware that I risk being taken for a neurasthenic prima donna when I explain to someone who wants "just a little" of my time that five minutes of the wrong kind of distraction can ruin a working day.

And, of course, I know Dickens wrote those particular lines I'm so fond of to an old, fat girlfriend he was trying desperately to avoid.

The first person to be buried in what is now called the Artists' Cemetery in our village was not an artist. He was a much beloved boy of eighteen, killed but a few days from his high school graduation. His parents, so taken by surprise by his abrupt cessation, could not imagine putting away his young body in a staid village plot. So they bought a hill and buried him under an uncut boulder and hoped wildflowers would grow around it and winds would keep the grasses moving. The boy's collie, killed while wandering home after visiting his master's grave, is now buried at his feet.

Later, some friends of the boy's parents asked to have their graves on the same hill. Something wild and lonely about the place attracted them more than the regular cemetery across the street. Some of these friends, but not all of them, were artists. Since that time, a lot of artists—because our village has a lot of artists—have come to be buried there. The message on one obelisk is written by the doctor buried beneath it: ". . . They rest here who added to the beauty of the world by art, creative thought, and by life itself."

In my peripatetic musings, up there among the graceful stones, I imagine those others wandering in the days when they were alive. Did they get the same message from the place that I do? That, yes, the artist may be separate during working hours but remains forever part of the life of humankind with its attendant dramas.

JANUARY, 1982

Partings

MARY CANTWELL

W as it on Wednesday or Thursday night—I can't remember now—that the *New York Post* ran ads for Grossinger's, the Concord and other less famous Catskills hotels where, for the price of a room and bath, two nights only, you could meet the man of your dreams? Or maybe he wasn't quite the stuff of dreams, but you'd reached the point where you were willing to settle. I would read them—on Wednesday or Thursday nights—sitting in the wing chair waiting for my husband, eavesdropping on my children, possessed by smugness and swollen with security. I read with a feeling akin to that of one listening to wind or rain or hail while cocooned in clean sheets, thick blankets and a radiator that thunked in the dark. I was dry, I was warm, I was not out there in the wet street with the blown-out umbrella and the wind crawling under my skirt and the mud freckling the back of my legs. I was safe, I was home, I was married.

And then one day I wasn't, and I signed the papers as if I were signing an execution order—on some day in February in some place in Mexico a connection will be terminated—and I found myself in that chill and streaming street.

Often I cried when, my hand in the supermarket bin for a roast, I realized that there were only three of us, and two of them small. For a long time I slept on the left side of the bed, the right being a vast and empty prairie. Sometimes, faced with the Saturday night trilogy—Archie Bunker followed by Bob Newhart followed by Mary Tyler Moore—I wondered if I would ever again spend an evening in the company of adults. And when I walked through Greenwich Village, past the houses we had lived in, I would grow sick and dizzy, mourning a marriage, mourning myself, mourning a boy. I never thought of myself as divorced, but as widowed. Widowhood leaves one more freedom to be sad.

But I managed. Pragmatic, conservative, blessed with a kind of tolerant affection for myself, I did nothing that would make a book, a short story or even an anecdote. Instead, I did all I could to come indoors. I made a home, I drew the curtains and I paid no attention to those who said that this was not living. What do they know, those people who tell you that risk is all? I would listen to them, perhaps, if they didn't usually speak from a cozy chair beside a flaming hearth. I know what risk is, everybody knows what risk is. Risk is getting up in the morning.

And now? Now I am fine. Sometimes I look for pain much as the tongue searches a dead tooth looking for sensation, but there is no shock left. There are occasional twinges though, messages from nerves I thought severed long ago, but they have more to do with myth than with anything I ever learned of reality.

For instance, I am not a churchgoer, but I do show up on Christmas, Good Friday and Easter. Good Friday is intensely private, but Christmas and Easter are for multiples, so then, and especially at Easter, I look at the nice Irish couples I see around me at St. Joseph's and I wish my husband were beside me and that we were going home to roast pork with onion gravy. It is silly; I am not all that Irish and certainly not all that Catholic, and he was none of those. But there is a picture in my head. It is a picture of a man and a woman and their two daughters, and they are seated at a dinner table. The man will never be more than thirty-five or the woman more than thirty-three, and the children will always wear hair ribbons, and the pork will never dry out. One can neither hear them speak, nor hear their silences. But what one sees is beautiful.

I have another picture. It is of a woman who has taken her children to Chinatown for dinner. They are a bit nervous because they don't really believe that a mother can head the table, order the meal, pay the bill and protect them from muggers. But, loyal, they have trailed her along Mott Street, eaten snails with black-bean sauce and are now terrified because how will she escort them unscathed on the subway, countless miles into the earth's bowels, that travels 14th Street? Well, she does. No problem. She would, however foolishly, fight anyone. But she is terrified, too, not because she doesn't trust herself but because she trusts God more. And God, to her, was her husband.

To rid herself of the analogy, she has to rid herself of God. And eventually she does, but not wholly, because she retains her faith in absolution. But it is hard, very hard, and there are many times when she'd like to embrace the old religion. She loves order, hierarchy, she thrills in French churches when the priest says, "O Seigneur." But there is no order, no one left to look up to, unless she casts herself in a Woody Allen movie and chants of Groucho, Flaubert and Brando. Too slick, too easy and, in the end, too cheap.

There is a third picture, of the woman at her older daughter's high school graduation. The woman is on one side of the auditorium, the child's father is on the other, and their younger daughter is flying between them like a carrier pigeon. He and she are not friends. One could, of course, call that childish; she prefers to construe it as a tribute to their previous relationship. If they were friends, she figures, they still ought to be married.

Still, she finds the day bizarre. There on stage is someone who is half he, half she; their blood, their genes. They created somebody: the woman is awed. As long as there is a she, the woman thinks, there is an us.

And a last picture. It is a diptych: one part painted from a letter in the February issue of *Gourmet*, the other from a letter in March. I read *Gourmet* every month, less for the recipes than for a world in which all restaurants are glazed in amber, as are all meals; all countries are as mysterious as the Fitzgerald movie travelogues of my childhood; and all travelers are middle-aged, blue-eyed people whose veins are beginning to knot about their shinbones.

One of those travelers wrote about staying in a place called the

Priory in Bath, where "the dinner was even better than claimed in your article!" My husband and I stayed in Bath once; we stayed in a lot of places. "We didn't know enough to make reservations," I'd say, "so there we were, desperate, when we stumbled across the most marvelous pub. . . ."

The other letter was from a woman excited about an after-dinner coffee that contained brandy and five liqueurs. My stomach turned when I read the recipe, but it brought back my first brandy Alexander, my first vermouth cassis, my first champagne cocktail. I disliked all of them, as did my husband, but he wanted me to try them, so I did. I wouldn't have tried many things, most things, without his prodding me.

So when I read about the couple at the Priory and the woman drinking her five-liqueur demitasse, I thought of him. I thought of us in Bath and of how we measured out the ingredients for cocktails with tablespoons. I remember when the world was an uncracked egg.

I don't know him now, nor he me, but reading *Gourmet* I had a sudden glimpse of what we'd be like. Both brown-eyed, heading toward middle age, putting on a little weight maybe, and sampling hotels and funny after-dinner drinks. Looking a bit alike by now, and more than a little bored with each other, and suffering that itch that precedes the settling-down for the last run. "Would that be enough?" a friend asked, a women for whom life is a perennially ascending escalator. I don't know, I said, but I think so.

MARCH, 1980

JANE ADAMS

Her son is leaving to live with his father. It is no orderly leave-taking, not a visitation according to decrees and orders and dispositions signed a decade ago, but an abrupt departure from the family constructed awkwardly with the leftovers of a marriage.

Her son is leaving to live with his father, futility and rage have shredded and thinned the ties of love between him and his mother, and the torment of his adolescence traps them both.

Her son is leaving to live with his father, a childish fantasy he abandoned along with the stuffed animals and the lacing shoe, the picture books and the plastic blocks. The small framed photograph disappeared from the boy's room years ago, unmentioned, after the birthdays that passed without cards or gifts, the phone calls that were not returned, the promises that were never fulfilled.

The last call was answered, the one dialed out of desperation. For nothing else works, not since the voice deepened, the shoulders broadened, the limits ignored. He is obstreperous and arrogant at school, constantly in small troubles that might be overlooked if he were at least using his excellent intelligence in ways that tests or teachers could determine. He is a trial in the neighborhood, trying the patience of everyone, even other parents who understand the problems of a fatherless fourteen-year-old—but after all, their kids surivived, and so did they.

He is most difficult at home, pushing, prodding, taunting, testing, flaying her with the edges of anger buried long ago. She is tired to her bones, trying to juggle his needs with hers, his anger with her confusion, his interruptions with her other child, her career, her life.

He is leaving to live with his father, and she was prepared to let go, but not quite yet. For ten years he has consumed her, as his father did, but this is much worse than the divorce. And the last few days before he leaves are heavy with silence.

He works in the yard finally, taking what ease he can from cutting and pulling and mowing. She washes and folds his clothes, darns holes in his sweaters, consumes hours in the small but chilling tasks; in the pediatrician's office she cries, and her tears blur the vaccination records required for entrance to a school she's never seen, whose principal she has never met, whose P.T.A. president will never know what an excellent fund-raiser she is, how dedicated a volunteer she has been.

The night before he leaves, they retire to their separate rooms, with perfunctory hugs and the tension of unsaid words heavy in the air between them. In the middle of the night, she hears him vomiting in the bathroom; she clenches her hands, but she does not go to him; this is for him to face without her. He is scared, she knows; he is frightened of the father he has not known all the days of his young life, and he wonders about him. She cannot tell him; she does not remember, either. In the darkness, she tries to call him up, to recall the qualities she once loved and respected, to take some comfort in the good memories and block out the others.

In the morning, they are strangers, withdrawn from the anger of the last few months, but withdrawn, too, from the love that is too painful to feel again. He has already left her; she can tell from the tiny, drawn lines around his mouth, the pale color in his face, the thin hunch of his shoulders. He is pulling himself together for the meeting that awaits him a thousand miles south of all that he has known and much that he has treasured these fourteen years. And she is chewing her lower lip, forcing back the tears. The ride to the airport is silent; both of them reach for the radio dial at the same time, and they laugh nervously, together.

She parks the car while he waits in the check-in line. He gets his seat assignment; always before, when he has flown alone, she has settled him in with books and toys, but this time she does not. She waits by the departure gate, at the window, straining to make him out through the cloudy porthole of the airplane. It departs, finally, but she does not leave until the last contrail disappears from the sky, and then she waits, with a cup of coffee, just in case. In case of what, she does not know; but just in case.

Relief is indistinguishable now from loneliness. There are no more tears; they collect, uncried, in the deep and aching void he has left in her. The space he filled is empty and accusing; not blame, or guilt, but sorrow that what she has given him was not enough. There is no anger, but that will come later, she knows; anger that his father, with the simple words, I want you, son, can do what she, who has loved and wanted him and loves him still, cannot.

Her son is leaving to live with his father. He is funny, and kind, and creative, and smart, this boy; underneath the anger and apart from the surging hormones that have changed him from a laughing, loving child to a silent, surly teenager is a son a father would be proud to call his own. And inside him, too, is the man he will become. She has taught him what she could, but this she cannot show him. This he will have to learn from someone else, someone she does not know anymore, someone whose ways are strange to her, whose life has taken turns and taught him lessons unfathomable to her. It's time I paid my dues, her ex-husband told her when they talked about their son; it's my turn to worry. She believes him, for she has no other choice. And the shrunken knot of that old pain, ten years dead now, expands and fills the void.

He is leaving to live with his father, and she does not know if he will return.

SEPTEMBER, 1980

JOAN GOULD

How rich, strange and tumultuous are the romances we conduct after death. I see myself—even before the condolence letters are acknowledged—crouching in the corner of what I still call our bedroom, pawing through my files, reassuring myself over and over again about the subject that intrudes like flesh among the funeral flowers: money. Time and time again, without cause, I add up the figures, as if some of them may have vanished during the night. I cannot stop myself from doing it.

And there, among checkbooks, bankbooks, partnership agreements, carbons of impeccably prudent letters, while looking for surety for the life that lies ahead of me, I find instead (I should say, in addition)—something. Never mind what. Surely checkbooks are the diaries of our time, and bank tellers our biographers!

It is nothing much, I add hastily, only a trifle. But it exists nonetheless, and what's more, it was meant to remain secret. The seamless wall is no longer seamless. Water can seep through this chink. A few moments ago, I was a widow, but suddenly I am transformed to wife again, an outraged wife at that. It feels good, this anger of mine, and, canny in the ways of grief by this time, I apply bellows to it, having discovered that anger is the only analgesic guaranteed to work every time.

All widows were married to saints, all divorcées to devils, a friend counsels me; but for me, it is no longer so. Where there was an empty space in the bed beside me, I summon a ghost whose shape I know so well, and try to flesh him out with more knowledge than I possessed in all those years. Well, we have plenty of time to get to know each other better, now that life no longer parts us.

Let me look back. Twenty-eight years is a long time that vanishes in the instant of a diagnosis. When my husband left the hospital after the operation, we entered a land where time is a liquid, rich and thick like honey, to be tasted drop by drop, for it is very probable there will not be enough of it to cloy the palate. We took our boy out to dinner; we took a Sunday walk through the Lower East Side; my husband took two months off from work for the first time since he left school over three decades earlier.

And all during that honeymoon, unable to help myself, I was having the roof fixed, getting the plumbing overhauled, taking care of things that had been neglected for years. Why? I'm not sure. Perhaps I was keeping myself, literally, from going to pieces; perhaps I was equipping myself with a dowry for widowhood.

Strange days, stranger nights. I remember one, not far from the end, when he awoke with his wound leaking over his bandage, pajamas, bed. I changed his bandage, changed the linens, gave him the urinal and cough medicine, tried to arrange his pillows since he could no longer sit up. Finally, I asked if there was anything else I could bring him. Asleep or nearly so, from the depth of his nature he answered, "Only my dancing shoes."

Did I delude myself, then, because there were moments of heroism and devotion, that we were heroic? Did I forget the fundamental enmity of the sick and the well, at 4 A.M., when the sick one needs to be heard and the well one needs to sleep, when the sick one knows this is it, and the well one knows this is not it, there are years ahead and someone has to fight with the plumber in the morning?

Of course I forgot.

And then there was the bit of folly that I discovered among the financial records. We quarreled, my ghost and I, and as usual his reasonableness won all the points. You kept a secret, I accused him. If so, there's proof I didn't choose to wound you, he answered. But a secret, deceit between *us*, I railed. You think you have the right to know every part of another human being, he countered, turn another person inside out? Is that what you'll do someday to our son? But that means you weren't completely happy in the marriage, I let out the truth at last. Only happy enough to sacrifice anything else for it, he said, and silenced me.

In that silence I heard a final lesson: If a secret existed, however small, then we two were not really one, and I was not in the grave as I imagined.

But my partner, my ghost, wasn't the only one with the right to reveal a new aspect during this late-blooming romance. I, too, was changing. Death is a great awakener.

Within this self of mine that had grown spiritually flabby during years of love and joint returns, I have discovered another self, one that I remember dimly from half a lifetime ago. It is leaner, more alert, warier, but at the same time more grateful for friendship, more suspicious of change and yet more convinced of the necessity to embrace it. It is a more supple self. Somehow it seems younger. When he left me, I was a middle-aged housewife. Now I am an adolescent widow, emotionally volcanic like all adolescents and convinced at times that I'm unnecessary, but alive, definitely alive.

I remember the day when one of my husband's clients who was divorced called for advice because he was worried. He had met a wonderful woman and wanted to remarry. Then why on earth was he worried? my husband asked. It seemed that she had been widowed twice. Both husbands had committed suicide, both by jumping out of windows, as it happened. "Get married, get married!" my husband counseled exuberantly. "But just to play safe, take an apartment on a low floor."

Not bad advice, it seems to me, this tempered buoyancy, though it needn't take the form of remarriage in my case. All of us over the age of forty, I find, suffer from bouts of self-pity. All of us, not just widows and divorcées, waste strength regretting the past, either because it was so good or because it was so bad, but only widows bear the special burden of our friends' pity, which implies that we're no longer the personages we used to be.

Of course we're not. We've changed, and so will our friends. The truth is that all of us—divorcées, widows and those whose time has not yet come—are going to have more than one life to live. Sooner or later we discover that we only rent our happiness or unhappiness, we don't own it, and we'd better be prepared to move out on short notice, carrying our own suitcases at that. After all, who ever promised us perpetual care?

That can be found in only one place, my ghost in dancing shoes tells me.

NOVEMBER, 1980

NOTES ON THE CONTRIBUTORS

ERICA ABEEL teaches literature at John Jay College, City University of New York. She is the author of *Only When I Laugh* and *I'll Call You Tomorrow and Other Lies Between Men and Women*, a collection of journalism including the "Hers" columns. Her forthcoming novel is *The Last Romance*.

JANE ADAMS lives in Seattle. Her most recent novel, *Good Intentions*, is based on the column on pp. 283–85.

SYBIL ADELMAN is a script writer for television and movies.

JENNIFER ALLEN is a writer who lives and works in New York.

BARBARA LAZEAR ASCHER practiced law with a Manhattan law firm before leaving in order to write full time. A collection of her essays will be published in 1986.

MARY KAY BLAKELY is a writer and a contributing editor to *Ms.* magazine. For many years a columnist for the Fort Wayne *Journal Gazette* in Fort Wayne, Indiana, she now lives in Connecticut.

MARY CANTWELL is a writer who joined *The New York Times* editorial board in November, 1980.

K. C. COLE is a columnist for *Discover* magazine. Her latest book is *Sympathetic Vibrations: Reflections on Physics as a Way of Life*.

LAURA CUNNINGHAM is the author of two novels, *Sweet Nothings* and *Third Parties*, and has written short stories and articles that have appeared in numerous publications.

LINDA BIRD FRANCKE, a former editor at *Newsweek* magazine, is the author of *The Ambivalence of Abortion* and *Growing Up Divorced*. She also collaborated with Rosalynn Carter, Jehan Sadat, and Geraldine Ferraro on their respective memoirs.

JOAN GELMAN is a television producer and a writer who is currently co-writing a book entitled *How to Set Up for a Mah-Jongg Game and Other Lost Arts*.

GAIL GODWIN'S most recent novels are *A Mother and Two Daughters* and *The Finishing School*.

JOAN GOULD has written articles and fiction for numerous national magazines during the past twenty years. Her next book, *Spirals*, will be a personal account based on her journals of a woman's perception of herself within her family. An avid sailor, she lives in Rye, N.Y., with her youngest son.

LOIS GOULDS novels include *La Presidenta, A Sea-Change*, and *Such Good Friends*.

ANN P. HARRIS is an advertising and freelance writer with a special interest in women and work. She has taught college English and worked as a journalist.

BARBARA GRIZZUTI HARRISON is the author of a novel, *Foreign Bodies*, and a collection of essays, *Off Center*. She is currently in Italy working on a book of nonfiction.

MOLLY HASKELL is a film critic and the author of *From Reverence to Rape: The Treatment of Women in the Movies*.

SUE HUBBELL, a writer and beekeeper, lives on a farm in Missouri. She is working on a book, *Living the Questions*, a natural history of her ninety acres of Ozark land.

SUSAN JACOBY is a writer who lives in New York. Her most recent book is *Wild Justice: The Evolution of Revenge.*

ANEES JUNG is a writer and editor who lives in Bombay and New Delhi. She is the author of a collection of essays on India, *When a Place Becomes a Person.*

MAXINE HONG KINGSTON, who resides in Hawaii and California, is the author of *The Woman Warrior* and *China Men.* Her shorter pieces are being collected in a forthcoming book, *Hawai'i One Summer.*

PERRI KLASS, a third-year student at the Harvard Medical School, writes a column for *Discover* magazine. Her fiction has twice been included in O. Henry Awards Prize Stories collections, and her first novel, *Recombinations,* is forthcoming.

DEIRDRE LEVINSON is a teacher and writer based in New York. Her first novel is *Modus Vivendi.*

JOYCE MAYNARD is a syndicated newspaper columnist and the author of the novel *Baby Love.* She is currently working on a book called *Domestic Affairs.*

A. G. MOJTABAI lived in Iran over twenty years ago. Her third novel, *A Stopping Place,* is set in the Islamic world. She now lives in Amarillo, Texas (home of the final assembly plant for all nuclear weapons in the United States), where she is completing a book of observations and reflections on nuclear realities.

FAYE MOSKOWITZ, a teacher and a Washington, D.C., writer, is the author of *A Leak in the Heart.*

PATRICIA O'TOOLE is the author of *Corporate Messiah: The Hiring and Firing of Million-Dollar Managers.* Her articles on working, business, and personal finance have appeared in many national publications.

293

NOTES ON THE CONTRIBUTORS

NELL IRVIN PAINTER is a historian who teaches at the University of North Carolina at Chapel Hill.

LETTY COTTIN POGREBIN, a writer and editor for *Ms.* magazine, has published five books, most recently *Family Politics.* She is currently at work on a book about friendship in America.

TOVA REICH is the author of the novel *Mara,* and of the just-completed *Master of the Return.* Her stories have appeared in many publications. Supported by a creative writing fellowship from the National Endowment for the Arts, she is at work on a new novel.

JILL ROBINSON is a writer who lives in London. Her latest novel is *Star Dust.*

BETTY ROLLIN is a writer and television correspondent. She is the author of *First, You Cry* and *Am I Getting Paid for This?.* Her forthcoming book is about a crisis in her family.

PHYLLIS ROSE is a professor of English at Wesleyan University and the author of *Parallel Lives: Five Victorian Marriages* and *Woman of Letters,* a biography of Virginia Woolf. A collection of her literary essays and reviews, *Writing of Women,* is forthcoming.

NORMA ROSEN has published a collection of stories and three novels. *At the Center,* her latest, deals with issues of abortion. She is at work on a new novel.

MAGGIE SCARF is the author of *Unfinished Business: Pressure Points in the Lives of Women.* She is currently at work on a book about long-term relationships.

ELIN SCHOEN, a resident of New York, is the author of *Tales of an All-Night Town, Widower,* and *The Closet Book.*

LYNNE SHARON SCHWARTZ is the author of three novels: *Disturbances in the Field, Balancing Acts,* and *Rough Strife,* and a collection of stories, *Acquainted with the Night.* She has received a Guggenheim Foundation Fellowship and, in 1985, a National Endowment for the Arts Fellowship.

GAIL SHEEHY is an author and journalist whose work *Passages* led to *Pathfinders.* She is at work on a book of reportage, memory, and nightmare about a survivor of genocide in Cambodia.

PHYLLIS THEROUX is the author of *California and Other States of Grace,* and *Peripheral Visions,* as well as of numerous articles and essays that have appeared in various magazines and newspapers. She is currently a columnist for *Parents* magazine and lives in Washington, D.C.

MARY-LOU WEISMAN is a writer and the author of *Intensive Care: A Family Love Story.* She is at present writing a feature movie for Paramount Pictures.

JUNE P. WILSON is a writer and translator living in New York who is at present writing a book of essays on the view at age sixty-nine.

About the Editor

Nancy R. Newhouse is the editor of the Living/Style Department of *The New York Times*. Previously she was a senior editor at *New York* magazine and at *House & Garden*. A graduate of Vassar College, she lives in New York City with her husband, Michael Iovenko, a lawyer.